THE ORIGINAL LETTERS FROM INDIA

THE ORIGINAL LETTERS FROM INDIA

ELIZA FAY, WALTER K. FIRMINGER

GYAN

Published by

GYAN

Gyan Publishing House
5, Ansari Road
Daryaganj, New Delhi-110002
Phone: 011-47034999, 9811692060
E-mail: books@gyanbooks.com

Distribution Network
gyanbooks.com
India, USA, Canada, UK, Australia

ISBN: 978-93-7133-108-1 (PB)

First Published, 1908

2nd Impression 2025

Printed at: Gyan Press, Delhi.

THE ORIGINAL LETTERS FROM INDIA

Author Eliza Fay, Walter K. Firminger

THE ORIGINAL LETTERS FROM INDIA

OF

Mrs. ELIZA FAY.

A NEW EDITION

WITH

INTRODUCTION AND NOTES

BY THE

REV. WALTER KELLY FIRMINGER, B.D., F.R.G.S.

Junior Chaplain on H. M. Bengal Establishment,
Editor of Bengal: Past & Present.

Published under the Auspices of the Calcutta Historical Society.

Calcutta:

MESSRS. THACKER, SPINK & Co.

1908.

INTRODUCTION.

Of the rare contemporary works, which throw light on the social life of the Calcutta of Warren Hastings and Sir Philip Francis, one of the most rare and certainly the most interesting is the *Original Letters* of Mrs. Fay. The book suddenly introduces Mrs. Fay and her husband to us on 18th April 1779, and in July 1795, the narrative leaves her, at a low ebb in her fortunes, in America. The second part of her book was written at Blackheath in 1815. The Registers of St. John's Church, Calcutta, show that she was buried on 10th September 1816 in one of our cemeteries (which no one now can say) by the Rev. H. Shepherd. On the occasion of her first visit, the City of Palaces, although boasting of a fine theatre, had but a mere apology for a church. Mrs. Fay survived to see Calcutta distinguished by a Cathedral. She had no doubt sat under Padre "Tally Ho Johnson," the last husband of that much "intermarried" Begum who could tell of the misfortunes of the English in Bengal in 1756, and of how her then husband (Watts) concealed in the palki of a purdah nasheen lady had entered Mir Jaffar's house at Murshidabad to arrange for the undoing of Suraj-ud-Daula. Mrs. Fay must have had some acquaintance with the old Begum, and she too must have known, howsoever distantly, that famous Mrs. Ellerton, who in the days of Lord Canning was wont to describe how she had seen Francis carried away "all bloody" after his duel with Hastings. The India of Mrs. Fay seems far remote in time from the India of to-day, and yet it is strange to think that my own mother, during her short stay in India, met with a lady, who, if she had not actually known Mrs. Fay, must probably have seen her, or at least known all about her.

Readers of Dr. Busteed, Archdeacon Hyde, Miss Blechynden, Sydney Grier, and Mr. H. E. A. Cotton are well acquainted with Mrs. Fay's prattle about Belvedere, the Harmonic, the beauty of Lady Chambers, the elegance of the second Mrs. Warren Hastings, the troubles of a Calcutta memsahib of the period, etc., etc., but few in late years have read—or indeed have had the opportunity of reading—Mrs. Fay's book from first page to last. It certainly deserves to be read as a whole, for although as a reviewer in 1818 wrote, "there is little magic in her style," the authoress was, as the same authority perceived, "a person of considerable acuteness and information." Indeed, apart from the context, Mrs. Fay's account of her visit to Belvedere cannot be quite valued for what it is worth: the context makes it clear that she was in a bad temper with her hostess. But the whole story of her first journey out to India—the gipsy-tour across France, over the Alps to Leghorn, the anxious journey through Egypt, the captivity at Calicut—is decidedly well worth reading.

It may indeed be wondered how it is that a book so often laid under contribution, so full of adventures, containing so many clearly cut descriptions of interesting persons and places, has been allowed to fall out of circulation. Well, in the first place, as it has been observed, Calcutta, being a place of frequent partings, is, in consequence, a place of short memories. When Mrs. Fay, in advanced years, returned to Calcutta, about a year before her death, and set to work to put her letters into print, I suppose there would have been but few here who would have remembered her on the occasion of her first visit, and perhaps the Calcutta of Warren Hastings' days had not for the men of that time the glamour which it has for us to-day. The Executors cut the book short where Mrs. Fay had left the printing of it; and after copies had been issued to the subscribers, its existence was forgotten until the Rev.

J. Long, in his articles in the *Calcutta Review*, began to draw upon it for picturesque quotations. Then, again, there is something about Mrs. Fay which fails to charm, something of a too conscious superiority which alienates sympathy in circumstances in which sympathy would not be grudged. When Mrs. Hastings hinted that our authoress had brought her troubles on herself "by imprudently venturing on such an expedition out of mere curiosity," although we see the injustice of the hint, yet after all we cannot help feeling that if Mrs. Fay would be so audacious, and would do things in a way which no ordinary woman would, or perhaps should, dare to do them, most people would feel inclined to share her critic's view of her sufferings.

For it is clear that the joint career of the Fays, from first to last, was a mad one. They started for India without obtaining the Company's permission to reside there. They plunge into France when the French nation was at war with our own. Eliza had been in France on no less than four previous occasions, but judge of her notion of the passage over the Alps from her *naïve* confession :—"On arriving near the Alps, it appeared that I had formed a very erroneous idea of the route, having always suffered that we had only one mountain to pass and that the rest of the way was level ground." (Another curious instance of Mrs. Fay's notions of geography will be found on P. 192, in regard to the highest mountains in the world.) The Fays make for Leghorn at a time when an English private trading ship would hardly dare to venture out of port unless protected by a convoy. Her own account shows how foolhardy (at least for a woman) was the journey through Egypt, yet we find the pair making for Suez, although they seemed to have been previously informed that the Turkish authorities had determined to close that port to European vessels. They arrive at Calicut to fall into the hands of Sudder Khan. Mrs. Fay has a dissipated and extravagant husband to look after: but are not her economies a little too drastic—those inns (recalling to our memory Sterne's last chapter of the *Sentimental Journey*) where beds (eight in a room) are procured at four sous a night, the tea which she calls a most "curious mess," etc, etc? Poor Anthony, we feel certain, will sooner or later revolt. There is, as college friends on long vacation tours find out, no severer strain on friendship than the strain involved in a tramp together through strange lands. The happiness of the journey depends so much on mutual give and take, on constant readiness to adopt what the other thinks the better way, forbearance with one another's faults in taste and temper, and on a generously tolerant view of one's friend's excesses both in economy and in expenditure. Mrs. Fay has good reason to know that she is "the better man of the two," and because her husband probably is made to realise this, he becomes pig-headed and obstinate. The pair are not friends, and we may feel certain that, sooner or later, they will part. It is, for instance, with scarcely suppressed amusement Eliza records Anthony's fatigue after he had boasted that the ascent of the Mount Cenis would have *for him* but few difficulties. It is little incidents such as this one which makes us see that the Indian experiment will never succeed.

I have been inclined to wonder whether Anthony Fay was such a fool as his wife has made him to appear. The fact that he started without the Company's permission to reside, and travelled by unusual routes and foreign ships, refused to call on the Judges, etc., etc., gives colour to the suspicion that he had really been sent out by some foe to prepare for that impeachment of Sir Elijah Impey on which ultimately we find him at work. If this were indeed the case, his wife, although deceived into believing that he seriously intended to practise as a Barrister, may to some extent have been misled by some of her husband's prejudices. The acerbity of her account of Hastings' wife has been noticed : of Hastings himself she writes : "He will never desert a friend, or forgive an enemy:" but it becomes clear that she changed her mind to some extent. She clearly came to see that her husband's attack on Sir Elijah Impey would extend to her benefactor, Sir Robert Chambers. In October 1778, Impey accepted the Presidency of the Sadr Diwani Adalat, and this was put forward as the taking of a bribe ; but Chambers, who had to some extent been regarded as a possible ally by Francis, followed suit by accepting the office of Judge of Chinsurah. This, I take it, is what Mrs. Fay alludes to when, in connection with the articles of impeachment, which Anthony Fay was drawing up, she writes : "the character of a highly revered friend is obliquely glanced at, and may be in the future more seriously implicated in the business."

The dates of Mrs. Fay's journey are as follows.—

1779 (April 10)—1783 (February 7).
1784 (March 17)—1794 (September 4).
1795 (August 2)—1796.
Unknown—Death 1816.

Of the last journey nothing is now known : in the second and third we have Mrs. Fay comparatively in "peace and prosperity." The business house she occupied is still in existence, but, as I write, it has fallen into the builders hand for alteration, if not for demolition. It stands in the corner formed by Church Lane and Hastings Street. From the records of St. John's Church I have been kindly permitted to extract the following letter.

"To the Rev. Mr. Blanshard, the Rev. Mr. Owen, Mr. Cockerell, Mr. Thornhill, Mr. Sealey, Mr. Johnson, members of the Church Vestry.

13th April, 1789.

"GENTLEMEN,

Pardon the freedom I use in making an application, which I flatter myself, however, will be attended with success having nothing for its object that can in the smallest degree injure the property of the Church.

"Permit me then to acquaint you that, about five years since, I became an inhabitant, and, sometime after purchaser of the house I now reside in, formerly the Post Office, and forms the south-west boundary of the old burying ground, now the compound of the New Church. At the period I mention, the lower floor was nearly as habitable as the upper one ; but shortly after, a considerable part of it was rendered almost useless, in consequence of a wall being built up against the window, so close as to prevent the accession of either light or air. There is also great reason to apprehend that from the accumulation of damp between the walls and the house, and the want of a free ventilation, walls of the latter will sustain material injury.

"Suffer me, therefore, to request, Gentlemen, that you will have the goodness to take the subject of this letter into consideration ; and be pleased to allow that part of the wall, which stands against my house, to be taken down ; or such openings to make in it, as may suffice to restore the premises to their former usefulness.

"I am, Gentleman,
"Your most humble servant,
"ELIZA FAY."

This letter supplies the reason for the name given to Old Post Office Street to a neighbouring street.

It is strange that, although on the occasion of her second visit to Calcutta, Sir Robert and Lady Chambers were still resident there, Mrs. Fay makes no mention to them. The references to the Chambers are some of the most interesting things in the book. Robert Chambers' name has been immortalised in many oftquoted passages of Boswell's *Life of Dr. Johnson*. He had been a member of the "Literary Club," that select coterie, which included among its members Burke, Reynolds, and Goldsmith. We all remember how on one occasion the Doctor left Chambers' rooms in the Temple. "Johnson could not stop his merriment, but continued it all the way till he got without the Temple Gate. He then burst into such a fit of laughter that he appeared to be almost in a convulsion ; and in order to support himself, laid hold of one of the posts at the side of the foot pavement, and sent forth peals so loud, that in the silence of the night his voice seemed to resound from Temple Bar to Fleet Ditch." This uncontrolable fit of jocularity is described by Boswell as "a most ludicrous exhibition of the awful melancholy and venerable Johnson." Alluding to Chambers' departure for Bengal the Doctor, in a passage, which Thackeray has instanced as an illustration of "the great wise benevolence, nobleness of heart of Dr. Johnson," writes : "Chambers you will find is gone far, and poor Goldsmith is gone much further. He [Goldsmith] died of a fever exasperated, I believe, by fear of distress. He raised money and squandered it by every artifice of acquisition and folly—but let not his failings be remembered : he was a very great man." At Goldsmith's funeral Chambers was one of the few mourners present.

In 1774, on the institution of the Calcutta Supreme Court, Chambers came to India with his young and beautiful wife and also his aged mother, who could not resign herself to a parting. He was the second judge, Sir Elijah Impey being the Chief Justice. In 1791 he became Chief Justice, and in 1799 he died at Paris. His body lies in the Temple Church. He had been one of the judges in the famous Nanda Kumar (Nuncomar) case. "Chambers," wrote Francis, "........in all their public opinions and decisions, particularly in the verdict against Fowke and the murder of Nuncomar, his deserting us in that manner and condeming us with an apparent reluctance, looked like the confession of a frend, and did us more mischief perhaps than the hostility of the others." Hickey in his scurrilous *Gazette* nicknames Chambers "Sir Viner Pliant," and Sir FitzJames

Stephen has in the severest terms commented on Sir Robert's manifest weakness in the Nanda Kumar case.* The first Earl of Minto described the Judge as a man "of mild and flexible character, although of great knowledge."

The beauty of Lady Chambers has been in no way exaggerated by her client, Mrs. Fay. Writes Johnson to Boswell (July 1773): "Chambers is either married, or almost married, to Miss Wilton, a girl of sixteen, exquisitely beautiful, whom he has, with his lawyer's tongue, persuaded to take her chance with him in the East." In *Hartley House* we have an account of her smart turn-out on the course: and Mrs. Fay tells us of Lady Chambers' cleverness: but she was something better than beautiful, smart, or clever. For twenty-five unbroken years she continued with her husband in Bengal, refusing to leave his side when he was ill, and going with him wheresoever he went with the constancy of Ruth. Her treatment of Mrs. Fay is in itself a monument to her kindness and most probably to her forbearance. She was a woman who well knew how to use the world without abusing it and go on her way rejoicing. It cannot, for one moment be denied, that the most helpful thing England can hope to offer to India is the type of noble womanhood so generously represented by Lady Chambers.

I have been unable to trace the house in which Mrs. Fay sought refuge beneath the Chambers' protection. Sir Robert, like Warren Hastings, seems to have been a keen speculator in landed property. He had property in Alipur, Cossipur and Bhowanipur, and the long row of godowns, now shops, which skirt the southern side of St. John's compound were at one time his property.

It is rather surprising to note that Mrs. Fay tells us nothing about the fate of the East Indiaman the *Grovenor*, on which poor little Thomas Chambers was sent home

---

* "Timid if not sneaking." Sir F. Stephen, *Nuncomar and Impey*, Vol. I., p. 178.

under the care of Mrs. Hosea. This is the more strange because Mrs. Fay was herself so anxious to secure a passage by that vessel. A contemporary account of the wreck of the *Grosvenor* and the consequent sufferings of the survivors has recently been republished in No. 3 of Vol. II of *Bengal: Past and Present*. We wonder whether Mrs. Fay ever came across Sir Robert's brother, William Chambers, the "Prothonotary and Persian Interpreter to the Supreme Court," who holds so distinguished a place in the history of Christian Missions to India, as a disciple of Schwartz, the translator (in part) of the Gospels into Persian, the associate with Charles Grant and David Brown in the North India Mission Scheme of 1786, and one of the ransomers of the Old Mission Church, when (on Kiernander's bankruptcy) the *Beth Topillah* came under the auctioneer's hammer. William Chambers died in 1793, and was buried in the tomb of his brother's children in the South Part Street Graveyard. It has sometimes been claimed that William Chambers was the first in modern times to translate any portion of the Gospels into Persian: this distinction, however, belongs to one of the early Jesuit missionaries, the Blessed Father Rudolph Aquaviva. It is interesting to note, that Sir Robert and Lady Chambers, with a Mr. Naylor, stood sponsor at the first recorded baptism of a Mahomedan of importance in Calcutta.

The reader will note that Mrs. Fay's manner of writing can scarcely be called a "style," and that she is none too careful of grammar. She frequently arranges her words in such an order that she is bound to get into trouble with her relative pronouns. In a very few instances I have taken the liberty of substituting full stops for commas, and when a sentence had to read over twice before Mrs. Fay's meaning became clear, I have made very slight alterations in the arrangement of her words. It will, however, be observed that Mrs. Fay could write very good English whenever she chose to do so.

The letters in the first part of the Book, it must be remembered, were written under the most trying circumstances imaginable. They reveal the fact that at nearly every halting place on the outward journey our authoress fell ill. She has given us what she wrote for her own family circle, and, as she tells us her tale in the way in which, in her circumstances, we might well have expected her to tell it, her chaotic punctuation remains as a sort of witness to the naturally distracted state of her suffering mind.

WALTER K. FIRMINGER.

ERRATA.

PAGE ix. Erase last sentence of para. "At Goldsmith's funeral" etc.

" 12. Footnote *for* "Layun" *read* "Lausun".

" 15. Line 17 *for* "Jaher" *read* "Jehu".

" 40. 2nd line of para. *for* "Brandly" *read* "Brandy".

" 146. 11th line from bottom *for* "desserts" *read* "deserts".

" 233 & 237. *For* "Echoes of" *read* "Echoes from".

ADDENDA.

PAGE 228. Note 2nd. The two Chevaliers were Pierre Mathieu Renault de St. Germaine, a godson of Dupleix, and Renault de Chilly. It was the latter who died in the desert.

" " Note 3rd. John Werner Vender Velden was a Dutchman and not (as Mrs. Fay says) a Dane. He had been one of the Dutch public servants at Chinsurah, but, getting into trouble there, escaped and secured British protection.

In the Note-books of Justice Hyde, preserved at the Bar Library of the Calcutta High Court, there are several references to Anthony Fay. He defended the notorious J. A. Hicky in the case brought against him by Warren Hastings.

ELIZA FAY.

From an Engraving of a Portrait by A. W. Devis.

ORIGINAL LETTERS

FROM INDIA;

CONTAINING A NARRATIVE OF A

JOURNEY THROUGH EGYPT

AND

THE AUTHOR'S IMPRISONMENT AT CALICUT

BY HYDER ALLY,

TO WHICH IS ADDED

AN ABSTRACT OF THREE SUBSEQUENT VOYAGES TO INDIA.

BY MRS. FAY.

PRINTED AT CALCUTTA.

1817

PREFACE.

THE volume now submitted to the public exhibits a faithful account of certain remarkable occurrences in the history of an individual whose lot has been to make frequent visits to several distant regions of the globe, to mingle in the society of people of different kindreds and tongues, and to experience many vicissitudes of fortune. At a time when fictitious representations of human life are sought for with so much avidity and constitute one of the principal sources of amusement in the hours of solitude, such a work as the present will, it is presumed, not be unacceptable. Those whose curiosity is attracted by the recital of incidents that never took place, or whose sensibility can be awakened by the description of emotions that were never felt, may perhaps derive a similar gratification from the following unembellished narrative of simple facts and real sufferings.

Five and thirty years ago it was the fate of the author to undertake a journey overland to India in company with her husband, the late Anthony Fay, Esq., who having been called to the Bar by the Honourable Society of Lincoln's Inn, had formed the resolution of practising in the courts of Calcutta. They travelled through France and over the Alps to Italy, whence embarking at Leghorn they sailed to Alexandria in Egypt. Having visited some of the curiosities in this interesting country and made a great stay at Grand Cairo, they pursued their journey across the Desert to Suez. After passing down the Red Sea, the ship in which they sailed touched at Calicut, where they were seized by the officers of Hyder Ally; and for fifteen weeks endured all the hardships and privations of a rigorous imprisonment.

When, after residing two years in India, the author on account of circumstances explained in the course of the work returned to her native country, she was repeatedly urged by several of her friends to publish some account of the events that had befallen her which it was supposed would engage the attention of the public, being connected with important circumstances in the lives of well known and respectable individuals, and illustrative of a potentate, whose movements were the subject of serious alarm in India. But at this period a woman who was not conscious of possessing decided genius or superior knowledge could not easily be induced to leave "the harmless tenor of her way", and render herself amenable to the pains and penalties then generally inflicted on female authorship, unless inspired by that enthusiasm that tramples on difficulties or goaded by misery which admits not of an alternative. Being utterly uninfluenced by either of these motives, and having all the fear of criticism and aversion to publicity which characterizes the young women of her day, the author at that time declined complying with the wishes of those she yet highly honoured, and never inquired further of the fate of her letters than to learn that they were duly received by those dear friends, to whom all her peregrination and the knowledge of her eventual safety could not fail to be highly interesting.

Since then, a considerable change has gradually taken place in public sentiments and its developments. We have not only as in former days, a number of women who do honour to their sex as literary characters, but many unpretending females, who, fearless of the critical perils that once attended the voyage, venture to launch their little barks on the vast ocean through which amusement or instruction is conveyed to a reading public. The wit of Fielding is no longer held over them *in terrorem* and the delineations of Smollet would apply to them in vain. The race of learned ladies ridiculed by these gentlemen is extinct. A female author is no longer regarded as an object of derision; nor is she wounded by unkind reproof from the *literary lords of creation*. In this indulgent era, the author presumes to deliver her letters to the world as they have been preserved by the dear sister to whom they were partly addressed, trusting that as this is, in its nature, the most unassuming of all kinds of writing, and one that claims the most extensive of allowances, they will be received with peculiar mercy and forbearance.

Since the period to which these letters refer, the author has made voyages to India, touching in the course of them at various places in all the quarters of the globe, and has been engaged in commercial and other speculations. Her trials and anxieties, however, have produced only a long train of blasted hopes and heartrending disappointments. An account of these subsequent occurrences is, therefore, subjoined in a series of letters drawn from the original journals and memorandums, and addressed to a lady whom the author has the happiness to rank in the number of her friends.

Shadows, clouds and darkness still rest on the remainder of her pilgrimage, which calls for the pilotage of kindness and the day-star of friendship. She has, however, by the blessing of Providence, been constantly enabled to rise superior to misfortune, will not now in the evening of her days derogate from the unostentatious energy of her character, or seek to solicit the pity of her readers by wearisome retrospect or painful complaints. With feelings acutely alive to kindness and truly grateful for every expression of it, she most thankfully esteems the generous patronage with which she has been honoured, and is rendered the more sensible of its value, because she is conscious that it was not meanly solicited or unworthily obtained.

To the inhabitants of Calcutta she begs more particularly to render her thanks. Long acquaintance, high esteem, and unfeigned affection call for this particular tribute. Five times has she visited this city, under various circumstances and with different feelings, yet never had cause to regret the length or danger of the voyage, secure of ever meeting here all that could increase the joys of social life in its happiest moments, or soothe the hours of languishment in the days of adversity.

CALCUTTA, *Anno 1816.*

LETTER I.

FROM MRS. F.—

Paris, 18th April, 1779.

I BELIEVE before I left England it was agreed that my letters should not, in general, be addressed to any one particularly, as they will be something in the style of journals; therefore, a contrary method would be rather embarrassing. I suppose you begin to think that I have forgotten you all; but it really has not been in my power to write till now, of which assertion an account of our route will furnish abundant proof. We reached Dover at about seven in the evening of the (in my eyes) ever memorable 10th April. The thoughts of what we all suffered on that day can never be banished one instant from my recollection till it shall please God to give us a happy meeting. My constant prayers are that we may be enabled to support this dreadful separation with fortitude, but I dare not trust myself with the subject; my heart seems to melt as I write, and tears flow so fast as to compel me to shut one eye while I proceed. It is all in vain, I must leave off. And must weeks, nay months, elapse before I can have the satisfact on of even hearing from you? How can I support this idea? Oh my dear Father! My beloved Mother! For your poor girl's sake, take care of your precious health; do not be unhappy. The Almighty will, I doubt not, preserve us to each other: something tells me that we shall meet again; and you have still two excellent children left to be your comfort. They, I know, will use every effort to keep up your spirits; happy to be so employed. But let me not repine; this trial is not permitted but for all wise purposes. I will now lay down my pen and endeavour to acquire a calmer set of ideas, for I must either write with fortitude or not at all. Adieu for a little while, I will try to take some refreshment and then resume my pen.

Half-past 4 P.M.—In vain I strive, the thoughts of home still prevail and totally preclude every other consideration. I know no better method of chasing these intruders than by proceeding with the narrative of our journey ; *allons donc.* We embarked at Dover for Calais on the 11th at 5 P.M. and had a most delightful passage of just three hours from port to port. I wished for a little sea sickness, but either the wind was not high enough, or I became too good a sailor, to expect benefit this way, for I remained perfectly well. I assure you that there is a deal of ceremony used here now. On coming within gunshot of the Fort, we hoisted a French flag and were permitted to sail up to the quay. We met the other packet coming out, which accounts for my not writing by that mail. I have neglected to mention that Mr. B—, the young gentleman whom Captain Mills recommended as a travelling companion, joined us before we left England. His appearance is by no means prepossessing : he seems a dissipated character and more calculated to shine in convivial parties than to render himself agreeable in the common routine of society ; whether this opinion be just or not time will discover. On landing we were all drawn up together and ordered to the Custom House, where we gave in our names, occupations, etc. ; they marched us about half a mile further to wait upon the Governor in order that he might put, any questions he chose to us. His Lordship not being visible we were forced to arm ourselves with patience and proceed to his Commissary, where we found it a mere matter of form, they asking us but what was known before. However, I assure you, we thought more than we dared to express on the occasion. Only imagine how disagreeable to be dragged about in such a manner immediately after a sea voyage instead of reposing ourselves. After all was settled, we took places in the Diligence for next day: then called on Mons. Pigault de l'Epinoye, to whom you remember I had been formally introduced. He received us with his usual kindness and hospitality. This gentleman is descended in a direct line from one of the six brave Citizens of Calais, who so nobly offered themselves as victims to save their beloved country from the barbarous sentence pronounced against it by our third Edward. He is much esteemed by his countrymen on this account.

This being my fourth visit to Calais, I must, of course, have formerly described everything worth notice there, so shall merely say we set out from thence on the 12th instant at 8 A.M. and reached Boulogne about noon. The sight of this place brought to my mind many pleasant recollections of the social hours passed there. I called on several friends, and was much urged to prolong my stay among them, but that, you know, was impossible. Indeed far rather would I, had time permitted, have taken one turn round the ramparts, to enjoy the melancholy satisfaction of once again beholding the white cliffs of my dear native land so frequently viewed from thence.

You must expect me to make frequent omissions and mistakes, for two men have just placed themselves under my windows with a humstrum; and indeed there is constantly some noise or other throughout the day or evening; sometimes two or three dancing bears; and a few hours ago they exhibited a poor little porcupine. I pitied the miserable animal from my heart. What can these unhappy creatures have done to merit being so tormented? (Now by way of parenthesis, I could almost wish that a London mob had possession of the two musicians, as possibly the discipline of a horse pond might be of use in teaching them for the future better employment on Sunday evenings)—but to proceed. We left Boulogne (a place I shall ever admire and perhaps regret), and about ten at night reached Montreiul, from whence we departed at three on Tuesday morning, dined at Abbeville, and by eight in the evening were set down at the same inn, where, you remember, we stopped when travelling this road before, but were hurried away before we had scarcely tasted a morsel, under the pretence of the Diligence being ready, and afterwards detained in the yard an hour, nor did our hostess in any respect deviate from her former character as you shall hear. As a lady in company and myself were greatly fatigued we chose tea, but, none being procurable there, were forced to use our own; the rest sat down to supper, which I had predetermined to avoid doing. Before they had a quarter finished, in came the woman; never did I behold such a horrible looking great creature. "Well," said she, "the coach is ready," and, on being asked if she wanted to get rid of us, replied that it was equal to her whether we went or stayed provided she was paid for her suppers! At last when compelled to relinquish her claim on that score from the lady and me she insisted on being allowed twenty-four *sous* for the hot water: this we complied with to comply, our hospitable country-woman (tell it not in Gath I blushed to acknowledge the claim) but persisted in remaining till on being summoned by the driver, nearly an hour afterwards, we set off and travelled sixty miles, without alighting, to Chantilly, where is a famous palace belonging to the Prince of Conde, but to my great mortification I was, through weariness, obliged to remain in the house while the rest of the party went to see it. Well, never mind, you can read better descriptions of it than mine would have been. From thence we proceeded to St. Denis, where I was fortunate enough to obtain a cursory view of the ancient abbey—a most magnificent structure, the burying-place of the kings of France. Such scenes naturally induce reflections on the vanity of all human grandeur and lead to a melancholy, rather soothing than otherwise, to minds wearied by exertion or irritated by disappointment. Having, however, little leisure to indulge in these reveries, we passed on to the Library, where, among other trophies, is deposited the sword of our illustrious Talbot; a pang shot across my heart at the exulting manner in which it was exhibited; in short, I felt, as an Englishwoman, a more severe degree of mortification than this memento of an event, so long gone by, seemed calculated to produce. The sacred relics were next displayed, amongst which are an eye of Thomas the Apostle, the shoulder blade of I forget what saint, and a small phial of the Virgin Mary's milk. At the sight of these absurdities I silently blessed God that my religious instruction had not been blended with such cunningly devised fables. If all the gems they showed us were genuine, the Treasury must be immensely rich for many of the shrine's were covered with them. We reached Paris about eight on Wednesday; and most dreadfully fatigued was I; nor will that appear strange when one considers that, for the last sixty miles, the carriage went as fast as eight horses could draw it over a rough strong pavement, never stopping but to change horses, and at St. Denis to repair a wheel. As the post went off next morning, I could not recover myself sufficiently to write by it; but now feel quite strong again; and, having brought you to Paris, may venture to take a little repose as it is past eleven.

19th, 7 A.M.—I have arisen thus early on purpose to finish my letter (which must be in the office before ten). I find little alteration in the place; the people behave as politely as if there were no war or even dispute between us. This, you know, is not the region of politics, therefore little can be mentioned under this head. I could communicate some observations, but as, perhaps, this may be inspected, judge it more prudent to suppress them. A variety of circumstances has contributed to detain us here longer than we intended. And I am fearful we shall not leave Paris before Thursday; however, this will be the only letter

I shall write until I can give you intelligence of our safe arrival at Marseilles, which will, I suppose, be in a fortnight. From thence to Leghorn we may coast in a *feluca*. So if you write by the mail of the 29th, addressed to me at the Post Office, Leghorn, your letter will be sure to reach me there. I have a thousand things more to say, but must reserve them for my next, for if I miss the post, it will, I am sure, make you very uneasy. God bless you.

Yours, etc., etc.

LETTER II.

Paris, 24th April, 1779.

BEING detained for want of our passports, I find it necessary for my comfort to hold the only communication now in my power with you. Last night we were at the Colissée, a place resembling our Ranelagh ; there were some brilliant fire-works to be exhibited, and as it is the custom for ladies to stand upon chairs to see them, a gentleman of our party, having placed us with our backs against a box, went to procure some. During his absence the Queen entered the box attended by the Duchess D'Alençon and several other ladies. I had seen her Majesty before at Versailles and thought her at that time very handsome, but had no idea how much better she would look by candlelight. She is delicately fair and has certainly the sweetest blue eyes that were ever seen, but there is a little redness, a kind of tendency to inflammation about them, and she is likewise slightly marked with smallpox ; both which trifling blemishes were then imperceptible and she appeared perfectly beautiful. On entering the box she sat down and pressed the Duchess to sit also, which the latter in terms of great respect declining, the Queen, in a tone of kindness that it is impossible to forget, said "Then you will oblige me to stand," rising as she spoke. The Duchess then complied and they conversed together very agreeably during their stay. Her Majesty seemed highly gratified by the entertainment and expressed her approbation, in what I could not help thinking rather too familiar a way for a person of her exalted rank, frequently exclaiming aloud, "Ah, Mon Dieu que c'est charmant ! ah, que c'est joli." The royal party soon retired, and we afterwards walked in the Rotunda than which a more brilliant spectacle can scarcely be imagined. The ladies were all splendidly dressed, and their heads adorned with feathers in greater profusion and far more lofty than is customary with us. But enough of this. I must now turn to a very different subject, having hitherto neglected to inform you of a singular conversation (and its result) which passed in the Diligence as we came to this place. We had among the passengers a Mr. H—, an English Jew, and two brothers named A—f, diamond merchants, who were just returning to their native country after a long residence in London. The former had left Paris some years and resided in a provincial town. Speaking of this circumstance, he observed that his principal reason for quitting the capital was his dread of assassination, to which he thought it probable his religion might render him more liable than other inhabitants, although he admitted that he had no proof that persons of his persuasion were among the more frequent victims. This statement, of course, excited both surprise and curiosity in us, who were foreigners, and the elder Mr. A—f, evidently mortified at such discourse and doubting a representation of facts from so prejudiced a quarter and about which it had not fallen in his way to inquire, stoutly denied the charge ; but the Jew would not give up his point. He said that in certain parts of the city, where there were many houses of ill-fame, it was but too common to rob and murder those who were inveigled into them and afterwards throw their bodies into the Seine ; when taken ou, they were conveyed to the Petit Châtelet to be buried, and that they who would ever take the trouble to visit that place would find that, out of the numbers desposited there, were very few (as reported) merely drowned persons, but evidently such as died by violence. This conversation ended (as that of man frequently does) by a wager between the parties, both of whom agreed to refer the matter to Mr. F—.

The Jew was to lose if, in one week, seven bodies under suspicious circumstances should not be exposed at the Petit Châtelet. I thought this a monstrous supposition, for though I had often heard of people being drowned in the Seine, and the explicit detail of Mr. H—led me to fear that the manner in which they met their fate was too truly described, yet I could not believe the number of victims to be so great. The result of Mr. F—'s researches has unhappily placed the fact beyond doubt. Within the last seven days ten miserable wretches have been exposed, who had marks of violence on their bodies, and of these there were two dreadfully mangled. But I will say no more on this shocking subject than merely to observe, that there must be either some radical defect in the police or a degree of ferocity in the people not to be repressed by the severe penal laws which, in other countries, are found adequate to the purpose. The slight degree of feeling expresed by the lower order in speaking of such things, even when pressed on their senses, evinces a hardness of heart approaching to absolute insensibility that, to me, seems quite revolting. I myself asked a young woman, who had been peeping through the gate at the Petit Châtelet, what was to be seen there? "Oh," replied she, with great apparent indifference, "seulement quelques bras et jambres" (only some arms and legs). I have wedden myself into a train of most uncomfortable thoughts, so lest I infect you with the gloomy ideas that fill my mind, the wisest way will be to say adieu ! shall no w soon be out of Paris.

Yours etc.

LETTER III.

Paris, 27th April, 1779.

MY DEAR SISTER,—As I do not propose sending this before Monday, I shall have full time to write every particular. I date once more from this sink of impurity, contrary to my expectation. We have been detained thus long that the Lieutenant d' Police might have time to make the necessary enquiries about us, but have at last obtained our passports, and, thank heaven, shall soon breathe a purer air. From the first place we stop at I purpose giving you a further account of our accommodations in the superb and elegant city of Paris, famous throughout the world for its superiority over all others, especially in the points of cleanliness and delicacy. I assure you that, so long as I before resided in France, I never till now formed an adequate idea of it but adieu for the present. I am going to drink tea. How do you think I make it? Why in an earthen pot an inch thick at the least, which serves the double purpose of tea kettle and teapot, so it is all boiled together and makes a most curious mess.

AUXERRE EN BURGOYNE.

130 Miles de Paris.

When I wrote the above I was in a great rage and not without reason, pent up as we were in a street scarce wide enough to admit the light; our chamber paved with tiles, which must never have been wetted, nor even rubbed, since the building of the house; add to this two *commodités* in the same state, on the stairs, and you will not wonder that my constitution was not proof against the shock; the very air I breathed seem pestilential. However, thank God, I escaped with one of my feverettes of four days' continuance. When I began this letter I was but just recovering; no creature to do the least thing for me in the way that I had been accustomed to; obliged to prepare for my departure the next morning though scarcely able to crawl; and, to crown the whole, a most extravagant bill for being poisoned with dirt. Well, we set off, another fresh country air soon restored me to myself: but I have not told you how we travel.

We found the route totally different from what we expected, and that we must be positively under the necessity of going by land to Chalons sur Soane, which is three hundred miles from Paris. Now, as we could get no remittances till our arrival at Leghorn, it did not suit us to take the Diligence, so after mature deliberation we determined on purchasing two horses and an old single horse chaise; but how to avoid being cheated was the question, for Mr. Fay did not care to depend on his own judgment in horseflesh. He made enquiry and found that there were many Englishmen employed in the stables of noblemen here; so, putting a good face on the matter, he went boldly to the Duc de Chartres' Castle and scraped an acquaintance with his head groom, who was very proud to see a countryman and immediately, on being told the affair, offered his assistance. Accordingly, they went next day to the cattle fair, where he pitched on an excellent draught horse, only a little touched in the wind, on which account he procured him for six guineas, so there cannot be much loss by him, even if he turns out amiss. But I dare say he will prove a most useful beast, for he has drawn Mr. B—r and myself in our chaise (which by the bye we bought for seven guineas) at the rate of thirty-five miles a day and does not seem in the least fatigued, though we had a heavy trunk at our back. So much for Azor; now for his helpmate Zemin. In the course of conversation with his new friend, Mr. Fay found that there was a very pretty mar› in the Duc du Lausanne's stables, which had been intended for the course but would not bear training, so he agreed to give eight guineas for her. Mr. B—was to ride her next week to a horserace in the Bois de Boulogne and we were to accompany him in a postchaise. But alas! poor man, it was an unfortunate attempt. It seems he had never been used to riding and was ashamed to own it (one of the weaknesses to which I really believe men are most invariably subject), so, wishing to pass for an excellent horseman, he mounted with pretended courage, but through actual fear reined her in so tight that Miss, knowing the weakness of her rider, reared up on her hind legs, threw him first and then fell backward over him. We thought, by the violence of the fall, that he must have been killed, but he came off with a few bruises; we had him bled immediately, put him to bed and left him in good hands till our return. Mr. Fay mounted Zemin and we proceeded to the course, where we were very agreeably entertained, only it grieved me to see so many beautiful English horses galloping about; I could hardly believe myself in France, for all the gentlemen were dressed after our manner. The Count D'Artois might very well have been taken for a jockey in his buckskin breeches and round hat. The bets were chiefly between him and the Duc de Chartres; the horses were all ridden by Englishmen; as to our little mare she could have fain been amongst them, but she had now a rider who knew how to manage her and is punished for her audacity; for Mr. B— has not the courage to mount her again and she is forced to carry Mr. Fay with a portmanteau of twenty pounds' weight. You will wonder at my temerity when I acknowledge having myself ventured to mount Zemin, after Mr. B—'s accident. I first, however, saw her tried by several persons, and, wishing to be able to vary the exercise by riding now

---

Duc de Lauyun?

and then during our journey, was induced to make the attempt. She performed twice very well; but on the third day, an umbrella being snapped close to her nose, just as I was going to set off, she began to rear, on which I instinctively abandoned both whip and reins, and, throwing my whole weight forward, clapped her round the neck with all my might: this sudden manœuvre fortunately kept her down; I seized the critical moment and alighted in safety with no other injury than a little fright and the consciousness of looking rather foolish. Nor has she ever been guilty of the like towards anyone; so that my character for horsemanship is completely established. We have been certainly lucky in our purchases: the horses perform well, and the chaise, without being particularly uneasy, seems very strong, I am told they will bring a good price in the South, but you shall hear.

I have nothing particular to say of the country; perhaps it may be national prejudice from which no person is entirely free, but, notwithstanding all their boasting, I do not think it equals my own dear England. It must be allowed that the present season is not the most favourable for making observations, for they cut the vines to the stumps in the winter, and, as they are not yet much sprouted, one sees nothing but a parcel of sticks in the manner of our hop poles, but not above thirty inches high, which gives an air of barrenness to the prospect. I do not know what my mother would do here, as she is not fond of wine; for there is nothing else to drink. For my own part, I believe I may answer for my companions, I cannot say that I find any great hardship in being obliged to put up with tolerable Burgundy at about fourpence a litre; it is not at all heady, so no creature thinks of drinking it with water. A pint every meal is the allowance of each. We have all necessaries with us, such as tea, sugar, bread, butter, corn for the horses, etc., so we have little to do with the inns, except at night, when we provide ourselves with meat for the next day. As to breakfast and dinner we fix on a place where there is water at hand and then sit down under the shade of a tree and make a fire, while the horses graze comfortably and eat their corn. Ask my dear father if he does not think this a good plan? At least we find it pleasant, and much more to our taste than spending time as well as money in the wretched public houses we have hitherto met with. I wish we were hardy enough to make the grass our pillows; but that is impossible, so we must submit to be disgusted and pillaged once a day. You may remember my remarking that I was afraid we should suffer during our journey, for the fineness of the spring which has proved to be the case. The weather has been excessively boisterous for the last fortnight, with much rain, than which nothing could be more disagreeable on a journey, especially conducted on such a plan as ours. We were, on account of the weather, obliged, to stop at Fontainbleau by which means we saw the palace and gardens and were almost wet through for our pains. It is an immense place; the chapel has been beautified, but the paintings are much injured by time. There is an elegant theatre which I was much pleased with. The apartments of the royal family are truly superb. We were shown the council chamber where the last peace was signed, and I, as an Englishwoman, beheld it with *great pleasure* you may be sure. We saw likewise the great gallery of *Stags*, famous for containing above a hundred stags' heads all arranged in order with an account when they were killed and by whom, and infamous (at least in my opinion) as being the place where Christina, Queen of Sweden, caused Monaldeschi, her chief chamberlain, to be beheaded, if not absolutely in her presence, at least while she remained in an adjoining room. I cannot bear that woman. She abdicated her crown from sheer vanity but retained that passion for despotism which showed what kind of feelings she had cherished while seated on the throne. I think that in her the faults of either sex were blended, to form a character, which, without possessing the firmness of a man or the gentleness of a woman, was destitute of virtues expected in both. Christina may have been an accomplished female; but she can never be called great, even by her admirers.

The gardens of Fontainbleau are all in the old-fashioned gingerbread style, ornamented with box in a thousand fantastical shapes. The Swiss, who showed us the Palace, was very thankful for a shilling, which is more than any person in the same situation would be in England for twice as much. The forest of Fontainbleau is thirty miles across, and nobody can hunt there without the King's permission; he comes here every season. We found the roads very heavy, but Azor was strong enough to go through them; however, we have given him a day's rest, and after dinner shall set off jeher like.

Now don't you envy all this pleasure? I assure you I should be very glad to go all the way in the same manner, for we travel without fatigue and the way of living suits me; for you know I always preferred wine to beer, but I would not have you to imagine that I can shake off all thoughts from home; they return but too frequently, and I really believe now that my illness at Paris was brought on principally by uneasiness of mind, but I find myself unequal to this subject. I must make a resolution never to enter upon it; for what service can it do to either of us to be continually recalling unpleasant ideas, especially when I have need of every possible consolation to support me in the arduous task which Providence has called upon me to undertake?

I have now literally exhausted my paper and must therefore leave you to imagine everything my heart says to all, and how truly,

LETTER IV.

Leghorn, 17th June, 1779.

MY DEAR SISTER,—I suppose you have long been uneasy at my silence, but indeed it is not in my power to write sooner. In my last I gave you reason to imagine we should arrive here in less than three weeks by way of Marseilles; but after we reached Lyons we were informed that this would prove a very uncertain and dangerous method, as between the English and French scarcely any vessel can pass free; therefore after mature deliberation, we determined, as we had still our carriage and horses, to push our way boldly through Savoy and cross the Alps to Italy. We stopped several days at Lyons, which, as you and all the world know, has long been famous for its incomparable silks and velvets. I think it ought to be so for its asparagus, which is the finest I ever tasted, and remarkably cheap. Being a vegetable I am very fond of, and having at all times found it beneficial to my constitution, I wished to eat it freely; but was almost disgusted by the manner in which it was constantly brought to table at the inn, covered with a thick sauce composed of eggs, butter, oil and vinegar. Having in vain remonstrated against this cookery, I at length insisted on seeing the cook himself, and when he made his appearance, arrayed as is customary in a white waistcoat, cap and apron with a meagre face almost as sharp as the large knife he held in his hand, I calmly represented to him that the sauce he had sent up wholly disagreed with my stomach and requested to have the asparagus simply boiled with melted butter. The poor man looked much distressed. "What, without oil?" "Yes." "Without eggs?" "Certainly." This answer completed his misery. "Ah ! Madame," exclaimed he, with clasped hands and uplifted eyes, "de grace un peu de vinaigre." Madame was inexorable and the shrug of contemptuous pity with which he retreated was ludicrous beyond expression.

On arriving near the Alps, it appeared that I had formed a very erroneous idea of the route, having always supposed that we had only one mountain to pass and that the rest of the way was level ground ; instead of which, when we came to Pont de Beauvoisin (50 miles from Lyons and the barrier between France and Savoy), we heard the agreeable news that we had a hundred and twelve miles to travel through a chain of mountains to the great Mont Cenis.

You may imagine how uncomfortable this information made us all : with what long faces we gazed on each other, debating how the journey was to be performed ; but being happily very courageous, I made light of all difficulties, and whenever there was a hill mounted Zemin, while the two gentlemen took it by turns to lead me as I had not a proper side-saddle, so poor Azor made shift to drag the chaise up pretty well and, in the descent, we made him pay for the indulgence. I forgot to mention that they were very particular about our passports at this barrier, and detained us while the Governor examined them minutely, though justice compels me to acknowledge that, in general, we were treated with very great politeness through France. No one ever attempted to insult us, which I fear would not be the case were these French people to travel in England. I wish I could say as much for their honesty ; but I must confess that they are miserably deficient : however my being acquainted with the language saved us from flagrant imposition.

Our method was this : we always, if possible, contrived to stop at night in a large town (as to dinner we easily managed that you know how), but never did we suffer the horses to be put into the stable till I had fixed the price of everything ; for they generally ask four times as much for any article as it is worth. If I found there was no bringing them to reason, we left the house. In particular at Chalons sur Saone, the first inn we stopped at, the woman had the conscience to ask half a crown for each bed. You may suppose we did not take up our bed there, but drove on to another very good house, where they showed us two rooms with excellent beds in them at the rate of four *sous* for as many as we wanted. So for once I committed an act of extravagance by paying for the whole; or we might perhaps have been disturbed in the night by strangers coming to take possession of those left vacant. For they are not very nice about such matters in France. I have seen rooms with six beds in them more than once during our route. I only mention the difference in price by way of showing what people may gain by chosing their houses, for we were really better accommodated at less than one-fourth of what we must have paid at the other house. Speaking of Chalons reminds one of a very unpleasant circumstance that occurred to us at the following stage. Mr. Fay had most unwisely, and contrary to my earnest entreaty, pinned our passports to the book of roads which he usually carried with him on horseback, and, as might be expected, they in a short time worked themselves loose, and we, on our arrival at the end of the next day's journey, were alarmed with the idea of their being entirely lost and that we should be compelled to return all the way to Paris to procure others happily Mr. Fay went back and found them at a place where we had stopped. I need not tell you what fright and vexation this folly and obstinacy cost us; but I hope it will have a salutary effect for the rest of our journey.

In further proof of my assertion on the subject of honesty, I must relate a little incident which occurred on our way to Lyons. Mr. Fay had changed as many guineas at Paris as he thought would be sufficient to bring us to Chalons, and received by weight twenty-four livres, ten *sous* for each, that is to say, sevenpence half-penny profit; well, the last day but one we finished our current money, but, as we were in a city, doubted not of being able to obtain nearly the value of our guineas. On inquiry we were recommended to a very religious goldsmith, who, by the landlord's account, spent almost all his life in acts of piety. After waiting an hour and-a-half till he returned from Mass, Mr. Fay delivered him a guinea confident of receiving its full value, when behold this conscientious gentleman, after the most minute inspection and weighing it in a pair of sugar scales, generously offered eighteen livres as a fair price, which so enraged Mr. Fay that he immediately left him and went to another shop, where the utmost they would give us was twelve livres. Only think, what wretches! since it was impossible for them to be ignorant of its real value. Mr. Fay declared that he would rather fast all day than submit to become such a dupe. This subjected us to great inconvenience; after discharging the reckoning we had only thirty *sous* remaining, and set out with a sum not sufficient to procure a single refreshment for our poor horses; so that at every inn we were obliged to represent our situation, but found none who had honesty enough to offer us a fair price for our guineas, or the charity to give us even a glass of wine or a morsel of bread. I leave you to guess if our appetites were not pretty keen by the time we arrived at Lyons. I shall never forget how foolishly we looked at each other all day: however a good supper obliterated all grievances, and the next morning we found a way to exchange our guineas for Louis d'Ors on equitable terms. So much for our starving adventure. To proceed on our journey.

On the 20th we reached Lanneberg*, a village at the foot of Mont Cenis, situated in what is called a valley, which, though really so with respect to the mountains that surround

*Lanslebourg.

it, is even with the clouds. I had a tolerable proof of its elevation, for the weather was so sharp, that I could not keep a minute from the fire. By the way I must observe that, having travelled through North Wales, I supposed myself to have acquired a tolerable idea of mountains and their appendages, such as cascades, torrents and apparently air-hung-bridges, etc., but the passage of the Alps set at defiance all competition, and even surpasses whatever the utmost sketch of my imagination could have pourtrayed.

The valley of Lanneberg is itself the most strange wild place you can conceive, in some parts grotesque, in others awfully terrible. The rocks rise round you so fantastically that you might think yourself transported to a place which Nature had made a repository of these stupendeous productions, rather with a view to fixing them hereafter in appropriate situations than of exhibiting them here. But above all the cascades throughout the road are charming beyond description, immense sheets of water are seen sometimes, falling from rock to rock, foaming, fretting, and dashing their spray from side to side; and descending in one grand flow of majestic beauty: in short, they went so far beyond any idea I had formed of such appearances in Nature, that they seemed to communicate new powers of perception to my mind and, if I may so express it, to expand my soul and raise it nearer to its Creator. The passage has been so ably described by various writers, that any formal account I could give you of it would rather waste your time than add to our information. I shall only tell you how I felt and acted, for I know your affection prompts the wish to travel in imagination with the sister you love. Come, then, let us ascend Mont Cenis together. After various deliberations it was concluded that I should go up across a mule as the safest way; both the gentlemen determined on walking, which Mr. Fay knew not to be very difficult, having made the experiment the evening before. I was strictly forbidden to touch the reins, being assured that the animal would guide himself, and that any attempt to direct him could hardly fail to prove fatal. Under this charge judge what I must have felt on my mule, in the very steepest part of the ascent, and when I became fully sensible of the "high and giddy height," all at once thought proper to quit the pathway and with great *sang froid* stalk out upon one of those precipitous projections, where only the foot of a wild goat or chamois ought to tread. What did I not suffer! I durst not touch the rein, durst not even call to the guide for help. Every instant appeared fraught with destruction, it seemed madness to die without an effort to save oneself, yet to make an effort was to invite the fate one dreaded. Happily this dreadful poise between life and death lasted not long; for the sagacious animal, calmly picking its way, fell into the track by a path which no human eye could discern, and the guides gave one great praise for my self-command—a praise I never desire to purchase again by a similar trial. If, however, anything could render a stranger easy in crossing the heights it would be the amazing skill and celerity which these people display. The road winds in a zig-zag direction; and in the most acute, and, of course, in the most dangerous turns they leap from crag to crag, as if they held their lives on lease and might safely run all risks till its term expired. The plain, as it is called, at the top of this mountain is six miles across. As we proceeded, we found "still hills on hills and alps on alps arise," for we continued to be surrounded by snow-topped mountains where reigns frost eternal. The heat of the sun had thawed the passage, so that we met with no inconvenience, but we passed great quantities of ice lodged in the crannies. There is a very large lake on the plain, said to be unfathomable; that I can tell nothing about but that it contains excellent salmon and trout, am well convinced, for we stopped at the inn, according to the laudable custom of all travellers, for the sole purpose of busting it. An inn, say you, at the top of Mont

Cenis! Yes, it is really a fact, not that I envy them their situation, but they are not the only inhabitants: for there are more than twenty farmhouses, where they make most excellent butter and cheese. Every spot around where it is possible for the hand of cultivation to scatter seeds for the use of man is treasured with care and nourished by industry: and you see gardens no bigger than a dining table and fields like a patch of carpet, from time to time, smiling beneath the rugged battlements of rocks like violets peeping in the hedges. Far among the apparently inaccessible heights of this "cloud capt" region, they pointed out to me a Chapel, vulgarly called *Dame de Neige*, and justly have they named her, for eternal snows designate her dwelling; if, however, these simple and sequestered beings can there draw near to God and experience the comfort of religious hope and providential care, this singular edifice has not been reared in vain, to bless such a region of desolation.

When you read an account of the road, it will readily be perceived that my fellow travellers must have found some difficulty in getting the horses over, as the poor beasts were not accustomed to such a rugged path; for you are to understand that the people in the neighbouring villages of Lanneberge and Navulese have no other means of subsistence than carrying passengers over the mountain. It is therefore their interest to render it impossible to any but themselves, so that whole passage of fifteen miles is covered with great pieces of rock which must be clambered over. The guides skip from one piece to another like goats, and go at the rate of five or six miles an hour; but my unfortunate companions could not proceed at this pace, so every ten minutes we had to wait for them. As I was carried down in an armed chair, fastened to poles and slung upon straps, in the manner of our sedans, between two men and in which I soon felt tolerably at my ease, I had the pleasure of seeing them continually, sometimes in the clouds, and at others nothing visible but their heads, which was rather amusing to me, especially as Mr. Fay had affected to make very light of it, and even said "I might walk very well if I chose it," but when we reached the bottom he told a very different tale and stormed violently at his own sufferings. The drollest part of our procession was that of the poor mule which bore our chaise in a kind of machine on its back; and another with the two wheels placed on each side in the oddest way imaginable. A good night's rest put us all into good humour, and we proceeded cheerfully forty miles along a very delightful road for the most part planted with double rows of trees to Turin, where we remained three days and were much amused; but having crossed the mountain, I must allow myself and you a little rest.

20th June.—I was more pleased with the Palace at Turin than any other I have met with during our journey, not for its external appearance certainly, for that is unpromising, but the inside simply atones for the deficiency. The rooms are all in long ranges, opening into each other by doors, which, by folding within the panels, become invisible. The furniture is beyond description rich and elegant, but the best part of every finely decorated house must ever be its paintings, and the Palace seemed to say: "You are already in Italy." Like a true Englishwoman, however, I looked more, I believe, at a picture of our Charles the First and afterwards at one by Vandyke of that unfortunate monarch's three children than at any other in the collection. The face of the king is exquisitely done, but his dress struck me as too fine, and withal so stiff, that I could not admire it. Poor Charles! We are tempted to forget the errors of the Prince in considering the amiable qualities and long sufferings of the man; nor is it possible to contemplate the benevolent melancholy of his countenance and credit every accusation of his enemies. I looked in his mild penetrating eyes till my own were suffused with tears. As to his children, they are the sweetest creatures I ever beheld; and to see them thus was perhaps the more pleasant from the consciousness that of its being the only period wherein they could communicate that sensation to a reflecting mind. There was no tracing the selfish and, eventually, callous libertine in Charles; nor the tyrant and bigot in James; all seems playful, graceful and dignified in James; all seems playful grace or dignified gentleness; and the painter appears to have given a kind of royal polish to the beauty (certainly far beyond nature) which he had so happily depicted in those unfortunate children. Among what I deemed the most curious portraits were those of Martin Luther and his wife. I have frequently meditated on this great character and always felt myself so much obliged to him (especially since my residence in a Catholic country) that I confess I was disappointed to see him a homely and rather vulgar looking man. I cannot believe that this is a good likeness; at least the one I saw of him in the abbey of St. Bertin at St. Omers left a very indifferent impression on my mind. The reformer might not be handsome in the common acceptation of the word, but surely penetration, courage and firmness must have stamped their expression on his features. Here is a terrible representation of another great man, though in my opinion deficient in the first mentioned quality (Sir Thomas Moore)—of his head rather, for it appears just severed from the body; his daughter has pointed at the horrible spectacle; and her complexion is so exactly what it should be that the whole scene appears natural and you feel too much for her even to offer her restoratives to life and misery. I would not live in the same room with such a picture for the world; it would be worse than the cave of Trophonious.

I was doomed to experience another disappointment in what is affirmed to be a faithful portrait of Petrarch's Laura, which I had fancied was the Venus of Apelles, an assemblage of all that was lovely and graceful in woman. You remember my saying that it was worth all the pains I took in learning Italian to read his sonnets in praise of this idolized being. So no wonder that I ran eagerly to seize on the features that had inspired such verses and awakened such tender constancy as Petrarch displayed. Judge then how disagreeably I was surprised at seeing a little red-haired, formal looking old maidish thing, no more like the beauty in "my mind's eye" than I do Hercules. Petrarch too was as ugly as needs be. Well, well, they are not the only couple seen to most advantage in their poetic dress. What further I have to say about the Palace must be very concise. I cannot help informing you though that we saw the King of Sardinia at mass with his whole family, but none of them seem to be remarkable for beauty. Though not esteemed rich, yet he lives in great splendour; the furniture of his state bed chamber even to the frames of the chairs is all of massive silver.

The theatre is a vast building and so magnificent in every respect that nothing you have seen can give you any idea of it; the stage is so extensive, that when they want to exhibit battles, triumphant entries, or any grand show they have room enough to produce the finest effect and really seem to transport you to the scene they would represent. It is not uncommon to have fifty or sixty horses at a time upon this stage with triumphal cars, thrones, etc., etc. The King's box is consistent with his superb Palace; it is as large as a handsome parlour and lined throughout with mirrors, which have a beautiful effect, as they reflect the stage and thus double the display of its grand processions, etc. All the boxes in this theatre are neat and commodious, furnished with chairs and curtains so that if the party chose to be retired they are at full liberty; and, as coffee and other refreshments are served, they frequently pay little attention to the stage, except when some celebrated performer or grand spectacle exercised their curiosity. There is a smaller theatre which opens when this is closed, but I did not see it. I visited the royal gardens but thought them very uninteresting, as all appear after those that surround the seats of our English nobility and gentry; and on running through another palace or academy and various other places nothing struck me as sufficiently novel to merit your attention. I have written such an intolerably long letter that I must conclude for the present, though I mean to bring you on my journey to-morrow, as I have not yet told you half that is in my mind; but there is such an uncertainty in my present movements that it is desirable not to lose a single day in forwarding a letter. Believe me, however and wherever I may be

Most affectionately yours,

E. F.

Leghorn, 28th June.

I RESUME my journal of yesterday which I shall enclose in this. I am still waiting a summons for departure, and anxious to say all I can to my dear friends before what may probably be a long adieu. From Turin we set out on the 20th ultimo to Genoa, a distance of 130 miles, and now I own my courage began to fail; for having been some days ill, I grew so much worse, from the motion of the chaise, that we were obliged to stop and get Mr. Fay s horse ready for me to ride, which was a great ease to me; but notwithstanding this relief, on the second evening I was seized with every symptom of fever, and that of the most violent kind. "Well," thought I, "it is all over with me for a week at least," but, thank God, I was mistaken, for at two in the morning, I fell into the most profuse perspiration I ever experienced, which, though it exceedingly weakened me, yet considerably abated the disorder, and although I felt ill, dispirited, and every way unfit to travel, yet I made a sad shift to pursue my journey.

Unfortunately, in coming out of Alessandria, the place where I had been so ill, we had a wide river to ford, and there was no way for poor miserable me to get over, but by Mr. Fay's taking me before him across the mare which was tolerably well accomplished. When he had landed me safe he went back, and with great difficulty whipped the old horse through ; he was up to the girth in water, and I expected every moment he would break the chain to pieces, for he frequently attempted to lie down. When we had overcome this difficulty, we continued in tolerable spirits, until our arrival next day at the Berchetta,* an Appenine mountain by the side of which Mont Cenis would appear contemptible ; it is nearly twenty miles over without any plain at the top, so that no sooner do you reach its summit than you turn short and descend immediately. Had the weather proved fine, the prospect from this prodigious eminence must have been glorious ; but so thick a fog enveloped us, that we could not distinguish anything of five yards distance and the cold was as piercing as with us in January. Never shall I forget the sense of wearisome, overbracing desolateness, which seemed to bow down my body and mind at this juncture. I felt a kind of dejection unknown before through all my peregrinations, and which doubtless tended to increase the unusual fears that operated on my mind when we arrived at the end of this day's journey. It was nearly dark ; the inn was little better than a large barn or hovel ; and the men we found in it so completely like all that we conceive of banditti and assassins, that every horrible story I had heard or read of instantly come into my head, and I perceived that the thoughts of my companions were occupied in the same painful way. Our looks were the only medium of communication we could use, for we were afraid of speaking lest we should accelerate the fate we dreaded. Everything around us combined

*Borchetta.

to keep alive suspicion and strengthen fear; we were at a distance from every human habitation: various whisperings and looks directed towards us continually passed among the men, and we fancied that they were endeavouring to find whether we had any concealed arms. When we retired for the night, worn out as we were, not one dared to sleep, and surely never night appeared so long. With the earliest dawn we departed, and as the people saw us set out, without offering us any injury, we are now persuaded that we wronged them; but yet the impression made upon our minds will not easily be effaced. We feel as if we had escaped some projected mischief.

We arrived early at Genoa, a grand but gloomy, disagreeable city, owing to the houses being very high and the streets so narrow that you might almost shake hands across them out of the window. It abounds with magnificent churches and palaces, principally built of the most beautiful marble; at least they are faced and ornamented with it. Their roofs flat, and rendered very agreeable gardens by flowering shrubs, little arbours covered with wood, vine and jessamine, elegant verandahs, awnings, etc. In these the ladies wander from morning to night. As far as I can hear or see, they are more remarkable for pride than anything else. Their dress costly but heavy and unbecoming, except so far as they manage their veils, which are so contrived as to give very good play to a pair of fine eyes. They wear rouge; but apply it better than the French ladies, who may be said to plaster rather than to paint; when the best, however, is made of this practice it is still a very hateful one in my opinion.

I went to view the Palaces of Daria, Doraggio and Palavicini, where are many fine pictures and statues; but the rooms are so large and so many of them are only half furnished, that they had on the whole an uncomfortable look. I was much pleased with several of the churches. The Cathedral is completely lined with marble, but I was attracted more by the Jesuits' Church on account of the painting; though, I have neither the health nor the spirit to enter into a particular description of them. The Assumption of the Virgin by Guido is a most delightful performance to my taste. I always admire his pictures, but being simply an admirer without knowledge on the subject, I seldom hazard a remark as to the manner in which a piece is executed.

The theatre here is large but not to be compared with that of Turin, the gardens are everywhere in the same style, all neat and trim, like a desert island in a pastry cook's shop, with garnish and fippery enough to please a Dutchman. There are many admirable chateaux in this city, but its chief boast, in my opinion, consists in being the birthplace of Columbus, who was undoubtedly a great man, and, from his talents, firmness, wisdom and misfortune, entitled to inspire admiration and pity. I often thought of him as I passed these streets and was ready to exclaim "You are not worthy of such a citizen." The velvets, goldwork and artificial flowers manufactured here are said to be unrivalled; but I have made no purchases for obvious reasons.

We saw a very grand procession on Corpus Christi day at which the Doge assisted, and all the principal nobility, clothed in their most magnificent habiliments, and each carrying a lighted taper. Several images also, adorned with jewels (as I was informed) to an incredible amount, were borne along to grace the spectacle. It is to be lamented that this noble city should disgrace itself by the encouragement given to assassination; for a man, after committing half a score of murders, has only to take a boat, which nobody prevents him from doing, and claim the protection of any foreign ship, which none dares to refuse, and there he remains in safety. Mr. Fay saw five of these wretches on board one vessel.

What you have heard of the custom of married women in

Italy being attended by their *cicisibeos* is perfectly true They speak of it with all the indifference imaginable. Surely, after all that has been sald the usage must be an indiscreet one if anything can be called so which tends to separate the affections of husband and wife, and *that* the constant attendance of another man must be likely to effect. Altogether it is a vile fashion, make the best of it, and I heartily hope never to see such a mode adopted in Old England.

We sold our horses at Genoa, for about three guineas profit and no more, as Mr. Fay embraced the first offer that was made him. You who know me will be well aware I could not part with these mute but faithful companions without a sigh. Far different were my sensations on bidding adieu to our fellow traveller Mr. B—r, who left us on our arrival at this place. My first impression of his character was but too just, and every day's experience more fully displayed a mind estranged from all that was praiseworthy and prone to every vice. He professed himself an atheist, and I am persuaded led the life of one. It is fortunate that his manners were as disgusting as his principles were wicked and that he constantly reminded one of that expression of the Psalmist "The *fool* hath said in his heart there is no God," as the comment "he was but a fool" rose to remembrance at the same moment.

We took our passage in a *feluca* from Genoa and arrived here in thirty-three hours. My first message was to the Post Office, where was only one letter for me, dated May 10th ; I am impatient for more, being daily in expectation of sailing, and it would be mortifying to leave any behind. I must now conclude ; believe me.

Ever most affectionately yours,

E. F.

P.S.—I open this to say our letters and remittances have arrived ; ten thousand thanks for your kindness, but I have not time to add another word.

LETTER V.

On Board *the Hellespont.*

OUTER MOLE, LEGHORN.

July 22nd, 1779.

MY DEAR FRIENDS,—You may perceive from this date that I have quitted Leghorn, but have I come to take up my quarters *here*, cannot be explained till the relation of some particulars which I must first notice in order to proceed regularly with my journal.

Our letter of introduction from Mr. Baretto, of London, to his brother, the King of Sardinia's Consul at Leghorn, procured us the kindest attentions from that gentleman and his family, indeed they were so friendly to us in every respect, that I soon felt all the ease of old acquaintance in their society and shall ever remember them with sentiments of the most cordial esteem. Through this kind family I saw whatever was worthy of note in Leghorn and its environs, but my increasing anxiety as to our journey took from me all power of investigation. When one sees merely with the eye and the wandering mind is travelling to the friends far left behind, or forward to the unknown clime whither its destiny points, few recollections of places and things remain on it. But how different will be its recognition of persons. When these have softened by an anxious hour by kindness, or relieved its irksomeness by smiles and gaiety, the heart will register their action and their image, and gratitude engrave their names on the tablet of remembrance. What a romantic flight. Methinks I hear you exclaim "But this is the land of poesy."

Surely I may be permitted to enter a little of its spirit. I shall never forget that Leghorn contains the Barettos and Francos. The latter are eminent merchants: the house has been established over a century. The eldest of the present family is above eighty years of age—a most venerable and agreeable old man, with more of active kindness and benevolent politeness than I ever met in one so advanced in life and who has seen so much of the world. He not only showed us every attention during our stay, but has given us a letter recommending us in the strongest terms to a Mr. Abraham, of Grand Cairo, which, should Mr. Baldwin (the East India Company's resident) be absent when we arrive there, may prove useful. At all events, we are equally indebted to Mr. Franco's friendly intentions.

We have often boasted of the superiority of the British flag, but alas! poor old England! her flag is here humbled in the dust. We have several ships in the Mole, but if one dare to venture out, so many French privateers are hovering round, that she must be taken in a few hours. I pity the poor captains from my heart, but the person for whom I feel most interested is a Captain Les—r, of the *Hellespont* (Mr. F—'s relation). I cannot express half what I owe to his civility. From the moment he knew of my probable connection with his family, he has uniformly shown us every possible attention. His situation is very disagreeable, to be forced either to abandon so fine a ship, or incur almost a certainty of being taken prisoner in her, as she must soon venture out; for she has already eaten her head-off by lying here a whole twelvemonth on expense, as such is the deplorable state of our commerce in the Mediterranean, that no one will now underwrite an English ship at any premium. I think the number lying here is seven, and believe they intend soon to make a bold push together; but it will all be in vain; they never can get through the Straits of Gibraltar unmolested.

At 4 o'clock p.m.

A Hard Gale Blowing.

I told you this morning what reason I had to esteem Captain L. He is now entitled to at least a double portion of my gratitude if estimated by the service done. As there was no likelihood of meeting with an English vessel, we engaged a passage in a Swedish one, called the *Julius*, Captain Norberg, for Alexandria, at £6 each. Cheap enough you will say; and had all in readiness. So last night I quitted the shores of Europe, God knows for how long; His will be done. Captain L., as his ship lay next but one to ours, and we were not to sail till daybreak, offered us his cabin, because, as he very considerately observed, we could not sleep confortably in our own, amid the noise of preparing for sea. I readily complied, well knowing the advantages of his proposal, having already dined several times on board the *Hellespont*, which is kept clean and in good order, equal to the nicest house I ever saw. This morning the *Julius* went out to the Road and we prepared to follow; but just at that time a sudden squall of thunder and lightning, succeeded by a very strong gale of wind; the poor *Julius* was forced to drop anchor, and there she lies, two miles off, pitching (driving piles Captain L. calls it), and has just struck her lower yards. She shipped one cable two hours ago, but the other brought her up. I see her now, and would not exchange cabins for a trifle.

Several vessels have been driven in in distress. One dashed directly against the *Hellespont* and snapped her bowsprit short. We had but just time to secure the poop lantern from the stroke of another. The iron was torn away, so you may guess it blows smartly, but I feel perfectly easy. I am luckily sheltered now, and no one shall persuade me to leave this ship till all is over and the weather settled again. I doubt we shall not be able to sail this day or two for the wind is rising; but so that we arrive, time enough to save our season at Suez, all be well. Tea is waiting, and they are tormenting me to death. Adieu. God bless you all, prays.

Your affectionate,
E. F.

LETTER VI.

Ship Julius at sea, 20th July 1779.

I hope my dear friends will safely receive my letter of the 2nd instant from Leghorn, wherein I mentioned the kindness of Captain L., and our situation in his ship. We remained with him till Sunday evening, when we embarked on the *Julius*, and the following morning sailed with a fair wind; but it changed in less than six hours and came on so strong that we were forced to put back again and cast anchor. The gale lasted till Wednesday evening; however, we made shift to ride it out, though we were continually paying out our cable (as it is called) and expected every moment to be driven on shore.

When the weather moderated, Mr. Franco sent off a letter to Mr. Fay, stating that he had just heard from Mr. Abraham of Grand Cairo, who was about to proceed to Europe with his family by the first ship, therefore to guard us against any future disappointment this kind gentleman enclosed a general letter to the Jewish merchants, Mr. Franco's name being well known throughout the East. Having already several letters of introduction to persons in Grand Cairo, we shall not, I imagine, have occasion to make use of this.

On Thursday, the 8th, we ventured to sail once more and have hitherto gone on pleasantly enough.

Tuesday, 20th July. Since my last date I have been a good deal vexed at an accident, which perhaps will appear very trivial. I had a pair of beautiful pigeons given me at Leghorn which furnished me with great amusement. These pretty little creatures, their wings being cut, ranged at liberty about the ship. At length one of them fell, or, rather, was blown overboard. I saw it a long while struggling for life, and looking towards the vessel as if to implore assistance; yet, notwithstanding my fondness for the poor bird and anxious desire to extricate it from its perilous situation, if such a thing were possible, I could not even wish that a ship, running eight knots an hour, should be hove to and a boat sent out after a pigeon. The widowed mate too only lived three days afterwards, never touching a morsel of food from the time the other disappeared, and uttering at intervals the most plaintive sounds which I could not avoid hearing, my cabin being upon deck. For you must know it is a regulation on board Swedish vessels that the whole ship's company join twice a day in devotional exercises; so Captain Norberg reserved this great cabin for the purpose of assembling them together, or we would willingly have engaged it. So much for my little favourites. I shall now advert to a more cheerful topic.

My voyage has been rendered very interesting and instructive by the conversation of one of our passengers, a Franciscan Friar from Rome, who is going as a Missionary to Jerusalem; and in my opinion no man can be better calculated for the hazardous office he has undertaken. Figure to yourself a man in the prime of life (under forty), full, well made and athletic in his person, and seemingly of a temperament to brave every danger: add to all these advantages a pair of dark eyes beaming with intelligence, and a most venerable auburn beard descending nearly to his girdle, and you cannot fail to pronounce him irresistible. He appears also to possess all the enthusiasm and eloquence necessary for pleading the important cause of Christianity; yet one must regret that so noble a mind should be warped by the belief of such ridiculous superstitions as disgrace the Roman Creed. He became extremely zealous for my conversion, and anxiously forwarded my endeavours after improvement in the Italian language that I might the more readily comprehend the arguments he adduced to effect that desirable purpose. Like other disputants, we used sometimes to contend very fiercely, and one day, on my speaking rather lightly of what he chose to call a miracle of the Catholic Church, he even went so far as to tell me that my mouth spouted forth heresies as water gushes from a fountain.

This morning (the 22nd) at breakfast, he entreated me to give up my coffee as a libation to the Bambino (Child) Jesus, and, on my declining to do so, urged me with the most impressive eloquence to spare only a single cup, which he would immediately pour out in honour of the Blessed Infant. Professing my disbelief in the efficacy of such a sacrifice, I again excused myself from complying with his request; upon which, declaring that he was equally shocked at my wilful incredulity and obstinate heresy, he withdrew to another part of the vessel and I have not seen him since.

23rd A.M. We are now off Alexandria, which makes a fine appearance from the sea on a near approach, but, being built on low ground, is, as the seamen say, "very difficult to hit." We were two days almost abreast of the town. There is a handsome Pharos or lighthouse in the new harbour, and it is in all respects far preferable; but no vessels belonging to Christians can anchor there, so we were forced to go into the old one, of which, however, we escaped the dangers, if any exist.

My acquaintance with the Reverend Father has terminated rather unpleasantly. A little while ago, being on deck together and forgetting our quarrel about the libation, I made a remark on the extreme heat of the weather. "Aye," replied he with a most malignant expression of countenance, such as I could not have thought it possible for a face benign like his to assume, "Aye, you will find it ten thousand times hotter in the devil's house (*nella casa di diavolo*)." I pitied his bigotry and prayed for his conversion to the genuine principle of that religion whose doctrines he professed to teach.

Mr. Brandy, to whom Mr. Fay sent on shore a complimentary letter, came on board to visit us. I rejoice to hear from him that there are two ships at Suez, yet no time must be lost lest we miss the season. This gentleman resides here as Consul for one of the German Courts, and may be of great use to us. We received an invitation to sup with him to-morrow. He has secured a lodging for us, and engaged a Jew and his wife to go with us to Grand Cairo as dragoman (or interpreter) and attendant. Should we proceed by water, which is not yet decided on, Mr. B. will provide a proper boat. I am summoned to an early dinner, immediately after which we shall go ashore with our dragoman, that we may have time to view whatever is remarkable.

24th July. Having mounted our asses,—the use of horses being forbidden to any but Mussalmans,—we sallied forth preceded by a janisary, with his drawn sword, about three miles over a sandy desert, to see Pompey's Pillar, esteemed to be the finest column in the world. This pillar is exceedingly lofty but I have no means of ascertaining its exact height, is composed of three blocks of granite (the pedestal, shaft, and capital each containing one). When we consider the immense weight of the granite, the raising of such masses appears beyond the powers of man. Although quite unadorned, the proportions are so exquisite, that it must strike every beholder with a kind of awe, which softens into melancholy when one reflects that the renowned hero, whose name it bears, was treacherously murdered on this very coast by the boatmen who were conveying him to Alexandria. His wretched wife stood on the vessel he had just left, watching his departure, as we may very naturally suppose, with inexpressible anxiety. What must have been her agonies at the dreadful event! Though this splendid memorial bears the name of Pompey, it is by many supposed to have been erected in memory of the triumph gained over him at the battle of Pharsalia. Leaving more learned heads than mine to settle this disputed point, let us proceed to ancient Alexandria, about a league from the modern town, which presents to the eye an instructive lesson on the instability of all sublunary objects. This once magnificent city, built by the most famous of all conquerors and adorned with the most exquisite productions of art, is now little more than a heap of ruins, yet the form of the streets can be still discerned. They were regular, and many of the houses (as I recollect to have read of Athens) had four courts bounded by dwarf walls, so much in the manner of our Lincoln's Inn fields, that the resemblance immediately struck me.

We also saw the outside of St. Athanasius' Church, who was Bishop of this diocese, but, it being now a mosque, we were forbidden to enter, unless on condition of turning Mahomedans, or losing our lives, neither of which alternatives exactly suited my ideas, so that I deemed it prudent to repress my curiosity. I could not, however, resist a desire to visit the palace of Cleopatra, of which few vestiges remain. The marble walls of the banqueting room are yet standing, but the roof is long since decayed. Never do I remember being so affected by a like object. I stood in the midst of the ruins, meditating on the awful scene, till I could have almost fancied I beheld its former mistress, revelling in luxury, with her infatuated lover, Mark Anthony, who for her sake lost all.

The houses in the new town of Alexandria, through which we returned, are flat-roofed, and, in general, had gardens on their tops. These in some measure, in so warm a country, may be called luxuries. As to the bazars (or markets) they are wretched places, and the streets exceedingly narrow. Christians of all denominations live here on paying a tax, but they are frequently ill-treated; and if one of them commits even an unintentional offence against a Mussalman, he is pursued by a most insatiable spirit of revenge and his whole family suffers for it. One cannot help shuddering at the bare idea of being in the hands of such bigoted wretches. I forgot to mention that Mr. Brandy met us near Cleopatra's Needles, which are two immense obelisks of granite. One of them time has levelled to the ground; the other is entire. They are both covered with hieroglyphic figures, which, on the sides not exposed to the wind and sand from the desert, remain uninjured; but their key being lost, no one can decipher their meaning. I thought Mr. B— might perhaps have heard something relative to them; he, however, seems to know no more than ourselves. A droll circumstance occurred on our return. He is a stout man, of a very athletic make and above six feet high; so you may judge what a droll figure he must have made of riding on an ass, and with difficulty holding up his long legs to suit the size of the animal, which watched an opportunity of walking away from between them and left the poor Consul standing erect like a colossus. In truth it was a most ludicrous sight to behold.

25th July. The weather being intensely hot, we stayed at home till the evening, when Mr. Brandly called to escort us to his house. We were most graciously received by Mrs. B. who is a native of this place; but, as she could speak a little Italian, we managed to carry on something like a conversation. She was most curiously bedizened on the occasion, and being short, dark complexioned, and of a complete dumpling shape, appeared altogether the strangest lump of finery I had ever beheld; she had a handkerchief bound round her head, covered with strings composed of spangles, but very large, intermixed with pearls and emeralds; her neck and bosom were ornamented in the same way. Add to all this an embroidered girdle with a pair of gold clasps, I think very nearly four inches square, enormous earings, and a large diamond sprig on the top of her forehead, and you must allow that she was a most brilliant figure. They have a sweet little girl about seven years of age, who was decked out much in the same style; but she really looked pretty in spite of her incongruous finery. On the whole, though, I was pleased with both mother and child: their looks and behaviour were kind, and to a stranger in a strange land (and this is literally so to us) a little attention is soothing and consolatory; especially when one feels surrounded by hostilities, which every European must as here. Compared with the uncouth beings who govern this country, I felt at home among the natives of France, and I will even say of Italy.

On taking leave, our host presented a book containing certificates of his great politeness and attentions towards travellers which were signed by many persons of consideration; and at the same time requesting that Mr. Fay and myself would add *our* names to the list: we complied, though not without surprise that a gentleman in his situation should have recourse to such an expedient, which cannot but degrade him in the eyes of his guests.

It being determined that we shall proceed by water, for reasons too tedious to detail at present, I must now prepare to embark. I shall endeavour to keep up my spirits. Be assured that I will omit no opportunity of writing, and comfort yourselves with the idea that before this reaches you, I shall have surmounted all my difficulties. I certainly deem myself very fortunate in quitting this place so soon. Farewell; all good be with you, my ever *ever* dear Friends, prays

Your own,

E. F.

LETTER VII.

GRAND CAIRO, *27th August* 1779.

MY DEAR FRIENDS,—In coming to this place, we were in great peril, and bade adieu to the sea at the hazard of our lives, the bar of Nile being exceedingly dangerous. Fourteen persons were lost there the day before we crossed it—a circumstance that, of course, tended to increase our anxiety on the subject and which was told me just before I closed my last letter, but for the world I would not have communicated such intelligence. Our only alternative to this hazardous passage was crossing a desert notorious for the robberies and murders committed on it ; while we could not have hope for escape and, from the smallness of our number, had no chance of superiority in case of attack. The night after we had congratulated ourselves on being out of danger from the bar, we were alarmed by perceiving a boat making after us, as the people said to plunder and, perhaps, to murder us. Our Jew interpreter, who, with his wife, slept in the outer cabin, begged me not to move our dollars, which I was just attempting to do, lest the thieves should hear the sound and kill us all for the supposed booty. You may judge in what a situation we remained while this dreadful evil seemed impending over us. Mr. Fay fired two pistols to give notice of our being armed. At length, thank God, we outsailed them ; and nothing of the kind occurred again during our stay on board ; though we passed several villages said to be inhabited entirely by thieves.

As morning broke, I was delighted with the appearance of the country, a more charming scene my eyes never beheld. The Nile, that perpetual source of plenty, was just beginning to overflow its banks ; so that on every side we saw such quantities of water drawn up for the use of more distant lands, that it is surprising that any remains. The machine chiefly used for that purpose is a wheel with earthern pitchers tied round it, which empty themselves into tubs, from whence numerous canals are supplied. Oxen and buffaloes are the animals generally employed in this labour. It is curious to see how the latter contrive to keep themselves cool during the intense heat that prevails here. They lie in the river by hundreds, with their heads just above water for hours together.

Rosetta is a most beautiful place, surrounded by groves of lemon and orange trees; and other flat roofs of the houses have gardens on them, whose fragrance perfumes the air. There is an appearance of cleanliness in it, the more gratifying to an English eye, because seldom met with in any degree so as to remind us of what we are accustomed to at home. The landscape around was interesting from its novelty, and became peculiarly so on considering it as the country where the children of Israel sojourned. The beautiful, I may say, the unparalleled story of Joseph and his brethren rose to my mind as I surveyed these banks on which the Patriarch sought shelter for his old age, where his self-convicted sons bowed down before their younger brother, and I almost felt as if in a dream, so wonderful appeared the circumstance of my being here. You will readily conceive that, as I drew near Grand Cairo and beheld those prodigies of human labour, the pyramids of Egypt, these sensations were still more strongly awakened; and I could have fancied myself an inhabitant of a world long passed away, for who can look on buildings reared (moderately computing the time) above *three thousand years ago*, without seeming to step back, as it were, in existence, and live through days now gone by and much in oblivion "like a tale that is told."

Situated as I was, the pyramids were not all in sight, but I was assured that those which came under my eye were decidedly the most magnificent. We went out of our way to view them nearer, and, by the aid of a telescope, were enabled to form a tolerable idea of their construction. It has been supposed by many that the Israelites built these pyramids during their bondage in Egypt, and I rather incline to that opinion; for although it has lately been proved that they were intended to serve as repositories for the dead yet, each being said to contain only one sarcophagus, this circumstance and their very form rendered them of so little comparative use that probably they were raised to furnish employment for multitudes of unfortunate slaves, and who more aptly agrees with this description than the wretched posterity of Jacob? I understand there is a little flat on the tops of the larger pyramids from which it is conjectured that the Egyptians made astronomical observations. The largest is said to be above five hundred feet high perpendicularly. The inclined plane must measure much more: the steps are nearly three feet distant of the pyramids. Though I very anxiously wished to have inspected them and the Sphinx, prudence forbade me from making the attempt, as you will allow, when I proceed further in my narrative.

On the 29th we reached Bulac, the port of Grand Cairo, and within two miles of that city, to my great joy, for on this river there is either little wind or else it comes in squalls so suddenly that the boats are often in danger overset, as they carry only, what I believe is called, a shoulder of mutton-sail, which turns on a sort of swivel and is very difficult to manage when the wind takes the wrong way. It seems indeed miraculous how we escaped.

Mr. Fay set out almost immediately to Mr. Baldwin's, who received him with much civility, and sent an ass for me, with directions to make all possible haste, as a caravan was to set off in three hours.

I must now give you a description of my dress, as my Jewess decked out, preparatory to our entering the great city. I had, in the first place, a pair of trousers, with yellow leather half-boots and slippers over them; a long satin gown with wide sleeves open to the elbows; and a girdle round my waist with large silver clasps: over that another robe with short sleeves: round my head a fine coloured muslin handkerchief closely bound, but so arranged that one corner hung down three-quarters of a yard behind. This is the dress for the house; but as I was going forth she next put on a long robe of silk, like a surplice, and then covered my face with a piece of muslin, half a yard wide, which reached from the forehead to the feet, except an opening for the eyes. Over all she threw a piece of black silk, long and wide enough to envelope the whole form; so thus equipped, stumbling at every step, I sallied forth, and with great difficulty got across my noble beast; but as the veil prevented me from breathing freely, I thought I must have died by the way. However, at last, I was safely housed, but found a great change had taken place. All thoughts of going were now laid aside. I dare not, at present, enter into particulars, and can only say that something was wrong, and that, on that account, we were kept in suspense until about a week ago, when just as we had determined to proceed, if possible by another way, matters were adjusted. So, to-morrow afternoon, we are to enter on the desert, and shall, please God, arrive at Suez most likely on Monday from whence I propose writing again. The season is so far advanced that a good passage cannot be expected. We have no hopes of reaching Calcutta in less than three months; but, at any rate, the voyage is preferable to going through the long desert, from Aleppo to Bassora.

When I write from India I will give a full detail of the affair to which I allude, though, as it is very important, you will most probably see the whole in the papers. Adieu for the present: it is bedtime.

28th.—Again I take up the pen to hold a little further

converse with my dear friends, while waiting the summons to depart ; and as health is the most important of all earthly subjects, shall begin with that. It will, I know, give you pleasure to hear that I have found scarce any inconvenience from the heat, though all of our party who have been in India agree that they have never felt the weather as oppressively hot as here, which proceeds from the terrible sandy deserts that surround the town, causing the air to smell like hot bricks. This, however, I could have borne, but just on our arrival, there broke out a severe epidemical disease with violent symptoms. People are attacked at a moment's warning with dreadful pains in stiff limbs, a burning fever with delirium and a total stoppage of perspiration. During two days it increases ; on the third there comes on uniformly a profuse sweat (pardon the expression) with vomiting which carries all off. The only remedies presented are lying in bed and drinking plentifully, even two gallons, of Nile water. No nourishment, not so much as gruel, is allowed until after the crisis. Not one has died of the disease, nor, I believe, one escaped : even the beasts have been affected. Mr. Fay had it three weeks ago, and among all I conversed with here, I remained the only healthy person, and really hoped to have proved the truth of what is asserted by physicians, that nervous persons are not subject to be attacked by contagious distempers, not even by the plague itself. However, this day, or night (?), I was seized with the most violent symptoms, so that at the three days' end my strength seemed entirely exhausted ; but I have, thanks be to Providence, recovered as surprisingly ; and am nearly well. It had every sign of the plague, except that it was not mortal. Do not be frightened at the name, but, I assure you, it is commonly called "la queve de la peste," and the general opinion is, that, had it arrived in the month of February, the living would scarce have been sufficient to bury the dead.

Grand Cairo by no means answers to its name at present,

whatever it may have done formerly. There are certainly many magnificent houses, belonging to the Beys and other rich individuals, but, as a city, I can perceive neither order, beauty, nor grandeur, and the contrast between the great, who seem to wallow in splendour and luxury, and the people at large, who appear to want the common necessaries of life, is not more than disgusting; because those who are raised above their fellows do not look as though they merited the distinction, either by brilliant manners, or even the most ordinary pretensions. The Christians (who are called Franks) live altogether in one street, which is closed at each end every night: a precaution neither unpleasant nor useless. An agreeable variety is given to the appearance of the town by the Mosques, or I should consider the whole wretchedly stupid. A wedding here is a gay and amusing spectacle from the procession which accompanies the bride in all her movements, drums, hautboys, and every other kind of noise and parade they can make: but the circumstance of completely veiling, not only the face, but the whole figure of the woman, in the enveloping mantle of black silk before described, gives an air of melancholy to these exhibitions. To show the face is considered here an act of downright indecency; a terrible fashion for one like me, to whom free air seems the greatest requisite for existence.

I must not conclude without mentioning a disappointment I met with. As the fertility of Egypt depends on the due increase of the Nile, persons are hired to go round Grand Cairo twice a day, and report how many inches the water has risen, returning solemn thanks to Almighty God for the blessing. This is continued till it gains a certain point when the dikes are broken down, and the river flows majestically into the canal formed for its reception, while the inhabitants hail its approach with every demonstration of joy. Such was the account I heard, and great was my anxiety lest I should not be permitted to see this *August* ceremony. At length the period arrived, but never, sure, were highly raised expectations more miserably deceived. For this famous canal, being dry nine months out of the twelve, and serving during the interval as a receptacle for the filth of a populous and not over cleanly city, I leave you to judge how beautifully *pellucid* its waters must appear : nor could St. Giles itself pour forth such an assembly of half-naked, wretched creatures as preceded this so vaunted stream ; crying aloud and making all sorts of frantic gentures, like so many maniacs. Not a decent person could I distinguish among the whole group. So much for this grand exhibition, which we have abundant cause to wish had not taken place, for the vapours arising from such a mass of impurity have rendered the heat more intolerable than ever. My bed chamber overlooks the canal, so that I enjoy the full benefit to be derived from its proximity.

I am now compelled, much against my inclination, to bid you adieu. For I have a thousand things to do, and this immense letter has left me very little time.

Ever yours truly,

Etc., etc.

P.S.—Not being able to enlarge on the only interesting subject has induced one to be diffuse on others, as I wished to convey some *information* by this, perhaps the last, opportunity, till our arrival in India, for it is doubtful whether I have any safe conveyance from Suez

LETTER VIII.

From Mr. F. To Mr. C.

On Boardship, in the Red Sea,
Near Suez.
September 1st, 1779.

Honoured Sir,—I seize the chance of three minutes to tell you that we yesterday arrived at Suez from Grand Cairo after a journey of three days over a most dreadful desert, where every night we slept under the great canopy of heaven, and where we were every hour in danger of being destroyed by troops of Arabian robbers. But, having a little party of English gentlemen and servants (among whom I held a principal command) well armed, and under the orders of Major Baillie and another military officer, we marched the whole way in order of battle, and though we could frequently see superior numbers, they never dared to molest us.

Your daughter behaved most courageously and is extremely well, considering the extraordinary fatigue she has undergone. There is another English lady and her husband on board, which promises to make it an agreeable voyage. The ship is a very fine one, and we have a handsome little chamber, and I hope in all things shall find ourselves well accommodated. We expect to sail in a few hours. The ship is called *Nathalia:* Captain—Chenu, a Frenchman, and apparently a very polite good-natured man—which is a great matter on a long voyage.

I, thank God, was never in better health and spirits, though I never slept during the whole journey on the Desert, and lived the whole time on bread and water, notwithstanding we had abundance of wine and provisions; but the heat being excessive, I found no other food agree with me so well, and Mrs. Fry, by adopting the same diet, preserved her health also; whereas all the rest were knocked up before we got half way over that confounded Desert. Some are now very ill; but I stood it as well as any Arabian in the Caravan, which consisted at least of five thousand people. My wife insists on taking the pen out of my hands, so I can only say God bless you all.

My Dear Friends,—I have not a moment's time, for the boat is waiting, therefore can only beg that you will unite with me in praising our Heavenly Protector for our escape from the various dangers of our journey. I never could have thought my constitution was so strong. I bore the fatigues of the desert like a lion, though but just recovering from my illness. We have been pillaged of almost everything by the Arabs. This is the Paradise of thieves. I think the whole population may be divided into two classes of them: those who adopt force and those who effect their purpose by fraud. I was obliged to purchase a thick cloak and veil proper for the journey, and what was worse, to wear them all the way thither, which rendered the heat almost insupportable. Never was I more happy than when I was on board, although, the ship having been for six weeks in the hands of the natives, the reason of which I cannot enlarge on here, is totally despoiled of every article of furniture. We have not a chair or a table, but as the carpenter makes them, for there is no laying in such things here. Our greatest inconvenience is the want of good water. What can be procured here is so brackish, as to be scarcely drinkable. I have not another moment. God bless you! Pray for me, my beloved friends.

LETTER IX.

MOCHA, *13th September, 1779.*

THANK GOD, MY DEAR FRIENDS, I am once more enabled to date from a place of comparative liberty, and, an English gentleman having promised me a safe conveyance for my packet, I shall proceed to give you a hurried and melancholy detail of circumstances of which it has been my chief consolation to know that you were ignorant. You are, of course, impatient to be informed to what I allude, take then the particulars : but I must go a good way back in order to elucidate matters, which would otherwise appear mysterious or irrelevant.

The East India Company sent out positive instructions some time ago to prohibit the trade to Suez, as interfering with their privileges ; but, as there was never a law made but means might be found to evade it, several English merchants freighted a ship (*Nathalia*) from Serampore, a Danish settlement on the Hooghly, fourteen miles above Calcutta, whose Commander, Vanderfield, a Dane, passed for owner of the ship and cargo. Mr. O'Donnell, one of the persons concerned, who had property on board to the amount of above £20,000, came as passenger, as did Mr. Barrington, the real supercargo, also a freighter, and two Frenchmen, brothers named Chevalier. They left Bengal on New Year's Day 1779 and came first to Calicut on the coast of Malabar, where they arrived in February : found English, French, Danish and Portuguese factors there and trade in a flourishing state so not apprehending any danger they entered into a contract with one Issacs, a rich old Jew who has great influence with the Government to freight them with pepper for Bengal on their way from Suez that being the greatest town on the coast for that commodity, the price was settled and £700 paid as earnest. This business arranged, they proceeded on their voyage ; and having luckily disposed of some part of the cargo at this place, reached Suez with the remainder in the beginning of June, landed their goods to the amount of £40,000, and prepared to cross the desert on their way to Cairo, the company besides those already mentioned consisted of Chenu, the second mate, with some officers and servants, in all twelve Europeans, strengthened by a numerous body of Arabian guards, camel drivers, etc., for the conveyance of their property—more than sufficient in everybody's opinion, for no one remembered a caravan being plundered, for although sometimes the wandering Arabs were troublesome yet a few presents never failed to procure a release from them. Thus were they lulled into a fatal security, each calculating the profits likely to accrue and extremely willing to compound for the loss of a few bales, should they happen to meet with any strolling depredators, not even once supposing their lives to be in danger or intending to use their firearms should they be molested.

On Monday, the 14th June, they left Suez, and next morning at daybreak had travelled about twenty miles (nearly one-third of the way), when the alarm was given of an attack, as they, poor souls, were sleeping across their baskets (or paniers). Captain Barrington, on awaking, ordered a dozen bales to be given to them immediately ; but, alas ! they were already in possession of the whole, for the camel drivers did not defend themselves an instant, but left their beasts at the mercy of the robbers, who after detaching a large body to drive them away with their burthens, advanced towards their passengers. Here I must request you to pause and reflect whether it be possible even for imagination to conceive a more dreadful scene to those concerned—particularly to Mr. O'Donnell, who from a concurrence of fortunate circumstances, had in less than four years realized a fortune of near £30,000, the bulk of which he laid out in merchandise on the prospect of getting 30 per cent., and, as his health was in a very weak state, proposed retiring to Europe. What must that man have felt, a helpless spectator of his own ruin. But this was nothing to what followed in their being personally attacked. The inhuman wretches, not content with stripping them to the skin, drove away their camels, and left them in a burning sandy desert, which the feet can scarcely touch without being blistered, exposed to the scorching rays of the sun, and utterly destitute of sustenance of any kind; no house, tree, or even shrub to afford them shelter. My heart sickens, my hand trembles as I retrace this scene. Alas! I can too well conceive their situation. I can paint to myself the hopeless anguish of an eye cast abroad in vain for succour! But I must not indulge in reflections: let me simply relate the facts as they occurred. In this extremity they stopped to deliberate, when each gave his reasons for preferring the road he had determined to pursue. Mr. O'Donnell, Chenu the cook, and two others resolved to retrace their steps back to Suez, which was undoubtedly the most eligible plan. Of the remaining seven who went towards Cairo, only *one* survived. Mr. Barrington, being corpulent and short breathed, sunk under the fatigue the second day; his servant soon followed him. One of the French gentlemen was by this time become very ill, and his brother perceiving a house at some miles distant (for in that flat country one may see a great way), prevailed on him to lie under a stunted tree, with his servant, while he endeavoured to procure some water, for the want of which the other was expiring. Hope, anxiety and affection combined to quicken his pace and rendered poor Vanderfeld, the Danish captain, unable to keep up with him, which he most earnestly strove to do. I wept myself almost blind as the poor Frenchmen related his sufferings from conflicting passion. Almost worn out with heat and thirst, he was afraid of not being able to reach the house, though his own life and that of his brother depended on it. On the other hand, the heart piercing cries of his fellow-sufferer that he was a dead man unless assisted by him, and conjuring him, for GOD'S sake, not to leave him to perish now they were in view of relief, arrested his steps and agonised every nerve. Unable to resist the solemn appeal, for some time he indulged him, till finding that the consequence of longer delay must be inevitable destruction to both, he was compelled to shake him off. A servant belonging to some of the party still kept on, and poor Vanderfield was seen to continue his efforts, till at last, nature being completely exhausted, he dropped and was soon relieved from his miseries by death. Nor was the condition of the survivor far more enviable, when having with difficulty reached the building, after which they had toiled so long, it proved to be an uninhabited shed. Giving himself up for lost, the French gentleman laid down under the shelter of the wall to await his last moment (the servant walked forward and was found dead a little further on). Now it so happened that an Arabian beggar chanced to pass by the wall, who seeing his condition, kindly ran to procure some water, but did not return for an hour. What an age of torture, of horrible suspense, for, if "hope deferred maketh the heart sick," the sensation must cause ten-fold anguish at a moment like this.

The unhappy man was mindful of his brother, but utterly unable to undertake the task himself, he directed the beggar as well as he could to the spot where he had left him with a supply of water. But, alas! all his endeavours to find the unfortunate men were ineffectual, nor were their bodies discovered. It is supposed that they crept for shelter from the sun into some unfrequented spot and there expired. The survivor, by the assistance of the beggar, reached the hut of a poor woman, who kindly received him ; and through whose care he was soon restored to strength and arrived safely at Cairo after as miraculous an escape as ever human being experienced.

The melancholy story had been mentioned by Mr. Brandy before I landed at Alexandria. O ! with what horror did I hear of this brief recital and the particulars I learned at Cairo ! The subject was, in fact, closely connected with my fears and sufferings at that place which I hinted at the impossibility of my then revealing. Neither could I, for the same reason, give you any account of the Egyptian Government, lest they should intercept my letter, although it is necessary that you should know a little of it for the sake of comprehending what I have further to relate concerning those unfortunate adventurers.

Egypt, then, is governed by twenty Beys, of whom one presides over the rest, but this superiority is very precarious; for he holds it no longer than till some other of the number thinks himself stronger enough to contend with him, and as they have here but two maxims in war, the one to fly, the other to pursue, these contests last not long. The vanquished, should he escape assasination, retires up-country, till fortune changes his aspect, while the victor takes his place. Thus do their lives pass in perpetual vicissitudes. To-day a prince, to-morrow a fugitive, and next day a prince again. These things are so common that nobody notices them, since they never disturb the inhabitants or compel them to take part in their disputes. In order to be a check on these gentlemen, the Grand Signor sends a Bashaw to reside among them, whom they receive with great respect and compliment with presents of value, pretending the utmost deference for his authority, but at the same time a strict eye is kept over him, and, on the least opposition to their will, he is sent in disgrace away ; happy if he escape with life, after refunding all his presents and paying enormous sums besides.

By the above statement you will perceive that the Beys are in reality independent, and likewise discern the hinge on which their politics turn, for as long as under colour of submission they consent to receive a Bashaw, it is in their power constantly to throw the odium of every disagreeable occurrence on his shoulders under the pretence of orders from the Porte. Now briefly to proceed with my little history. Some time after the fatal robbery, another ship called the *St. Helena* arrived at Suez, under Danish colours, with the real owner, a Mr. Moore, on board. He, justly apprehensive or a similar fate, refused to land his cargo till the then Chief, Armrath Bey, had accorded him a solemn permission or rather protection under which he reached Cairo, disposed of his effects, and prepared for his return with a fresh cargo. But in the interim Mr. O'Donnell had been advised to present a memorial to the Beys by which he reclaimed his property as an Englishman, threatened them with vengeance of his nation if not immediately redressed, and declared himself totally independent of the Danes. This rash procedure alarmed the people in power, who, however, still continued apparently friendly in hopes of a larger booty, till the 30th July, when they threw off the mask, seized the caravan, and made Mr. Moore a prisoner. You may recollect that in my letter from Cairo, I told you what a hurry Mr. Fay was in to fetch me from Bulac, not having, as he then thought, time to spare. It so happened that I arrived within an hour after the seizure of the caravan ; and, when the gentlemen concerned were in the first transports of that indignation, which such a daring outrage could not fail to excite, at once exasperated by the treacherous behaviour and alarmed lest some new crime should be committed against them.

Everyone is of opinion that their design was to cut us all

off, had we gone out ignorant of the seizure of the caravan. I had scarcely sat down in Baldwin's parlour, when this terrible news, which seemed to involve the fate of every European alike, burst upon me like a stroke of lightning. Never shall I forget the terrors I felt. In a few moments the room was filled with Europeans, chiefly English, all speaking together, calling out for their arms and declaring they would sell their lives dearly; for not one appeared to entertain a doubt of their being immediately attacked. In the midst of this confusion, Mons. Chevalier (the poor man who escaped from the desert) cast his eyes upon me, exclaiming "Oh, Madam, how unhappy you are in having come to this wretched place." This drew the attention of the rest and "what shall we do with the lady?" was every-one's question. At last they resolved on sending me to the house of an Italian physician as a place of safety. Thither I was instantly taken by a native, who even in the distress and confusion of the house, and although the Italian was only a few steps distant across a narrow lane, felt greatly shocked because my veil chancing to be a little loose, he could see one corner of my eye, and severely reprehended the indecency of such an exposure.

On reaching my expected asylum a scene of more serious alarm (if possible) than I had left at Mr. Baldwin's awaited me. The lady and her daughter were wringing their hands and crying out in agony that they were utterly ruined; that all the Europeans would be murdered; they even appeared to think that receiving another of the proscribed race increased their danger. Imprisonment and massacre in every shape were the sole objects of their conversation and so many terrible images did their fears conjure up and communicate to my already disordered mind, that there were times when the reality could have been scarcely more appalling. Oh, England! dear England! how did I apostrophise thee, land of liberty and safety! but I must not review my thoughts: a simple narrative is all I dare allow myself to write.

For several days we remained in this harassing state of suspense and alarm. At length news arrived that the two ships which had brought those ill-fated adventurers to Egypt's inhospitable shore were seized by the Government three days before they took possession of the caravan. Their prisoners indeed we already virtually were, not being allowed to quit the city. I should have mentioned that the Bashaw was the tool made use of on this occasion; he pretended that he had orders from Constantinople to seize all English merchandise and confiscate the vessels, suffering none but the East India Company's packets to land at Suez. This *firman* was said to be obtained of his Sublime Highness by the English Resident at the Porte on behalf of the East India Company. Whether this report was true or false we could never learn. Many other reports were propagated as must always be the case in a country under arbitrary government there being no certain rules to judge by, every one pronounces on the event as his hopes or fears dictate. Sometimes we were all to be sent prisoners to Constantinople; then we were assured that after a general plunder of our effects we should certainly be released; and once it was confidentially reported that the *bowstring* would be secretly applied to prevent our telling tales.

What added to our mortification and justified our fears was that all Christians belonging to our ship were, on the 10th August, dragged to Cairo in the most ignominious manner, having previously suffered, during their imprisonment at Suez, every species of hardship which barbarity and malice could inflict. The people also at whose house we lodged behaved to us continually with marked disrespect: if asked a question they seldom deigned to reply, and took care to enlarge perpetually on their condescension in suffering themselves to be incommoded with strangers. To be thus treated, at a time when perpetual solicitude and terror had unbraced my nerves and subdued my spirit, seemed so cruel that it absolutely hurt me more than ever our detention—a detention which was certainly harder upon us than any other Europeans in one sense, since we had no connection whatever with the parties who were coming from a different quarter of the globe, not concerned with trade and unknown to those who had visited their country on that account. No demon of avarice had led *us* into their power, nor could we afford a prey to theirs. These considerations, however evident, made no impression on our host: they were rather motives of exultation over us, and what enhanced our misfortune, it was irremediable, for we could not change our abode without going into another street, where we should have been unprotected.

All the Christians live in one part of the town as I before noticed. During the time when the plague rages, they visit each other by means of bridges thrown across the streets from the tops of the houses; and this is a convenience they often resort to at other times as it saves them from insult which they often meet below. I find I have written myself into a strange humour that I cannot proceed methodically; but I must try to arrange my thoughts and go forward better.

At length the Beys, enchanted by that deity whose bewitching attractions few mortals can resist, whether on the banks of the Nile or the Thames; in other words, influenced by the promise of three thousand pounds and an absolute indemnification by Mr. O'Donnell gave us leave to proceed on our voyage in defiance of the tremendous order of their master, and thus ended this most disagreable and distressing business. I will release you from this wearisome letter. I shall have time at Mocha to continue my journal. Adieu till to-morrow.

Ever most affectionately yours,

E. F.

LETTER X.

(*Enclosed in the Foregoing.*)

MOCHA, *15th September 1779*.

MY DEAR SISTER,—I resume my pen in order to give you some account of our passing the Desert, which being done by a method of travelling totally different from anything in England, may afford amusement, and even without the charms of novelty, could not fail to interest you, as the narrative of one so nearly and dearly connected.

When a caravan is about to depart, large tents are pitched on the skirts of the city, whither all who are proposing to join it repair. There they are drawn up in order by the persons who undertake to convey them. Strong bodies of Arabian soldiers guard the van and rear; others flank the sides, so that the female passengers and merchandise are completely surrounded and, as one would hope, defended in case of attack. Each gentleman of our party had a horse, and it is common to hire a camel between two with panniers to carry their provisions, etc. Across the panniers, which are of wicker, a kind of mattress is thrown, where as they take it on turns to lie and court repose during their journey. Females, who can afford the expense, are more comfortably accommodated. These travel in a kind of litter called a *tataravan* with two poles fastened between two camels one behind, the other before. The litter has a top and is surmounted by shabby, ill-contrived venetian blinds, which in the day increase the suffocating heat, but are of use during the nights which are cold and piercing. Every camel carries skins of water, but before you have been many hours on the Desert, it becomes the colour of coffee. I was warned of this and recommended to procure small goblets of porous earth, which after filling with *purified* water, I slung to the top of my *tataravan;* and these with water melons and hard eggs proved the best refreshments I could have taken. The water by this means was tolerably preserved, but the motion of the camels and the uncouth manner in which the vehicle is fastened to them, made such a constant rumbling sound among my provisions as to be exceedingly annoying. Once I was saluted by a parcel of hard eggs breaking loose from their net and pelting me completely: It was fortunate that they were boiled or I should have been in a pretty trim. To this may be added the frequent violent jerks occasioned by one and the other of the poles slipping out of its wretched fastening, so as to bring one end of the litter to the ground. You may judge how pleasing this mode of travelling must be.

At our first outset, the novelty of the scene and the consolation I felt on leaving a place which had been productive of much chagrin and so many too well grounded apprehensions wrought an agreeable change on my harassed feelings; but, when we had proceeded some distance on the Desert, when all traces of human habitation had vanished, when every sign of cultivation disappeared, and even vegetation was confined to a few low straggling shrubs that seemed to stand between life and death as hardly belonging to either, when the immeasurable plain lay round about me, a burning sun darted his fierce rays from above, and no asylum was visible in front, my very heart sunk within me. I am sure you will do justice to my feelings, the late catastrophe being deeply imprinted on my mind, and indeed never absent from it. For all the world you should not have known what was passing there when I made so light of it in my letter from Grand Cairo.

In the midst of these soul-subduing reflections, the guides gave notice of a body, apparently much larger than our own being within reach of us. All the sufferings related by the poor French gentleman my active imagination now pourtrayed was about to be inflicted on me. My dear parents, my sisters cried I, will never see me more! Should they learn my fate what agonies will they not endure! But never can they realise the terrible realities that I may be doomed to undergo? Happily, for sure, my fears outwent the truth. The party so dreaded turned off in pursuit of some other prey, or perhaps intimidated by our formidable appearance, left us unmolested.

It is impossible, even amidst fear and suspensee, not to be struck with the exquisite beauty of the night here. A perfectly cloudless sky and the atmosphere so clear that the stars shine with a brilliancy infinitely surpassing anything I witnessed elsewhere. Well might the ancient Egyptians become expert astronomers, possessing a climate so favourable to that study; nor were we less indebted to those Heavenly luminaries, since by their refulgent light and unvarying revolutions the guides cross these tractless deserts with certainty, and, like the mariner, steer to the desired haven.

You will perceive that my boast of having crossed the Desert, like a lion, was not literally just; but then remember it was his strength, not his courage, to which I alluded: for it is true that, considering how much I had suffered in Cairo, I really did perform the journey well, and, on the second day, convinced by the behaviour of some around me, how greatly dejection increased the actual evils of our situation, I rallied my spirits to the utmost, and, lifting my heart up in gratitude to the Almighty for having thus far supported us, I determined to trust in His goodness and not desert myself.

On this day I was exceedingly effected by the sufferings of one of our party, Mr. Taylor, going out as an assistant surgeon on the Bengal Establishment. He complained of illness when we sat out and seemed overwhelmed with melancholy. He had been plundered of all by the Arabs, had sustained various misfortunes, and, of late, appeared to be consumptive. The extreme heat of the weather so overpowered him that he resigned all hope of life; and at length, in a fit of despondency, actually allowed himself to slide down from his horse, that he might die on the ground. Mr. Fay, seeing him fall, ran to assist him in regaining his seat, but he earnestly begged to be left alone, and permitted to die in peace. It was impossible to inspire him with hope, and, as he appeared to have so little strength, I did not believe that, with so strong a predilection for death, he could have been kept alive. Yet to see a fine young man, a countryman and fellow traveller, expiring amongst us, without striving to the last to preserve him, would have been inhuman. Thank God, our cares so far prevailed that he is still with us, though his disorder is now confirmed, and his melancholy but little abated. He thanks us for his life, as if grateful for our attention, but not for the gift. I fear his heart as well as his constitution is breaking.

When my mind was a little relieved on poor T—'s account I had leisure to think of the horses. You recollect how partial I ever was to these noble animals. We had several with us of such singular beauty and docility that they would have attracted the attention of the most indifferent spectator. The wretched creatures suffered so much from heat and thirst that their groanings were terrible, and added to this an involuntary rattling in the throat as if they were on the point of expiring, so that one heard them with a mixture of compassion and horror extremely painful to bear. Yet, notwithstanding that this continued for many hours, we were so fortunate as not to lose a single horse in the caravan. With the dogs we were less successful. Three very fine ones set out with us, but none of them survived. One of them was the most beautiful Italian greyhound I ever beheld: he cost seven guineas at Venice. The first day he got tolerably well forward, but during the second his strength failed, and he appeared to suffer excruciating pain from the heat. When he was in the most frightful state, his tongue hanging out of his mouth, his eyes wildly staring and altogether presenting the idea of madness, his master, Mr. T., had the modesty to bring him to me, and request that I would admit him into my tartaravan, I hope no person will accuse me of inhumanity for refusing to receive an animal in that condition : self-preservation forbade my compliance; I felt that it would be weakness, instead of compasson, to subject myself to such a risk, and you may be certain my sympathy was not increased for its owner when he solemnly assured me that it would cost him a less severe pang to see his own father thus suffering then he then felt. I was induced to credit this assertion, knowing that when last in England he had remained there seventeen months without visiting that old gentleman, though he acknowledged having been within 150 miles of his residence. A very short time after this, the poor creature dropped down gasping, but ere he breathed his last, a brutal Arab cut him to pieces before his master's face ; and on his expressing anger at his cruel behaviour, ran after him with a drawn scymitar. You may judge from this incident what wretches we were cast amongst.

We found Suez a miserable place, little better than the Desert which it bounds, and we were, as probably I have already told you, impatient to get on board, where we found every portable necessary of life had been carried off. We had been pretty well pillaged ourselves, and could therefore sympathise with the losers as well as lament our own personal inconvenience. However, thank Heaven that we escaped as we did. If they ever catch me on their desert again I think I shall deserve all they can inflict.

Our passage down the Red Sea was pleasant, the wind being constantly favourable, but afforded no object of interest save the distant view of Mount Horeb, which again brought the flight of the children of Israel to my mind, and you may be sure I did not wonder that they sought to quit the land of Egypt after the various specimens of its *advantages* that I have experienced. The only vessels we saw were those built for the conveyance of coffee, for which this port is famous. They are so bulky, clumsy and strangely constructed that one might almost take them for floating mountains. I cannot be expected to say a great deal of my shipmates, having been so short a time together, but, to own the truth, I do not look forward to much comfort where the elements are so discordant. However, as we are to touch at Calicut on the coast of Malabar, you shall from thence have the particulars: for by that time we shall be well familiarised with each other. May the details be more agreeable than my present ideas warrant me in supposing.

Let me now proceed to say a few words of Mocha, which is a pretty considerable place, walled round and guarded by soldiers. It appears to a great advantage after Suez, being plentifully supplied with fruit and vegetables ; the provisions not bad and the water excellent. The worst I know of it is the excessive heat, which is even beyond that of Cairo. Our sailors have a proverb that there is only a sheet of paper between that and another place too shocking to be mentioned. I should yet say there were many sheets, for we have really met with so much kindness and hospitality here as to make us almost forget the heat.

The principal trade is carried on by Banians and Rajputs (as they are called though I cannot tell why), who come here from India, make comfortable little fortunes and return. A family of the former, consisting of three brothers named George, has shown us every possible attention ever since we landed, and the Chevalier de St. Lubin, a French gentleman of elegant manners and superior information, has treated us in the same style. It is whispered among the English here that Mons. de St. L. has been on a mission from the French Court to Hyder Ally for the express purpose of sowing seeds of discord between him and the English and that he has, to a great degree, succeeded. How far this is true we cannot yet say, but so entirely was Mr. Fuller, one of our passengers, persuaded of the fact, that he just now proposed that we should arrest the Chevalier, who is about to proceed, in a day or two, to Europe. How far Mr. F. may be politically right I cannot tell, but my heart revolted at the idea of receiving every mark of attention from a man one hour and, on bare suspicion, making him a prisoner the next; and most truly did I rejoice when this scheme was overruled. There should be very sufficient reasons for conduct so despotic and apparently ungrateful, and we were certainly not in possession of documents to authorise such a procedure. I am much better pleased that this gentleman should return peaceably to his native country and forward my letters to you—which he has promised on his *honour* to do and to secure them amongst his private papers. I might have written twice as much if I chose.

And now, my dear friends, I must again bid you adieu. I trust my next accounts will be more pleasant than this sad detail must prove, and that I shall meet letters at Calcutta with good news of you all. My heart aches with thinking of the distance between us; and, after surmounting so many difficulties and happily escaping from them after so many dangers, I feel inspired with hope for the future.

Ever most affectionately yours,

E. F.

LETTER XI.

ON BOARD THE NATHALIA,

AT SEA, *28th October*, *1779*.

MY DEAR FRIENDS,—I wrote you from Mocha, in date the 18th September, by the Chevalier de St. Lubin, who has most solemnly engaged to forward my letter and I trust will keep his word.

We have now been six weeks at sea and in the course of a few days I hope to reach Calicut. Our passage across the Indian Ocean we found very pleasant. The Monsoon being against us made it tedious, but no boisterous seas had we to contend with as in the Mediterranean. All has been calm, easy and free from alarm hitherto. Fortunate indeed may we deem ourselves in having experienced such fine weather, for our ship is not half laden and has not cargo enough to keep steady; you will now expect me to say something of those with whom we are couped up, but my account will not be very satisfactory, though sufficiently interesting to us—to being there.

The woman, of whom I entertained some suspicion from the first, is, now I am credibly informed, one of the very lowest creatures taken off the streets in London. She is so *perfectly* depraved in disposition that her supreme delight consists in rendering everybody around her miserable. It would be doing her too much honour to stain my paper with a detail of the various artifices she daily practices to that end. Her pretended husband, having been in India before and giving himself many airs, is looked upon as a person of mighty consequence whom no one chooses to offend. Therefore Madam has full scope to exercise her mischievous talents, wherein he never controls her, not but that he perfectly understands how to make himself feared. Coercive measures are *sometimes* resorted to. It is a common expression of the lady: "Lord bless you, if I did such or such a thing, Tulloh would make no more ado, but knock me down like an ox." I frequently amuse myself with examining their countenances, where ill nature has fixed her empire so firmly, that I scarcely believe either of them smiled unless maliciously. Miss Howe's description of Solmes in *Clarissa Harlowe* recurs to me as admirably suiting this *amiable* pair —to that I refer you.

Chenu, the Captain, is a mere "Jack in office." Being unexpectedly raised to that post from second mate by the death of poor Captain Vanderfield and his Chief Officer on the fatal Desert, he has become from this circumstance so insolent and overbearing that every one detests him. Instead of being ready to accommodate every person with the few necessaries left by the plundering Arabs, he constantly appropriates them to himself. "Where's the Captain's silver spoon? God bless my soul, Sir, you have got my chair: must you be seated before the Captain's glass?" and a great deal more of this same kind; but this may serve as a specimen. And although the wretch half starves us; he frequently makes comparisons between *his* table and that of an Indiaman which we dare not contradict while in his power. Tell me now should you doat on three such companions for a long voyage? But I have a fourth who at least merits to be added to the triumvirate, his name I——Hare, Esq., barrister-at-law, a man of the very first fashion, I assure you, and who would faint at the thought of anything plebeian. T— was one day showing him a very handsome silver-hilted sword, which he greatly admired, till chancing to cast his eye on the scabbard he read "Royal Exchange." "Take your sword," said he, "it's surprising a man of your sense should commit an error; for fifty guineas I would not have a city name of any article of *my* dress. Now St. James or Bond Street has a *delicious* sound : don't you think so, my friends?" Now, would anyone suppose this fine gentleman's father was in trade and he himself brought up in that very City he affects to despise? Very true nevertheless. Quadrille he would not be thought to know—it is only played by the wives and daughters of tradesmen in country towns! I want to make you see him. Figure to yourself a little mortal, his body constantly bent in a rhetorical attitude as if addressing the Court, and his face covered with scorbutic blotches. Happily, from an affectation of singularity, he always wears spectacles. I say happily as they serve to conceal the most odious pair of little white eyes mine have ever beheld. What Butler says of Hudibras, that

" He could not ope
His mouth, but out there flew a trope"

may literally be applied to this Heaven-born Orator, who certainly outdoes all I ever heard in the use of strained compliments and far-fetched allusions. But with all these oddities, were he only a good-natured, harmless simpleton, one might pity him. At first he took so much pains to ingratiate himself with us that he became a sort of favourite. So many confessions of superior abilities in Mr. Fay, such intreaties to spare him when they should practise in the Courts together, a studied attention to me in the minutest article, effectually shielded him from suspicion till his end was answered, of raising a party against us, by the means of that vile woman, who was anxious to triumph over me, especially as I have been repeatedly compelled (for the honour of the sex) to censure her swearing and indecent behaviour. I have, therefore, little comfort to look forward to for the remainder of the voyage.

It is, however, only justice to name Mr. Taylor as an amiable, though melancholy, companion, and Mr. Manesty, an agreeable young man, under twenty, just going out as a writer on the Bombay Establishment, from whom I always receive the most respectful attention. Mr. Fuller is a middle aged man : it is easy to see that he has been accustomed to gentle society. How different his manners from those of Hare ! Poor man, he has, it seems, fallen into the hands of sharpers and been completely pillaged. He has the finest dark eyes I ever met with. His trip to Bengal is, I doubt not, a last resource. May it prove successful. I have no enmity towards him, for, though he has joined the other party, it is evidently with reluctance. Mr. Moreau, a musician going out to India to exercise his profession, is very civil and attentive.

Dissensions run very high on board. The very day we sailed from Mocha, a sudden quarrel arose between the Captain and Mr. Hare, the Barrister ; on which the ship was ordered about, and they were going ashore in a great hurry to decide it, but, by the interposition of friends, they were prevailed upon to curb their wrath till their arrival at Callcut, as, in case of an accident, no officer remained to supply Chenu's place. About a month after, they were reconciled, and so ended this doughty affair.

I had almost forgotten to mention Pierot, the purser of the ship, a lively, well-informed little Frenchman, full of anecdotes and always prepared with a repartee—in short the soul of the party. He sings an excellent song and has as many tricks as a monkey. I cannot help smiling at his sallies, though they are frequently levelled at me, for he is one of my most virulent persecutors. Indeed, such is our general line of conduct ; for, having early discovered the confederacy, prudence determined us to go mildly on, seemingly blind to what it was beyond our power to remedy. Never intermeddling with their disputes, all endeavours to draw us into quarrels are vainly exerted. I despise them too much to be angry.

During the first fortnight of our voyage my foolish complaisance stood in my way at table, but I soon learned our genteel maxim "catch as catch can." The longest arm fared best, and you cannot imagine what a good scrambler I have become. A dish, once seized, it is my care to make use of my good fortune : and now provisions running very short, we are grown quite savages : two or three of us perhaps fighting for a bone, for there is no respect of persons. The wretch of a Captain, wanting our passage money for nothing, refused to lay in a sufficient quantity of stock ; and, if we do not soon reach our Port, what must be the consequence, Heaven knows.

After meals I generally retire to my cabin, where I find plenty of employment, having made up a dozen shirts for Mr. Fay out of some cloth I purchased at Mocha to replace part of those stolen by the Arabs. Sometimes I read French and Italian and study Portuguese. I likewise prevailed on Mr. Fay to teach me shorthand, in consequence of the airs Mr. Hare gave himself because he was master of this art and had taught his sisters to correspond with him in it. The matter was very easily accomplished. In short, I have discovered abundant methods of making my time pass usefully and not disagreeably. How often, since in this situation, have I blessed God that He has been pleased to endow me with a mind capable of furnishing its own amusement in despite of all means used to discompose it.

4th November.—We are now in sight of the Malabar Hills, and expect to reach Calicut either this evening or to-morrow. I conclude this letter and shall send it under charge of Mr. Manesty to forward it from Bombay. I am in tolerable health, and looking with a longing eye towards Bengal, from whence I trust my next will be dated. The climate seems likely to agree very well with me. I do not at all mind the heat, nor does it affect either my spirits or my appetite.

I remain,

Ever affectionately yours,

E. F.

LETTER XII.

CALICUT,
12th February, 1780.

MY DEAR FRIENDS,—It was my determination never to write to you during the state of dreadful captivity in which we have been held, but, having hopes of a release, I think, I may now venture to give you some account of our sufferings, which have been extreme, both in body and mind, for a period of fifteen weeks, which we have spent in wretched confinement, totally in the power of barbarians.

I must premise that, such is the harassing confusion of my mind and the weakness of my nerves, that I can merely offer you a simple statement of facts, and even that must necessarily be incorrect, for incessant anxiety and constant anticipation of more intolerable evils have totally unhinged my faculties. God knows whether I may ever recover them! At present all is confused and clouded. Reflections on our speedy arrival in Bengal which so many circumstances had contributed to prevent, and the apprehension lest our delay should afford time to raise serious obstacles against Mr. Fay's admission into the Court as an advocate had long been as so many daggers piercing my vitals. Add to this, the heart-breaking reflection what immense tracts lie between me and those dear *dear* friends whose society alone can render me completely happy! Even were the most brilliant success to crown our future views, never could I know comfort till the blessed moment arrive when I shall clasp you all to my fond heart, without fear of a future separation, except by that stroke, to which we must all submit and which has been suspended over my head as by a single hair. I trust that I have been spared to afford me the means of proving more substantially than by words absence has made you how inestimably precious in my sight. Well may it be said that the deprivation of a blessing enhances its value; for my affection rises now to a pitch of enthusiasm, of which I knew not that my heart was capable, but which has its consolation, amidst all the horrors of imprisonment and sickness, with no congenial mind to which I could declare my feelings sure of meeting with sympathising affection as I so delightfully experienced in the company of my beloved sister. But I forget all this, while you are impatient to hear how we fell into so distressing a situation——! take then the particulars.

I told you in my last that we expected to reach Calicut very shortly, and, accordingly on next day, on the (to me ever memorable) 8th November, we anchored in the Roads, and to our great concern saw no English Flag up. In a short time we were surrounded by vessels which approached us with an air of so much hostility that we became seriously alarmed, with one exception, this was the redoubtable Mrs. Tulloh. She had frequently, in the course of the voyage, expressed a violent desire for some romantic danger, on which she could descant hereafter; and, far from congratulating herself on having arrived at Grand Cairo, when the caravan was setting off in safety, she ever expressed a wish that *she* had been present during that period of terror and confusion, of which she envied us the participation. On hearing Chenu declare that he feared he must make a *show* of engaging, notwithstanding the deficiencies under which he laboured, and which evidently rendered the idea of resistance on our part a mere farce (since we had neither arms, ammunition, nor men on board sufficient to abide the contest), she positively insisted on having a chair brought up on deck in which she was determined to sit and see the engagement; observing that it was the next best thing to escaping from shipwreck. Having no ambition to play the heroine in this way, I resolved on going below, and exerting (should it be necessary) my limited abilities in assisting Mr. Taylor, who had agreed to officiate as surgeon, not feeling myself inclined to brave horras of this nature for the mere love of exhibition. Most probably had the matter become serious, she would not have been permitted to indulge her fancy, but by degrees our suspicious visitants sheered off without venturing to commence an attack, seeing us so well prepared to resist them ; and we flattered ourselves that our fears had been altogether groundless.

The next morning, Hare and two others, going on shore to reconnoitre, brought back intelligence that we might all be safe at the Danish Factory on condition of our passing for Danes, as a misunderstanding actually subsisted between Hyder Ally and the English. Mr. Passavant, the Danish Consul, had been on board meanwhile, and given us pretty nearly the same information, and from others we learnt a circumstance, which confirmed our apprehension that some mischief was brewing. This was the departure of Mr. Freeman, the English Consul, who had left the place some weeks before, taking with him his furniture and effects —a positive proof that he supposed hostilities were about to commence, and, as it has been a common procedure in these cases for Asiatic Princes to begin a war by imprisoning the ambassadors or residents, of course, wise men will fly when the storm blows.

Now, our most worthy fellow-passengers had privately agreed to continue their journey by land, and rejoiced in the opportunity of leaving us in the lurch. They, therefore, accepted Mr. Passavant's invitation immediately without consulting us. At first this behaviour affected me a good deal, and I resolved to follow them, Mr. Fay concurring in my opinion. But, on calm reflection, we judged it most prudent to learn what reception they met with, before *we* ventured on their slippery ground. On Sunday, Chenu dined on board, and appeared very earnest for our quitting the ship; but we did not attend to his persuasions. The gunner, who had charge of the vessel, was a very respectable man, and we had lately held many conversations with him. He had a vile opinion of the Captain, believing that money would tempt him to commit *any* act however atrocious, and he had resolved, in case an armed force was seen approaching the ship, to cut and run down to Cochin with all the sail he could set. But alas! before Chenu left us, this day he ordered all the yards to be struck, saying he should stay six weeks. This was doubtless done to frighten us and to induce us to go on shore; but, having taken our resolution, we were not to be moved, especially as he dropped some dark hints respecting the situation of those who were there, insomuch that we had reason to think that our only chance of escaping imprisonment was by remaining where we were. Meantime intelligence reached us from various quarters that disputes ran high between the Captain and his passengers about the remaining half of their passage money. As they proposed leaving the ship there, he demanded payment, which they refused till they should arrive in Bengal.

On the 8th, came Lewis, Hare's servant, for his own clothes. He brought news that a challenge had again passed between his master and Chenu on the occasion of his master's trunks being stopped for the passage money: he left them on the point of deciding it when he came off. You may suppose we became exceedingly anxious to learn the event, but we soon had other matters to engross our attention.

During the three days we stayed here, after every one else departed, boats full of people were continually coming on board, by permission of our *worthy* Captain, under the pretence of viewing the ship. We thought this rather odd, but John, the Gunner, being, as I observed before, a prudent steady man, we trusted to his discretion. About four on Monday afternoon, I was sitting in the Round House at work, when a large boat came alongside with *more* than twenty *armed men* in her. One of them showed a written *chit*, as he called, it from Chenu. Notwithstanding which John insisted on their leaving their arms behind them : this they at length complied with and were then permitted to enter. I ran down half-frightened to Mr. Fay, who was reading in our cabin, and told him the affair. "Pho," said he, "it is impossible they should mean any harm. Are we not under the protection of the Danish flag?" This silenced me at once, and he went upon deck to see the issue. All this while our visitors feigned to be mighty ignorant and inquisitive, peeping into every hole and corner, as if they never saw such a sight in their lives—purposely dallying on the time till just dark, when, to my great joy, they departed. A heavy squall came on, which they sheltered from under the ship's stem. There another boat met them, and, after some parley, they both (as I thought) went away.

But, in a few minutes, down came Mr. Fay. "You must not be alarmed," said he, "I have news to tell you. We are to have a hundred and fifty seapoys on board to-night." "Seapoys : for what?" "Why the English are coming to attack Calicut. Chenu has promised Sudder Khan, the Governor, his assistance and he has sent these troops for our defence." "O Mr. Fay," replied I, "this is a very impossible story. For GOD'S sake, suffer not these people to enter the ship, if you can avoid it : otherwise we are ruined. I see plainly this is a second Suez business." For by the same treacherous pretext they gained the possesion of the ship there. At that instant all that those unfortunate men had suffered coming fresh into my mind, I really thought that I should have fainted. Seeing that I was rendered more uneasy by being kept in suspense, he now acknowledged that, under favour of the night, a large party headed by a Captain Ayres, an Englishman in Hyder's service, had already made good their entrance. The Commander had, indeed, related the same nonsensical tale to our Gunner, as an excuse for his proceeding, but did not seem himself to expect it would gain belief. Being, however, nearly destitute of arms and ammunition (the Arabs had taken care of that) what could we do but recommend ourselves to the Divine Protection, which, I may say, was never more earnestly solicited by me? When the redoubtable Captain Ayres had settled everything upon deck, he favoured us with his company below. As this gentleman is in great power and has a large share in the subsequent transactions I must devote a few moments to giving you a little sketch of his history.

He was born in London; and, at the usual age, bound apprentice to a saddler: but, being a lad of spirit, associating himself with other promising youths of similar talents and courage, he soon found employment more suited to his active genius. In a word, he became a "Gentleman Collector on the *Highway*." This post he maintained several years, and, if we may credit what he relates in a boasting humour, performed many notable exploits. It is true he sometimes got inclosed in the hard grip of the Law but he always found means to liberate himself from it; till, on one unlucky trial, proofs ran so strong against him, that, in spite of money and of friends (which in his case were *never* wanting), he was *capitally convicted*, though afterwards pardoned on condition of transport for life. This induced him to enlist for the East Indies, where he exercised his former profession, and was twice imprisoned at Calcutta on suspicion, but having acted cautiously, nothing positive appeared against him. So, by way of changing the scene, he was draughted off for Madras, where, finding his business rather slack and his pay insufficient to support him without it, our Hero determined on deserting to Hyder Ally, which resolution he soon found means to put in practice, carrying with him two horses, arms, accoutrements, wearing apparel and everything else of value he could lay hands on to a pretty considerable amount. This show of property, no matter how acquired, gave him consequence with Hyder, who immediately promoted him to the rank of Captain. Being a thorough-paced villain, he has during, these seven years taken the lead in every species of barbarity. He even advises his General, who is governor of this province, to massacre all the natives by way of quelling a rebellion, which has arisen. The least punishment inflicted by him was cutting off the noses and ears of those miserable wretches, whose hard fate subjected them to his tyranny. In short a volume would not contain half the enormities perpetrated by this disgrace to human nature. But to proceed, at the sight of him I shuddered involuntarily, though, at that time, ignorant of his real character—such an air of wickedness and ferocity overspread his features. The Sergeant, who accompanied him was (always excepting his master) the most horrid loathsome creature I verily believe in existence. From such anoth er pair the Lord defend me! Ayres told me, with the utmost indifference, that the people at the Factory had all been fighting duels, that Mr. Passavant, the Danish Chief, had sent for a guard to separate them, and that the Governor (finding the ship had no owner, as all these disputes arose about dividing the spoil) had thought proper to take possession of her in the *Nabob's* name, until matters were inquired into after which he faithfully promised to restore her, without the least embezzlement—the love of justice alone inducing him thus to act.

Though we perceived the fallacy of these pretences, yet, as it was useless to argue with this vile instrument of oppression, we only requested to be set on shore with our effects. This he engaged for, and even offered to take *charge* of any valuables or money. You may be sure we pleaded poverty, declaring that (except our clothes, which could be of no object in a country where so few are worn) a guinea would possess all that we possessed. In the meantime, we requested a guard to protect our persons from insult. Having pledged his *honour* for our security, the Captain departed. You will believe that sleep did not visit our eyelids *that* night. The fright had disordered me so much that a violent retching came on, succeeded by a strong fever, which occasioned dreadful pains in my limbs. In the midst of these excruciating tortures, I heard Ayres tell his Sergeant that orders were come to plunder the ship, and all the officers and prisoners in the Round House.

Can anything be imagined more distressing than my situation without means of relief, no possibility of obtaining advice, and no female from whom I could look for succour or assistance? This was about two in the morning—these words sounded like the signal of death in my ears. Immediately a party of armed men surrounded our cabin and demanded entrance, I clung round my husband and begged, for God's sake, that he would not admit them. For what could be expected from such wretches but the most shocking treatment! All this while there was such a noise without of breaking and tearing to come at their plunder as convinced me that we should at once lose sight of our little property. *Everything was lost:* at first they were pacified at being told that I was asleep; but soon grew out of patience, brandished their scimitars, and one man, who spoke a little English, threatened with horrible execrations to murder us, if we did not instantly comply with their demands and open the door. Mr. Fay drew his sword on this declaration, swearing solemnly that he would run the first man through the body who should presume to enter his wife's apartment. His air of resolution and menacing actions had their effect so far as to prevent them breaking open the door, the top of which being smashed I beheld through it their terrific countenances, and heard them incessantly calling *Ao, Ao* (in English "come"). This word made an impression upon me which is indescribable. I can never hear it pronounced on the most common occasion without trembling—but to return. Mr. Fay now entreated me to rise if possible, being fearful he could not much longer keep them at bay. I endeavoured to comply, but the agonising pains I suffered and the extreme weakness brought on by fever, rendered it impossible for me to stand upright. There was, however, no other remedy. So by degrees I got my clothes on. [I recollect now that I must have been above an hour employed on this business.] Through the glass door I could see the villains outside use menacing gestures and urge me to make haste—vowing vengeance on me, if I kept them longer waiting.

Expecting a strict search and being desirous of rescuing something from the general wreck, Mr. Fay contrived to conceal our watches in my hair, having first stopped their going by sticking pins in the wheels; and the little money we possessed and what articles I could take without exciting suspicion, were concealed about my person. Thus equipped I crawled out, *bent double*: in an instant, the cabin was filled with seapoys. I must here pause and allow my sister to imagine herself in my situation at that dreadful moment. No language I can find would do justice to my feelings.

But, when I came on deck, the scene which presented itself would have appalled the stoutest heart. Mine, already weakened by grief and apprehension, I could not withstand it. A sudden burst of tears alone saved me from fainting. The poor sailors were so distracted that many of them could scarcely be restrained from jumping overboard to escape slavery—sometimes crying for their wages and asking the officers to pay them, who, incapable of affording any consolation, walked about like men bereft of reason—no wonder since this fatal event would, to say the least, occasion them the loss of twelve months' pay—exclusive of their private

venures

We were immediately ordered on shore, together with the carpenter and ship's steward. We demanded our luggage but in vain. At length, having represented the necessity of a change of linen, a person was sent down with me, in whose presence I put up a few common things in a handkerchief, not being allowed to take anything of value. But having laid out a silk gown the day before to put in a case I went ashore, I begged hard for that, and obtained it, though my husband was not suffered to take a second coat or even to change that he had on. Our beds were likewise refused lest they should contain valuables, and upon the deck the bundle was again examined in search of hidden treasure. But finding nothing, they, contrary to my expectations, searched no further but permitted us to leave the vessel unmolested, except that they had the cruelty to toss several half-extinguished *blue lights* into the boat, the smoke of which, from the rancid oil and abominable rags used in their composition, almost stifled me. At this time it rained hard and continued to do so the whole day, which forced me to creep under the shelter of a kind of half-deck where I sat bent double for two long hours, and then a remarkably high surf prevented large boats from landing. We had no remedy but to go into a canoe, scarcely bigger than a butcher's tray and half full of water, so that we reached the shore dripping wet. Compare this account with the many cheerful and flattering conversations we have held together on the subject of my arrival in India. What a striking difference! It is true we were in the hands of the natives, but little did I imagine that any power on this continent, however independent, would have dared to treat *English* subjects with such cruelty as we experienced from them.

As if to aggravate our miseries by every species of insult, they compelled us to walk above a mile, through a heavy sand, surrounded by all the mob of Calicut, who seemed to take pleasure in beholding the distress of white people—those constant objects of their envy and detestation. When we had proceeded about half way, our guards detained us nearly an hour in an open square till the Governor's pleasure should be known. He sat all the while smoking his *hooka* and looking down upon us: when, having sufficiently feasted his eyes, he ordered us to be taken to the English Factory. How I dragged on my weary aching limbs I know not. The rain still poured: as we went a lad, who had deserted from Madras and was then a sergeant in Hyder's service, seeing a country-woman in such distress, offered to procure me an umbrella, but could not prevail on the barbarians to stop while he ran for it though he was their officer. I thanked the lad for his kind intention, and Mr. Fay insisted that I should take his hat, while he walked on bare-headed to the place of our confinement. But here I cannot describe the horror which seized me on finding that we were totally in the power of wretches, who, for, ought I knew, intended to strip and murder us. Why else were we sent to an empty house? Not a single chair to sit on, or any other bed but the floor! These were my heart-breaking reflections, as I threw myself on a window seat, worn out with fatigue and want of nourishment; without the means of procuring even a draught of water to assuage my thirst, which grew excessive; for the offer of a bribe would have been dangerous.

In this miserable condition we remained till two o'clock, when Mr. Passavant, having heard of our misfortune, sent us a dinner, but his messenger had very great difficulty in obtaining admittance with even this temporary relief. From him we learned that the other passengers were hitherto unconfined, but expected every moment to be made prisoners. After Mr. Fay had dined (for my anxiety continued so great, that exhausted as I was, I could not touch a morsel of what was brought), I besought him to look round for some place into which I might crawl and lie down unseen by the seapoys that guarded us. He was averse to this lest they should imagine that we were seeking to escape and make that a pretext for ill-usage; but, perceiving that the sight of these prevented me from taking that repose so necessary to recruit my poor worn-out frame, he complied with my request, and, having discovered a lumber-room leading out of the verandah, which surrounded the house, he assisted me into it. Here, with my little bundle for a pillow, I stretched myself on the floor amidst dirt and rubbish, and enjoyed a fine sleep of more than three hours, when I awoke refreshed and entirely free from the dreadful tortures, which had racked me the whole night. I did not even feel any symptoms of pain.

Surprised and thankful for the change, I joyfully went down to Mr. Fay, declaring that I would continue to make use of the lumber-room to sleep in, and, as Mr. Passavant had, during my nap, sent me a rattan couch, though, by the by without either mattress, pillow, or mosquito curtains, I was just going to have it conveyed there, when the place was found to be swarming with venomous reptiles—perhaps a hundred scorpions and centipedes. Happily I slept too soundly to feel them, and I remained unmolested, but had I moved hand or foot what might have been the consequence?

The next morning we had a visit from Mr. Hare; less, it appeared, to condole with us on our unexampled suffering than to embrace the occasion of displaying his own eloquence, for which having a very strong passion, it was no wonder if he thought the misfortunes of others proper subjects to expatiate on. Mounting his rhetorical hobby-horse, the orator harangued a long while though to little purpose, endeavouring to turn our situation into ridicule. He offered to convey letters for us to Bengal, pretended to be in raptures with the fine view of the sea from our verandah, which I hinted he might still have time to admire at his leisure though he affected to be certain of leaving Calicut in a few hours. At length he concluded by advising me to address a *tender* memorial to Hyder Ally, whose general character for gallantry would not admit of his refusing any request made by a *fair* lady. This was wonderfully witty in the speaker's opinion, as you may conceive how *fair* the lady in question looked. How a man could break a jest on a creature so bowed down by affliction I know not, but I envy not his feelings.

I forgot to tell you that the duel between the captain and the orator was prevented by the guard, doubtless to the regret of these heroes. It seems the day they went on shore, Ayres accompanied by another captain of a pretty similar description, named West, made Mr. Passavant a visit to look at the strangers. Now as it was of the utmost importance that they should remain undiscovered by such dangerous people, and, as their visitants, though illiterate, were sufficiently acute, all perceived immediately the necessity of being guarded. Accordingly they every one spoke French, and this together with their long wide coats and *preposterous* hats, which had just then become fashionable in England, effectually shielded them from suspicion. When, behold, a sudden fit of patriotism, aided by an irresistible fondness for exhibition, rendered the great Mr. Hare incapable of persevering in the deception. "What," exclaimed he, "shall *Englishmen* harbour distrust of each other? Perish the ignoble idea! Be the consequences what they may, I will no longer restrain myself from embracing my beloved countrymen." At the conclusion of this heroic speech, "suiting the action to the words," advancing theatrically, he grasped the hand of Ayres and shook it with such violence as if he meant to demonstrate the excess of his joy and confidence by dislocating the shoulder of his newly acquired friend.

The most unreserved intimacy immediately took place between these two congenial souls, and it is asserted that, unable to keep any secret from his bosom confidant, Hare was really so mad (I may say so cruel), as absolutely to acknowledge the ship to be English property. I could not have believed his folly and imprudence would carry him so far. This much is, however, undoubtedly fact that the man in the spectacles is continually pointed out as the author of every mischief which followed. It is surprising how often we find weakness and malignity united, or rather let us say that Providence has thus ordained it for the benefit of mankind. Probably the former induced Hare to injure the party to which he had attached himself; the latter undoubtedly led him to visit us, for he could not conceal his exultation at the circumstance of our accidental capture in the vessel seeming to involve us exclusively in her fate. This unfeeling wretch availed himself of this to lay a scheme, which had it been adequately seconded, must have brought on our destruction.

Ayres was first prevailed on by large presents to dissuade the Governor from confining *them*. That point gained, he pushed their interest forward thus: "These gentlemen," said he, "have no concern here of any kind; besides, as they are people of the highest consequence, their detention would bring half India on our back, so take my advice and let them go." "Well but," replies Sudder Khan, "what must I do with my prisoners?" "Oh keep them by all means," replies *Beelzebub*, "the man is a stout fellow, and after a little breaking in, will make a most excellent soldier. Send him and his wife up the country: there feed them on dry rice, he will soon be glad to enlist I warrant you. Th chief of the other party, Mr. Hare, is a brother lawyer, so you need not fear. He will be glad enough to get rid of him. Indeed he owned as much to me privately and pledged his honour that no ill-consequence could possibly arise from the transaction—the person in question not being of sufficient importance for the English to reclaim him solemnly, especially as he came here without leave." You will wonder how I came by all this information. Have patience, you shall know in time.

The Governor heard this argument calmly, promised fair and acted so far agreeably to his professions that, while *we* were closely confined and miserably situated, our worthy fellow-passengers enjoyed full liberty to walk about and amuse themselves as they pleased. This procedure could not fail to vex us excessively though we were then ignorant its real cause, and whenever we ventured to expostulate on our unreasonably harsh treatment with Ayres, or any other who chanced to call the only answer we could obtain was (with a shrug of affected compassion) " Why did you stay on board? Nothing can be done for you *now*. You must abide the event." These insinuations created fears that a distinction would really be made in our eventual disposal as much to our disadvantage as the present state of things, but we had no remedy All the avenues to relief were closed.

think I told you that our watches were concealed in my hair, being secured with pins to prevent them from going. One of the pins, however, came out at the very time I was set on shore. Never shall I forget what terrible sensation the ticking of the watch caused! I think had it continued long I must have completely lost my senses, for I dared not remove it from fear of worse consequences, but happily it stopped of itself. When we were fixed in our prison, Mr. Fay took these watches (we had three you know) and all the money we had power to secure in chequins, which are easy of conveyance (about twenty-five pounds), and putting them into his glove hid them in a snug place, as he thought, about the verandah. The day after we were taken prisoners, a most dreadful hurricane of rain and wind came in (it was the break up of the monsoon,) and next morning we found to our extreme grief that the place where Mr. Fay had concealed our treasure, to which alone we could look for means of escape, was entirely blown down, and no vestige of our little property remaining. Mr. Fay was in despair from the first: yet after he had told me, I searched diligently all round but in vain. At length it struck me that, from the direction in which the wind blew, if I could make my way into an enclosure at the back of the house, it might possibly be found there. The seapoys guarded the front, but there being only one door at the back, they seldom took the trouble of going round. I did not tell Mr. Fay of my scheme, for there was nothing he opposed so strongly as the appearance of seeking to escape ; but, when he was completely absorbed in contemplating this new misfortune, I stole to the back door. There was a large lock and the key inside, and to my surprise, when I had turned this, my passage was clear to the stairs leading to the enclosure, and not a soul in sight. The grass was excessively high and wet, but I struggled to make my way through it, and waded about determined at least not to leave an inch unexplored. Imagine my joy, when in the midst of a deep tuft, I found the old glove with its contents safe and uninjured. What a treasure it seemed! How many are there who ever felt such a true delight on receiving a magnificent fortune, as we experienced in again beholding this sheet anchor of our hopes thus unexpectedly restored.

But alas! the little unlooked for liberty I had regained was too tempting not to be enjoyed again, and a day or two afterwards, as I was walking about in the grass, I spied a seapoy coming round. I was not certain that he saw me so I endeavoured to reach the house unobserved. At the moment I turned round to fasten the heavy door, he ran to it, pushing it against me with such violence that the large key, which had unfortunately a very long shank, by this means struck directly against my right breast and gave me the most excruciating pain. I fainted through excessive agony, and was with difficulty recovered. Much I fear the consequences of this accident will embitter my future life. Having no other nurse than my poor husband, who was not only ignorant of what ought to be done, but totally without the necessaries for any kind of emollient application, my case was truly distressing so that even Ayres, who chanced to call, expressed some concern for me, and sent plenty of milk which I used as an embrocation with success. I believe he punished the seapoy for his insolence, but this could not repair the mischief.

At the very time when this painful event took place in the cheerless monotony of our prison days, the cruel designers, who had assisted in dooming us to this dreadful abode, fell completely into the pit which they had digged for us. The evening before, Ayres, Tulloh and Hare had called on us together: the former was (according to his general *policy*) endeavouring to discover whether we had any concealed property, on which I exclaimed: "Captain Ayres how should we have anything left, except the baggage in the vessel which is of little value, as the Arabs pillaged us to the utmost of their power. We were altogether a set of poor creatures when we came to Calicut and you are well aware that we have received nothing since." "Answer for yourself, Mrs. Fay," cried Hare, "for my *own* part I feel happy in saying that I am *not* poor: I have property—*valuable* property, and shall not shrink from avowing that I possess it." I marked the eye of Ayres during this bombastic speech, and have since found that I was not deceived in its expression.

Sudder Khan, induced by this and other stories, which the passengers had told of their own consequence, determined to frighten them into the payment of a large sum of money. Accordingly next morning (the 13th) he sent a large party of seapoys to the Danish Factory who peremptorily demanded them as the Nabob's prisoners. Mr. Passavant at first refused, but, on their threatening to fire into his house, was constrained to yield to this outrageous violation of the most sacred rights, and delivered his guests to slavery. God forbid that I should, generally speaking, be capable of rejoicing in the miseries of my fellow creatures, even where they merit punishment, but I must own (blame me if you will) that for a short time I *did* feel satisfaction in this state of retributive justice, in as far as regarded the Tullohs and Hare, for the vile conduct of these people and the malevolence of their disposition, had steeled my heart against them.

It was certainly a curious sight to behold them, after all their airs of superiority, reduced to take up their residence with us, whose situation when singular had been the object of their ridicule and contempt. The scene was, however, now changed. Although *they*, like many others in the world, were able to support their neighbours' misfortunes with stoical firmness, and even to render them a source of amusement, each readily discovered, when personally attacked by a similar calamity, that close imprisonment is by no means a proper subject on which to exercise wit, and that people when in distress are not precisely in the humour for relishing the pleasantry of others on their troubles. Tulloh fortunately understood Moors, which is the general language among the military throughout India. By this means he got his trunks on shore the day after the seizure, and saved them from the violent storm, which came on next morning, wherein every one imagined the ship must have been wrecked. How we wished to see her drive on shore especially when Sudder Khan, the Governor, who is Hyder's brother-in-law, was seen walking about in great perturbation on the beach anxiously watching the vessel, praying to Mahomet, and from time to time casting up the sand to Heaven with earnest invocations and entreaties that she might be spared as a present to the great Hyder; very probably fearing that some blame might attach to him in case she were lost.

As it happened, however, all things went wrong for us. The cabin and steerage where we had been placed were soon filled with water, and everything—books, wearing apparel, beds, with laces, buckle rings, etc.,—was either stolen or totally spoiled. These latter I might have saved when we were brought on shore, but unfortunately the trunk, which contained my clothes was just *without* the cabin door, and two of the wretches, who watched us, sat on it so that I could not remove an article This disaster left us nothing but our lives to be anxious about. Why do I say anxious since life on the terms we held it was hardly worth preserving? The other passengers' luggage was injured but not like ours; for we not being favourites, had been forced to keep our packages at hand during the voyage, as we had no one to get them up when wanted, whereas the rest had theirs stored away in the hold and consequently very little damage befell them. Many ships perished in this terrible hurricane. The *St. Helena*, which left Mocha a week after us, met with it, and suffered so much that she was forced to put into Cochin (a Danish settlement in latitude 10) with the loss of her masts; and so greatly shattered besides as to be compelled to undergo thorough repairs. If this happened to a fine new vessel, what must have become of us had we continued five days longer at sea, badly found in all respects and worse manned, not half the people enough to work the ship properly even in good weather? Was not this another hairs-breadth escape, think you, though by a dreadful alternative? The ways of Providence are inscrutable! But to revert to my main subject, and glad shall I be when it is concluded, for I detest matter-of-fact writing. Yet this story must be told in my own way or told not at all.

When the gale ceased, the whole cargo was landed and deposited in the Governor's warehouses, where he caused the gentlemen's luggage to be opened; and, like a child pleased with gee-gaws, every article which struck the eye was instantly condemned as his booty. Poor Hare's trunks were stuffed with knick-knacks like a pedlar's box. Judge then what agonies he appeared in when the fatal moment of examination approached lest they should become, as might be expected, objects of desire to the Governor. Not a single toothpick case, knife, or knee-buckle was produced but what he declared had been received as a pledge of friendship from different relations—parents, sisters, male and female cousins to the utmost verge of propinquity, all put in their claims with success. Tulloh serving as interpreter until he was perfectly weary of the office, ashamed of pleading trifling causes, and only deterred from throwing up his post by the earnest entreaties of Hare, who continued stamping, exclaiming and fretting, as if his life depended on the issue. At last a small paper bundle fell into the searcher's hands. He then became outrageous. "For Heaven's sake," cried he (almost breathless with apprehension,) "my dear friend, for Heaven's sake endeavour to preserve this parcel for me. Should it be taken I am an undone man, for I shall never be able to replace the contents. Let them take my clothes, my law-books, everything except my music books, all that I can yield without a sigh." Tulloh imagining that the contents must be of immense value to him from his extreme agitation, earnestly interceded for the parcel, but obtained it with great difficulty, as curiosity and avarice were awakened by the convulsive eagerness with which the owner pleaded for it. The former was soon gratified and the latter consoled, for Hare, tearing open the parcel, discovered to the astonished spectators neither more nor less than an exquisite assortment of Venetian fiddle strings!! But ah! dire mischance! the remorseless waves, which are neither respecters of persons nor things, had pervaded this invaluable treasure and rendered it wholly useless. To complete his misery the next thing that presented itself to the sad owner's eyes was a most expensive and finely toned tenor violin purchased at Venice, for which the precious strings were intended, broken all to pieces! I leave you to form any ideas you may think proper on the subject of that extravagant sorrow such a character was likely to exhibit; I pass on to matters more interesting.

The general introductory letter which as you may recollect Mr. Franco gave us at Leghorn had remained in Mr. Fay's pocket book from that time till we reached Calicut. We had been told that Isaac, the Jewish merchant, who agreed to freight the *Nathalia* and received £700 as earnest on that account, was immensely rich, and had great credit with the Government of which he held several large contracts for building ships, etc., besides a very great one with Sudder Khan. Everyone also, even Ayres, spoke highly of his general character. But our introduction to Mr. Baldwin had been productive of, or at least connected with, so many misfortunes that my confidence was lost, and I dreaded making further applications lest similar events should ensue. This was very foolish reasoning you will say, and I am ready to acknowledge it : the only excuse to be made is that my mind was weakened by calamity. However, after Tulloh and the rest of these people joined us, our situation became, if possible, still more distressing, and we anxiously sought every practicable mode of relief. Mr. Fay, therefore, petitioned the Governor for leave to go out under a guard, which being granted, he immediately delivered his letter to Isaac, who seemed highly gratified at hearing from Mr. Franco, whom he had personally known at Constantinople, where they were both young men, about *sixty years* ago, for, like him, he enjoys a full possession of his faculties, both bodily and mentally, being equally remarkable for temperance and sobriety. Mr. Fay could not speak to our strangely acquired friend except by an interpreter so that no confidential conversation could take place. He was apparently touched with pity for our sufferings, especially on hearing how much I was afflicted with illness. My spirits were raised by the account my husband gave of his visit, and soon after his favourable report was confirmed by a present brought to the Factory by a servant belonging to the benevolent Jew which in our situation was truly valuable, consisting of a caddy of fine tea, a teapot, and a tea-kettle. Although these things were expressly sent to me, yet Mrs. Tulloh and her party seized the last mentioned article and forcibly kept it, so that I was forced to make my tea by boiling it in my teapot. Ah! my dear sister, I was ill enough at this time to be laid up on a sick bed and carefully nursed, yet I was thankful for such food as I should have once loathed, and I still continue on my rattan couch, without pillow, or any covering except my clothes, and surrounded by people whom my very heart sickened to behold.

I will here by way of relaxation transcribe a few passages from my journal, as nothing happened for some time worthy of a particular recital, reserving for myself, however, the option of resuming the narrative style, whenever I shall deem it necessary.

14th November, 1779.

Mr. Fay was sent for, this morning, to the Governor, who asked him what he wanted. He replied "Liberty." There was no observation made on this answer, nor can we conceive what Sudder Khan can mean by the detention of so many persons who never bore arms. They gave Mr. Tulloh 30 rupees for our support. All we are able to procure is tough, lean, old beef, goat flesh and a not unpleasant rice cake but too sweet to be palatable with meat: we preserve either with difficulty from our perpetual visitors the crows, having no cupboard or place to put our vessels on. Of all existing creatures the crows are surely the most voracious and the most persevering. I have seen one with his eye fixed for a full hour on a person, and, the instant that person's eye was averted, pounce on the bread or whatever had been prepared and bear away the prize. Mem.—Ayres is remarkably like these crows, he has the same *thievish* expression of countenance and form of his head resembles theirs.

15th November, 1779.

The gentlemen waited all day at the Governor's house, being promised their baggage, but he thought proper to disappoint them. Received 10 rupees subsistence money.

18th November, 1779.

A most impudent message brought from the Governor requiring all the gentlemen to enter into Nabob's service which they unanimously refused, with every mark of contempt, and were in consequence closely confined. One of Mr. Fay's trunks were brought on shore containing wearing apparel and law books probably much damaged, yet certainly most valuable to him, as he had none remaining. Made application for it but without success. Tulloh received 20 rupees.

20th November, 1779.

Received notice to prepare immediately to set off for Seringapatam, a large city about three hundred miles distant, where Hyder Ally usually resides. How can I support this journey over the mountains! Mr. Fay is about drawing up a petition representing the bad state of my health, and entreating permission for me to proceed to Cochin. We hope to prevail on Issac to present it.

21st November, 1779.

Discover that the journey to Seringapatam was merely a vile plot of the Governor's to put us off our guard and thereby gain possession of what property had hitherto been concealed. Thank God! this feint miscarried. A letter reached us from Mr. O'Donnell stating the arrival of the *St. Helena* at Cochin. He laments our misfortune and promises to take such methods as shall compel the Nabob to do us speedy and effectual justice. Heaven speed his endeavours. This life is horrible.

22nd November, 1779.

The gentlemen waited five hours at the Governor's for their effects, but returned without them. He takes evidently a satisfaction in seeing them like slaves attendant on his nod. Five ships supposed to be English passed in front of our prison. How peculiarly disagreeable did I feel this sight.

23rd November, 1779.

Mrs. Tulloh being taken ill of a fever, application was made to the Governor for medicine, but this happening to be a high festival, he, like the Pharisees in Scripture, refused to profane it by doing good. Should the woman die in the interim what cares he?

24th November, 1779.

This morning got some medicines from the ship's chest. Many flying reports of hostilities having actually commenced between Hyder Ally and the English. Should this really prove true our fate will be sealed *for life*. Little did I think when pleading the cause of the Chevalier de St. Lubin at Mocha, that he had been raising a storm, whose effects would so materially involve us. Mem.—The lady is well again.

28th November, 1779.

It is now certain that the Nayhirs have laid siege to Tellicherry, a settlement of ours about a degree to the northward. Seven miles nearer lies Mahey, which the French held till we took it from them in March last, but not finding it worth keeping, have since evacuated it, after dismantling the fortifications.

29th November 1779.

Suddér Khan is about to march a thousand troops into Mahey, under the pretence of resuming it in the Nabobs' name; but everyone guesses this to be merely a feint to cover his real intentions of privately assisting the Nayhirs. Should they succeed in their attack, Hyder will throw off the mask and declare war: but if the English conquer, he will disown the whole affair.

30th November, 1779.

I have now a lamentable tale to relate. We were this morning hurried away at a moment's warning to the Fort, crowded together in a horrid dark place scarcely twenty feet square, swarming with rats, and altogether suffocating for want of air. Mr. and Mrs. Tulloh secured a small room to themselves: but my husband and I were obliged to pass the night among our companions in misery—rats continually gnawing the feet of my couch and their perpetual squeaking would have prevented sleep had our harassing reflections permitted us to court its approach.

1st December, 1779.

Luckily discovered a trap-door, which led to some rooms or rather lofts, where no human foot had trod for many many years. These had been the storerooms of the Pirate Angria and they certainly contain "a remnant of all things"—broken chairs, looking glasses, books: even a spinnet was among the articles but beyond all repair, and vast quantities of broken bottles, which had been filled with liquors of all kinds; but the rats in their gambols had made havoc among them. I remember when I should have shuddered at the thought of sleeping in such a wretched place, but now privacy gave it irresistible charms. So, having with difficulty obtained leave to occupy it, we exerted every nerve to get a spot cleared out before dark for my couch and likewise so to arrange some lots of canvas which were among the spoils as to form a sort of mattress for Mr. Fay. Here we lay down comparatively happy in the hope of enjoying a tolerable night's rest, my husband being provided with a long pole to keep off the rats. Never, surely, were mortals so completely disappointed, and for my part I may add terrified. No sooner was the light extinguished than we heard a fluttering noise attended at intervals by squeaking. By degrees it approached the beds, and we felt that several creatures were hovering over us, but of what description we were totally ignorant. Sometimes their wings swept over our faces, seeming to fly heavily: then again they would remove further off, but still continued squeaking. Good God, what horrors I felt. Mr. Fay protested that whole legions of evil spirits had taken possession of our apartment and were determined to expel the intruders. The rats also acted their part in the comedy, every now and then, as we could hear, jumping towards the beds. However, Mr. Fay on these occasions laid about him with his pole and thus kept them at bay. Our winged adversaries were not so easily foiled. They persisted in their assaults till daybreak, when what should we find had caused all this disturbance, but a parcel of poor harmless bats whose "ancient solitary reign we had molested." To any one accustomed to see or hear these creatures our terror must appear ridiculous, but to me who had never chanced to meet with any such, the idea never occurred, nor did even Mr. Fay suggest any probable or natural cause of alarm. We cannot help laughing very heartily at it ourselves now and you are at full liberty to do the same.

2nd December.

Ayres called to tell us that two ships of the line and a frigate had just passed towards Tellicherry. We shall soon hear news from thence. Oh! may it change our hard destiny! The Governor marched at the head of his troops towards Tellicherry.

10th December.

Application was made this morning to the Lieutenant-Governor through Mr. Isaacs, who, I am convinced, is our true friend, representing that, this air disagreeing with me, I requested permission to remove to Cochin, and that my husband, on account of my extreme ill-health, ought to accompany me. He promised to consult Sudder Khan upon it. The Quelladar, or Governor of the Fort, spent some time with us this morning. He is a fine old man with a long red beard and has altogether a most interesting appearance. Here I may as well give a short description of this place.

Calicut, then, is situated on the coast of Malabar in 11° north latitude and 75° east longtitude. It was formerly a very considerable town governed by a Zamorin, who also held the adjacent country, but it has been some years in possession of Hyder Ally, of whom you must have heard on the occasion of his wars with the English in 1770. They would certainly have put an end to the reign of this usurper had he not discovered a method of influencing the principal persons in power, in consequence of which he obtained a peace much more honourable and advantageous to himself than to those who granted it. Having acquired by his genius and intrepidity everything that he enjoys, he made his name both feared and respected so that nobody chooses to quarrel with him. I have indeed heard a comparison drawn between him and the King of Prussia, though I think much to the disadvantage of the latter as supposing their *natural* abilities to be equal. The great Frederick ought infinitely to surpass a man who can neither write nor read, which is the case with Hyder. The lawful prince of the country which he has usurped, the government is held by him in actual confinement, though with every outward show of respect, by which means he prevents the people from rising, lest their legitimate sovereign should fall a sacrifice to his resentment.

The Fort must have been formerly a strong place, but is now in a dilapidated state. The walls are very thick, and they mount guard regularly, which was one inducement to send us here, as Ayres told the Governor it was not worth while to keep a hundred sepoys watching us when they were wanted elsewhere and that the Fort was quite good enough for us to live in. These arguments prevailed, and here we were sent. When I first arrived I was so extremely ill as to be scarcely sensible of what passed for some hours; but I remember Hare burst into a flood of tears, declaring that we were all doomed to death by our removal to this wretched spot, which being completely surrounded by stagnant water, could not fail to produce some of those disorders so fatal to Europeans. We have not, however, hitherto experienced any complaint. The loft we sleep in is indeed disgusting beyond belief, and the Quelladar, I suppose at the suggestion of Ayres, has ordered the easier of the two ways of entrance, that discovered by Mr. Fay, to be blocked up, so that there is no way left but by means of a ladder placed almost in a perpendicular direction. There is a rope by which to hold, or it would be impossible for any person to descend, but even with this assistance I have great difficulty to reach the bottom.

11th December.

Peremptorily ordered to make ready for a journey to Seringapatnam. By the Governor's desire delivered an inventory of our losses. He promises full restitution, but has given no answer to my request. I am full of solicitude on this subject, but would submit to anything rather than remain in this wretched place.

12th December.

Mr. Fay waited twice on the Lieutenant-Governor, but without effect. What can he mean by thus trifling with us? Is it merely a wanton exercise of power, or intended to hide some dark designs. These perpetual surmises distract me. Mem:—Tulloh received 144 rupees to pay *all* our debts, but took especial care not to let us have a single rupee. What wretches we are cast among! My very soul rises at them.

13th December.

Mr. Fay was sent for by the Governor, who told him that we might both have permission to go to Cochin whenever we thought proper, that he would furnish us with a boat and pay every incidental expense, besides making entire satisfaction for damages sustained. Can all this good news be true? How suspicious I grow! What a change from being credulous! Yet where is the wonder after being so frequently deceived?

14th December.

Preparations are going on briskly all day with our fellow-passengers, who are eager for their departure, as well they may. Everything which was taken from them on shore has this day been returned, but the things left in the ship are irrecoverable. Of course, we benefit nothing by this restitution. Mr. Fay could not obtain our promised license to-day. These delays weigh down my spirits and increase all my complaints. I have still much pain in my breast. Oh! that I fear will prove a fatal blow. I shall have a great loss in Mr. Taylor.

15th December.

The Governor still with holding our license, under the pretence of business, I advised Mr. Fay to insist on being *immediately* despatched, or, in the case of refusal, by all means to declare himself ready to accompany the others. For I saw clearly that should they once leave us, it must then be entirely at this fellow's option whether we went all or not, and who would rather not run even the risk of dying of fatigue on the journey than hazard remaining at the mercy of such wretches. I dread lest this should be part of the old plan of which I have since never heard, and had almost forgotten it. It is much easier to practice against two individuals than a whole company.

16th December.

The doolies (a kind of shabby palanquin in which a person sits upright and is carried between two men) arrived this morning about ten. The gentlemen went to take their leave, when Tulloh earnestly represented our case, to which the Governor replied that he could not possibly attend to other matters till they were gone, but pledged his word that nothing should arise on his part to detain us a single hour afterwards. Everyone agreed with me how dangerous it was to trust such fallacious promises. On my knees I entreated Mr. Fay to persue the method I had before pointed out, but my advice was despised. At nine in the evening the party commenced their journey, having just first stripped the place of provisons and everything else which, having been bought out of the general purse, we had an undoubted right to share. They even took my tea kettle, but luckily the man who had it in charge forgot it amidst the hurry of departure. My heart sunk within me at seeing them quit the Fort, not from motives of esteem or regret (as you may suppose), for it was impossible to grieve for the loss of some of the company. We parted with as much indifference as absolute strangers, after a fellowship in misfortune sufficient to have united almost any other society more closely than an intercourse of years under common circumstances. I went to bed, but in spite of every endeavour to calm the agitation of my mind, passed a sleepless night.

17th December.

Rose in extreme anxiety, which was far from being diminished by a message from the Governor ordering Mr. Fay not to attend him till the evening. Accordingly at four o'clock he sat out, and as I felt extremely ill, the certain consequence of the fretting and want of rest, I lay down and had just sunk into a dose, when my poor husband flew into the room like a madman, uttering a thousand extravagant expressions. Starting up in new and indescribable terror, and wringing my hands, I begged only to know what had happened. "Happened!" cried he, "why we are betrayed, ruined, utterly undone. You must leave this place instantly, or you may be made a prisoner here for ever." "Where are we we to go?" I very naturally asked. I *heard* not the answer. My head swam, and I dropped on the floor completely overpowered. Whatever happened at that *fearful* moment I forget and endeavour to banish from my mind as the effect of insanity. How he accomplished it, I know not but Mr. Fay actually carried me in his arms down that almost perpendicular ladder, which I had described, and placed me on a kind of bier. I was in this manner conveyed to my former habitation. I opened my eyes and became for a few moments sensible of the motion, but soon fainted again and did not recover till I found myself once more entering the English Factory as a prisoner.

I now inquired what was the cause of this change in our abode, and learned that Mr. Fay, being refused leave to depart had became so exasperated as wholly to lose all self-command and rushing up to the *musnud* (throne) of the Lieutenant-Governor had actually seized him peremptorily insisting on the immediate fulfilment of his promise. Such conduct might have been expected to bring down *instant* destruction, but fortunately every one present was persuaded that grief and vexation had literally turned his brain. They are not only terrified at every species of madness, but, from their religious prejudices, regard sufferers under these complaints with a superstitious awe. Swayed by these mingled emotions the wicked Governor condescended to temporise with my husband acknowledging that he had no power to release us without the Nabob's order which in consideration of my ill-health he would endeavour to procure. To pacify him further, he permitted our return to this place, where we are certainly in this respect more comfortably situated. But these concessions went little towards allaying the fever of passion which his continual and cruel delays had executed. Thence arose the alarm which I experienced and which for a time so materially affected my health.

19th December.

Received 5 rupees for subsistence money, which we were informed were the last we should ever have. I cannot conceive what they mean to do with us or what will be our fate at last.

21st December.

The Governor sent for Mr. Fay to offer him a commission in the Nabob's service, and, on his absolute refusal, swore that he might subsist how he could, that his master's money should no longer be lavished on idlers. Then in a rage he ordered palanquins. "You shall go to Seringapatnam" said he, "they will soon teach you better manners there." Mr. Fay joyfully acquiesced in this mandate. We provided necessaries for our journey, which was fixed for the 24th. The other knew better than to keep his word. So this, like all our former views and expectations ended in smoke—shall I say?

26th December.

A very melancholy Christmas-day passed yesterday. My dear friends little imagined they were drinking the health of a poor prisoner. For I know you did not forget us: neither were we forgotten here, if empty compliments can be styled remembrance. All the Europeans and several of the natives attended our levee. But alas! what relief can mere ceremonious visits afford to misfortune? say rather that *aided by recollection* such shadowy comforts add keeness to affliction's sting. I feel my mind insensibly raised whenever I attempt to expatiate on any subject which tends to revive the ideas of our separation. Even now I tread forbidden ground. For your sakes as well as my own, let me hasten to escape by skipping over this dangerous season of Christmas. I therefore pass on.

10th January 1780.

The little money saved was nearly expended, and we must soon have been reduced to our last mite, had not Providence sent us relief from a quarter little dreamed of. Mr. Fay wrote about a week ago to Mr. Church, Governor of Tellicherry enclosing a memorial of our case, which he requested might be translated into the language of the country and proper methods used for its safe delivery to Hyder Ally himself. This morning brought in reply a most generous humane letter from Mr. Church, which, after acknowledging himself honoured by our application and promising his utmost concurrence in every measure we may think necessary, concludes thus: "My heart bleeds for your distresses and those of Mrs. Fay. She, in particular, must have suffered greatly. I have taken the liberty to accompany this letter by an order for two hundred rupees to serve *present* occasions. Any sum you may in future require, a line to me shall always command it, as I know the difficulties of procuring remittances where you are. Englishmen ought to feel for each other. We are not without our share of troubles here, and I verily believe Hyder is at the bottom of all." Now, pray does not this letter deserve more than I have said of it? Just thus would my dear father have treated a distressed countryman. Methinks I see his benevolent heart venting itself in tears of sympathy at this recital. Precious tears! Why am I not permitted to mingle mine with them? For they will flow in spite of my endeavours to restrain their course.

11th January.

Having now money to bribe with, we began to think of an escape. For besides the silence observed on the fate of our companions, though near a month has elapsed since their departure, we live in continual dread of being forced up country and perhaps massacred there. Every one who leaves this places must first obtain permission from the Governor, but as these passes only mention generally *so many people*, and are granted indiscriminately to whoever applies for them (provided they be not suspected persons), one can easily be procured under feigned pretences. It is a matter frequently done. A Friar belonging to the Portuguese convent usually manages these affairs when properly instructed. This information we have from a native Portuguese, named Pereira, an officer in Hyder's service, with whom Mr. Fay commenced an intimacy while we were in the Fort, and who is now quartered here at his special request. Though I must confess, I cannot like this man, yet I am obliged to trust him. The visits we receive from Ayres are terrible trials to one who loathes dissimiluation as I do. This wretch has once or twice mentioned a cow that annoyed him by entering the little garden or paddock in which it appears is house his placed. This morning he entered the factory with his scymitar in his hand unsheaved and bloody. With an expression of dilabolical joy he informed me that he had just caught the animal entering, and, being armed, had completely chined her. "You cannot imagine," said he, "how *sweetly* the sword did the business." My heart shuddered with horror and indignation, yet I dared not give vent to those feelings. I doubt not he would murder me with as much pleasure as he killed the cow with, and have no reason to suppose he would be punished for the act.

12th January.

Some quarrel unknown to me has certainly taken place between Pereira and Mr. Fay. The looks of the latter alarm me. His dark scowling eye is frequently directed towards him with an expression of dreadful import. Yet he appears desirous of forwarding our escape. He has introduced us to Father Ricardo, who engages to provide us for all things for our departure to Cochin.

13th January.

The priest breakfasted with us, and promised to set about the business without loss of time. He is to receive twenty rupees on our setting from thence, and twenty more on our arrival at Cochin or Tellichery, through the medium of Isaac, on which the order from Mr. Church was drawn, by which means we received it without suspicion.

14th January.

A license or passport is procured for us as two Frenchmen going to Mahey. We have paid twenty rupees boat-hire to a smuggler. These are commonly very courageous men: which is some comfort to me. Under Mr. Fay's protection and his, I will endeavour to think myself secure. His house is admirably situated for that purpose, close by the river side. This is to be our place of rendezvous. The precise time is not yet fixed upon. The intervening hours! How anxiously they will pass.

15th January.

The boatman called to desire we would be at his house at six this evening. We gave him our little luggage (we had been obliged to purchase many necessaries) and four rupees to buy provisions. When it grew dark, Mr. Fay put on a sailor's dress, and I equipped myself in a nankeen jacket, a pair of long striped trousers, a man's night cap and over that a *mighty* smart hat, with a pair of Mr. Fay's shoes tied on my feet, and stick in my hand. In this dress Mr. Fay declared I was the very image of my dear father, which highly gratified me. I had tied the clothes we took off in a handkerchief. With that in one hand, and brandishing my stick in the other, I boldly sallied forth, taking care, however, to secure a retreat in case of accidents—a most fortunate precaution as the event proved. Father Ricardo met us at the smuggler's, according to appointment, and we paid him twenty rupees, and gave him security for another twenty. When this was settled, nothing remained, as we supposed, but to step into the boat. When, behold! news was brought that the sailors had made their escape no one knew whither. After waiting two hours in that dangerous situation to see if they would return, and raving in all the folly of angry disappointment against those who had misled me, we made a virtue of necessity and trudged back to our prison, where we luckily effected an entrance without exciting suspicion.

17th January.

Had all arranged for our escape last night, but so many people were about us, that we dared not make the attempt.

19th January.

Father Ricardo has once more arranged all things for to-night. We must give more money, but that is no object. Once free and we shall doubtless find means of proceeding on our journey.

5th February.

Every day has this wicked priest contrived some fresh scheme to amuse us with false hopes of escaping. Every night have we lain down in the full persuasion that it was the last we should pass in confinement, and as constantly have we awoke to meet bitter disappointments. This continued alternation of hope and fear preys on my spirits and prevents me from gaining strength, but yesterday I received a serious shock from the behaviour of Pereira which excited more alarm than almost any circumstance that has occurred to me.

I had long marked his hatred to Mr. Fay, and dreaded his revenge. I was sitting at work when he, naked from the middle, entered the room just as Mr. Fay was going into the next room. His strange appearance and the quick step with which he followed my husband caught my attention, and I perceived that he held a short dagger close under his arm nearly all concealed under his handkerchief. The exigency of the moment gave me courage. I sprang between him and the door through which Mr. Fay had just passed, drawing it close and securing it to prevent his return, and then gently expostulated with Pereira on the oddness of his conduct and appearance. He shrunk away, and I hope will never trouble us again, especially as he has adopted another mode of revenge which may be equally effectual, though more slow in its operation. He went to Ayres and informed him that we had endeavoured to escape, mentioning every particular of our scheme, and, as far as I can learn, telling the whole truth; but fortunately naming a different evening from the one on which our unsuccessful attempt really was made: on which Ayres exclaimed: "Well, Pereira, you have made up a very fine story but without a word of truth. For on the very night you mention, Fay was sitting with me over a bottle of wine. I'll take my oath of that, for it was my birth night." This was true likewise, so we were saved for the time; but, as Ayres knows that, escape is in our heads; he will, I fear, guard us with a redoubled vigilance, and so far Pereira's design has taken effect.

6th February.

Mr. Fay has completely detected the pious Father Ricardo and his worthy colleague, the smuggler, and sorely against their will, compelled them to refund his money all to about twenty-three rupees, which they pretend has been disbursed. We now discovered that, although our offers might tempt their avarice and lead them to deceive us, yet they dared not persevere in assisting our escape, as the consequences of detection would to them be inevitable death.

10th February.

At length I begin to cherish hopes of our speedy release, as Sudder Khan returned last night from Seringapatnam, but is encamped without the town, waiting for a lucky day, till when he dares not enter his own house. So how long we may still be detained, Heaven knows. Mr. Fay and our friend Isaac propose paying him a visit to-morrow.

13th February.

They went on Friday and again to-day, but have not yet been able to obtain an audience, and thus we may perhaps be led on a fortnight longer by his ridiculous superstitions. Mr. Isaac, however, assures my husband that from all he can learn it is really intended to release us, which makes me comparatively easy: yet it is impossible not to feel severely this delay at such a critical period: for should Hyder commence hostilities against the English whilst we remain in his power, not all Isaac's influence will be sufficient to extricate us from it. Our doom must be sealed for life.

14th February.

Our indefatigable advocate walked out with Mr. Fay—(I should have mentioned that the distance is about three miles), but they were again disappointed, Sudder Khan being still closely shut up at his devotions, which are to continue six days longer at least. How very distressing to be kept in all this horrible suspense. Our friend still comforts us with the assurance that all will be well. He really behaves to me like a father, and as I have now acquired some knowledge of Portuguese, we are enabled to converse fairly well. I do not recollect having described his person, and will therefore endeavour to give you some, though a very inadequate, idea of it. Isaac, then, is a fine venerable old man, about eighty-five, with a long white beard; his complexion by no means dark and his countenance being yet majestic. I could look at him till I almost fancied that he resembled exactly the patriarch whose name he bears, were it not for his eye which is still brilliant. His family, I find, according to ancient custom in the East, consists of two wives, to whom I am to have an introduction.

15th February.

Saw a letter to-day from Mr. Tulloh to Mr. Passavant, the Danish Factor, dated 19th January which mentions that they were fifteen days on their journey to Seringapatnam, and twelve more confined in a shed, half-starved to death, as no one was permitted to assist them except with the coarsest food in small quantities. At length the Nabob granted them an audience, when having listened to their complaints, he sent for Sudder Khan to answer the charge. "Three successive days," says Tulloh, "we were all sent for and confronted with him, when Hyder commanded him to make instant restitution. However, we have, as yet, received nothing, except that yesterday on taking leave His Highness presented us with five hundred rupees for our journey to Madras, besides ordering our palanquins, carriages for our baggage, and every other convenience, likewise a guard of a hundred seapoys to conduct us into the English bounds. I spoke to him for Mr. and Mrs. Fay, and obtained an order for their release also. Whether the ship will be returned or not, God knows. We are just to set off." Thus far Tulloh. Now the man who brought this letter saw them all go, and remained at Seringapatnam ten days afterwards without hearing further; so I hope we may conclude they are now out of *their* troubles. Mrs. Tulloh has now seen enough, poor woman, to satisfy her taste for adventures.

From all I can learn, it would have been utterly impossible for me to have supported the various hardships of their journey in my precarious state of health. Poor Mr. Taylor, how sincerely do I pity him.

17th February.

Mr. Isaac called by appointment about two o'clock, and took my husband with him to wait *once more* on the Governor. He seems to entertain no doubt of bringing back the order for our release. I endeavour to be calm and to rest with confidence on his assurance; but when I contemplate the dreadful alternative, should he meet a peremptory refusal, and recollect the deep machinations that have been practised to keep us here, my heart recoils at the idea. It is now eight in the evening: everything is packed up and ready for our departure: yet they return not. Some obstacle must I fear have been thrown in their way by that vile Sudder Khan to prevent our liberation and we are destined to remain his wretched prisoners. How shall I support this intelligence? Heaven inspire me with fortitude! I can neither write nor attend to anything.

LETTER XIII.

COCHIN, *19th February, 1780.*

THANKS be to Providence that I am at length permitted to address my beloved friends from this land of liberty towards which my wishes have so long pointed. After wading through my melancholy journal, you will perhaps be enabled in some measure to form an idea of the joy that fills my breast on contemplating the contrast between my present situation and that from which I have so recently escaped. I will not, however, indulge in reflections, but hasten to proceed with my narrative, which broke off at a most interesting period in my last letter, when I was every instant expecting the news of our release.

I was not relieved from suspense till near twelve on Thursday night, when the gentlemen returned bringing with them the so-anxiously desired passports for ourselves and such trifling articles as remained in our possession. More than this, I find they could not obtain for us, though absolute promises of restitution and remuneration have been frequently held out. This, however, seemed a slight evil with what even *one* day's detention might produce. We, therefore, abandoned all thought of further application on the subject, and on Friday, 18th February, at 5 A.M., joyfully quitted our detested prison, and repaired to the house of our steady friend and benefactor Isaac, when we found one of his sloops prepared to convey us to Cochin, with every refreshment on board. Thus, by the indefatigable exertions of this most excellent man, we are at last released from a situation of which it is impossible for you to appreciate the horrors. To him we are indebted for the inestimable gift of liberty. No words I can find adequate to the expression of my gratitude. In whatever part of the world, and under whatever circumstances my lot may be cast, whether we shall have the happiness to reach in safety the place to which all our hopes and wishes tend, or are doomed to experience again the anxieties and sufferings of captivity, whether I shall pass all the remainder of my days in the sunshine of prosperity, or exposed to the chilling blasts of adversity, the name of *Isaac the Jew* will ever be associated with the happiest recollections of my life; and, while my heart continues to beat and warm blood animates my mortal frame, no distance of time or space can efface from my mind the grateful remembrance of what we owe to this most worthy of men. When we were plundered and held in bondage by the Mahometan robbers amongst whom we had fallen, when there was no sympathising friend to soothe us among our Christian fellow-captives, when there was no hand to help us, and the last ray of hope gradually forsook the darkening scene of our distress, kind Providence sent a good Samaritan to our relief in the person of this benevolent Jew, who proved himself an Israelite indeed. Oh my dear sister! How can I, in the overflowing of a grateful heart, do otherwise than lament that the name of this once distinguished people should have become a term of reproach! Exiled from the land promised to the seed of Abraham, scattered over the face of the earth, yet adhering with firmness to the religion of their fathers, this race, once the boasted favourites of Heaven, are despised and rejected by every nation in the world. The land that affords shelter denies them a participation in the rights of citizenship. Under such circumstances of mortifying contempt and invidious segregation, it is no wonder that many of the children of Israel in the present day evince more acuteness than delicacy in their transactions, and are too well disposed to take advantage of those from whom they have endured so much scorn and persecution. It gives me, therefore, peculiar pleasure to record their good deeds, and to proclaim in *my* limited circle, that such men as a FRANCO and an ISAAC are to be found among the posterity of Jacob. These sentiments are not overstrained but the genuine effusions of a thankful heart : as such receive them.

19th February, 1780.

This morning, about eleven, we arrived at our long-wished-for Port, and were landed close to the house of our good friend Isaac which is pleasantly situated by the river side, about a mile from Cochin, and rendered in every respect a most delightful residence. Here we were welcomed by the two wives of Isaac who were most splendidly dressed to receive us, rather overloaded with ornaments yet not inelegant. Indeed I think the Eastern dresses have infinitely the advantage over ours. They are much more easy and graceful ; besides affording greater scope for display of taste than our strange unnatural modes. They were extremely hospitable and very fond of talking.

I mentioned before having learned a little Portuguese during my imprisonment which was of great advantage to me here ; for, except Malabar, it is the only language they speak, and a miserable jargon indeed is what they call Portuguese here. However, we contrived to make ourselves mutually understood so far as to be convinced that each was kindly disposed towards the other. Had I been differently circumstanced, it would have given no great pleasure to have accepted the pressing invitations of these ladies to pass some time there. The entire novelty of the scene would have amused me. Novel I may well call it in more respects than one. We were entertained with all the profusion that wealth can command and generosity display. Though religious prejudices banished us from *their* table, ours was loaded with every delicacy—all served on massive plate. Among many articles of luxury which I had never seen before were numbers of solid silver *peekdanees*, which serve the purpose of spitting boxes (excuse the term). They stood at each end of the couches in the principal room. Some of them were nearly three feet high with broad bottoms; the middle of the tube twisted and open at the top, with a wide mouth for the convenience of such as had occasion to expectorate. These are not what *we* should call indulgences in England, but in a country, where smoking tobacco and chewing betel are universally practised, they must be allowed to be necessary ones.

You will judge what a change these apartments were to me when contrasted, not with our prison in the Fort of Calicut (for our residence there was undoubtedly the acme of wretchedness), but with the house in which I had so long lived without any furniture at all save my unmattressed couch, an old table and three broken chairs, and where many a time the poor Portuguese lad, who served us, had entered at the hour of dinner empty-handed, exclaiming that the dogs had carried off all that had been provided. My own face I never saw during the whole period, there not being so much as the fragment of a looking-glass to be obtained.

The younger wife of Isaac attached herself to me in such a manner as I never before experienced, and really appeared as if she could not bear to part with me even when I went to see the town of Cochin, which is truly a very pretty romantic place. What was far more to my satisfaction, we luckily found there Mr. Moore, who proposed sailing the next day, and kindly offered us a passage on the *St. Helena* which you may be sure we gratefully accepted. On our way back we were accosted by a Captain Richardson, whose ship is under repair here, and will be ready in about six weeks. He shook hands with us as country folks, and directly offered us both a passage to Bengal with every accommodation in his house during our stay here—a most liberal proposal was it not? And which would have been very fortunate for us had we missed the *St. Helena*. In the present case, his offer was, of course, declined; but I shall ever recollect the kindness, which dictated it, and trust that opportunities will be afforded to evince my gratitude.

On the 21st, at 5 A.M., Mr. Fay left me with my new friends, promising to return for me in about half an hour, to the great grief of the fair Jewess who was become so fond of me. Alas! I waited hour after hour, and no husband returned. I was in the greatest anxiety and consternation imaginable, dreading lest some new disaster had overtaken us and that our ill-starred journey was again stopped short in its course. It is impossible for you to conceive what I suffered during his absence and how my mind was harassed by various tormenting conjectures. Those only who have been subject to such cross accidents as I have so frequently experienced can judge of my feelings. At length, about noon, he made his appearance, and very calmly began unpacking his chest as if to replace the things at his leisure. I asked, of course, what had occurred, and if Mr. Moore had changed his intention. "Why," answered he, "Moore and all the rest are gone on board, but somehow I don't think he will sail to-day for all that." This reply almost bereft me of my senses, knowing the consequence of being left behind would be a journey by land to Madras—(for he would never have the patience to wait till Captain Richardson's ship was ready)—the expense of which alone must amount to eight or nine hundred rupees, not to mention the intolerable fatigue of travelling in this country. Aware that if I did not exert myself all was lost, I took a hasty leave of our kind friends, and we proceeded to Cochin with our little baggage, and sent for a boat, but, by this time, the afternoon breeze had set in, and the sea ran so high that none would venture over the Bar. At last a man agreed to provide a large boat and take us off for sixteen rupees. When we came to the water side, what should this mighty boat prove but a narrow canoe, with paddles, scarcely big enough to contain us and our four rowers. I hesitated. The people ran round me on all sides intreating me not to venture, and assuring us both by words and gestures that the danger was imminent. Captain Richardson, who was among them, declared that it would be next to a miracle if we escaped; indeed every moment evidently increased the risk. Mr. Fay, now seeing the error of his delay, swore to run all hazards rather than stop any longer at Cochin—a common practice with most people who have brought themselves into difficulties by their imprudence and who seek to regain by obstinacy what they have lost by folly. Pity such cannot always suffer alone. Finding him positive, I commended myself to the protection of the Almighty and stepped in; all the spectators seeming to look upon me as a self-devoted victim. Yet how was it possible to avoid going? Had I refused, Mr. Fay would constantly have upbraided me with whatever ill-consequence might have resulted from the delay, and who could wish for life on such terms? "No," thought I at the moment, "rather let me brave death in the line of my duty than have my future days embittered by reproach however unmerited." As we proceeded the waves gradually rose higher and higher, and began to break over us. One man was continually employed in baling out the water, though his only utensil was a bamboo, which hardly held a quart. Never shall I forget what I felt on looking round in this situation; every wave rising many feet higher than the boat and threatening to overwhelm us with instant destruction. I sat at first with my face towards the stern, but afterwards moved to the front, and when I saw a wave coming bowed my head to receive it. We were a mile from the shore, and at least two from the ship. Was not this sufficient to appal the stoutest heart? Yet I can truly say that my mind was perfectly composed, conscious of the rectitude of my intentions. I could look boldly up to Heaven for protection. Mr. Fay will tell you how frequently I begged him not to entertain the least doubt of our safety. "We have never," said I, "been conducted thus far by the hand of Providence to perish. Remember my dear parents: is not *their* happiness involved in *our* safety? Depend upon it we shall be preserved to become the humble instruments of rendering their declining years happy."

While I was speaking a tremendous wave broke over us and half filled the boat with water, on which, thinking it would be presumptuous to proceed, we ordered the men to make for the nearest land. This the wind would not permit, so we were obliged to keep on, and had reached within a mile of the ship, when she began to spread her sails, and in a few minutes got under weigh with a fair wind. Our people now wanted to quit the pursuit, as she gained ground considerably, but we kept them in good humour by promising more money, and putting a white handkerchief on a stick waived it in the air. After some time we had the pleasure to see her tack about and lie to. So, in another half hour, we came up with her, having been three hours in the condition I have described—wet through and nearly frightened to death, being every moment in the most imminent danger. To describe my joy or my impatience to quit the boat is impossible. Without waiting for the chair to be lowered, I scrambled on board, and, had I not been relieved by a violent burst of tears, must have fainted.

Everyone in the vessel blamed Mr. Fay exceedingly for running such a risk by his delay, as the other passengers, who went on board in the morning, did not experience the least inconvenience. Mr. Moore luckily came in the provision boat, which was six hours in getting on board. This circumstance was the means of saving our passage.

When we reached Ceylon the wind became contrary—which, together with a strong current, kept us upwards of three weeks beating off the Island before we could weather Point de Galle. This will account to you for my letter being scarcely legible. I am at this moment writing on my knees in bed; and, if I had not been contented with this method all the way, I could not have written at all. My father well knows a vessel has not a very agreeable motion when beating up in the wind's eye.

4th April.

At length, thank Heaven! We are at anchor in the Madras Roads, having been six weeks making a passage that, with a fair wind, we could almost have performed in as many days. Happily for me our society has been very different from the last I was condemned to mix with on shipboard. Of these Mr. Moore and Mr. O'Donnell are of the utmost importance to us. Our acquaintance with them commenced in Egypt, and as they were indeed (though innocently) the cause of all we suffered there, a very agreeable fellowship has naturally taken place between us. The latter is now obliged to return to India to begin life again (his losses on the Desert having been followed by many unavoidable expenses as you will learn from my narrative), and seek a competence under all the disadvantages an injured constitution, added to a deep sense of disappointment and injustice, subject him to. You may be sure we have had many conversations on the sad story of the Desert and the last moments of those who perished there. A boat is just come to take us ashore, so adieu for the present. The roads are very full. There are eight ships of the line and above sixty other vessels which form a magnificent spectacle.

6th April.

I was exceedingly alarmed yesterday by the surf. We got safe over it, but another boat upset just afterwards; however, fortunately, no lives were lost. Sir Thomas

Rumbold is hourly expected to embark, which is all that detains the Fleet, so that, perhaps, I may not be able to write ten lines more.

6 P.M. As far as I can judge, I feel pleased with Madras, and gratified by the reception I have hitherto met with. I shall, of course, write to you again from hence, being likely to remain here a week or two. At present I must close my letter; but as a matter of curiosity shall just mention the astonishing celerity of the Indian tailors. Yesterday evening Mr. Fay, not being *overstocked* with clothes to appear in, ordered a complete suit of black silk with waistcoat sleeves which they brought home, *before nine* this morning, very neatly made, though the whole must have been done by candle light.

I cannot conclude without saying that, although I feel rather weak, my health is improving, and that the pain I suffer from the accident which befel me at the Factory is not so violent as formerly. God grant I may soon be relieved from apprehensions on that score.

The Governor is gone on board. Captain Richardson, of the *Ganges*, under whose special charge this packet (containing the whole of my narrative from Mocha) will be placed (as I had no safe opportunity of forwarding it from Calicut or Cochin), has sent for it. The perusal will cost you many tears, but recollect that *all is over*, and my future communications will, I trust, be of a very different complexion. May this reach you safely and meet you all well and comfortable. Adieu. God Almighty preserve you, prays your own.

E. F.

LETTER XIV.

MADRAS, *13th April.*

MY DEAR FRIENDS,

Agreeably to my promise, I take up the pen to give you some account of this settlement, which has proved to me a pleasant resting place after the many hardships and distresses it has lately been my lot to encounter, and where, in the kind attentions and agreeable society of some of my own sex, I have found myself soothed and consoled for the long want of that comfort; while my health has reaped great advantage from the same source.

There is something uncommonly striking and grand in this town, and its whole appearance charms you from novelty as well as beauty. Many of the houses and public buildings are very extensive and elegant. They are covered with a sort of shell-lime which takes a polish like marble, and produces a wonderful effect. I could have fancied myself transported into Italy, so magnificently are they decorated, yet with the utmost taste. People here say that *chunam*, as it is called, loses its properties when transported to Bengal, where the dampness of the atmosphere prevents it from receiving that exquisite polish so much admired by all who visit Madras. This may very likely be the case.

The free exercise of all religions being allowed, the different sects vie with each other in ornamenting their places of worship, which are, in general, well built; and from their great variety and novel forms afford much gratification, particularly when viewed from the country, as beautiful groups of trees intermingle their tall forms and majestic foliage, which with the *chunam* and rising spires, communicating such harmony, softness and elegance to the scene as to be altogether delightful—rather resembling the images that float on the imagination after reading fairy tales or the *Arabian Nights'* entertainment than anything in real life. In fact Madras *is* what I conceived Grand Cairo to be before I was so unlucky as to be undeceived. This idea is still further heightened by the intermixture of inhabitants, by seeing Asiatic splendour combined with European taste exhibited around you on every side, under the forms of flowing drapery, stately palanquins, elegant carriages, innumerable servants, and all the pomp and circumstance of luxurious ease and unbounded wealth. It is true that this glittering surface is here and there tinged with the sombre hue that more or less colours every condition in life. Yea, behold Europeans, languishing under various complaints, which they call incidental to the climate (an assertion it would ill become a stranger like myself to controvert), but respecting which I am a little sceptical, because I see very plainly that the same mode of living would produce the same effects even "in the hardy regions of the North." You may likewise perceive that human nature has its faults and follies everywhere, and that *black* rogues are to the full as common as white ones, but (in my opinion) more impudent. On your arrival you are pestered with Dubashees and servants of all kinds, who crouch to you as if they were already your slaves, but who will alway cheat you in every way possible; though in fact there is no living without one of the former to manage your affairs as a kind of steward, and you may deem yourself very fortunate if you procure one in this land of pillagers who will let nobody cheat you but himself. I wish these people would not vex one by their tricks, for there is something in the mild countenances and gentle manners of the Hindoos that interests me exceedingly.

We are at present with Mr. and Mrs. Popham, from whom we have received every possible civility. He is a brother lawyer and a countryman of my husband, and she is a lively woman. Her spirits have, in some measure, restored mine to the standard from which those amiable gentlemen, the Beys of Egypt, Sudder Khan with his co-adjutors—Ayres and my unworthy shipmates, had so cruelly chased them.

We have made several excursions in the neighbourhood of Madras, which is everywhere delightful—the whole vicinity being ornamented with gentlemen's houses built in a showy style of architecture and covered with that beautiful chunam. As they are almost surrounded by trees, when you see one of these superb dwellings encompassed by a grove, a distant view of Madras with the sea and shipping so disposed as to form a perfect landscape, it is beyond comparison the most charming picture I ever beheld or could imagine. Wonder not at my enthusiasm—so long shut up from every pleasing object, it is natural that my feelings should be powerfully excited when such are presented to us.

Nothing is more terrible at Madras than the surf, which, as I hinted before, is not only alarming but dangerous. They have two kinds of boats to guard against this great evil, but yet, notwithstanding every care, many lives are lost. One of these conveyances called the massulah boat is large, but remarkably light, and the planks of which it is constructed are actually sewed together by fibres of the cocoanut. It is well calculated to storm the violence of the surf, but for greater safety it requires to be attended by the other, called a catamaran, which is merely composed of bamboos fastened together and paddled by one man. Two or three of these attend the massulah boat, and, in case of its being upset, usually pick up the drowning passengers. The dexterity with which they manage these things is inconceivable, but no dexterity can entirely ward off the danger. The beach is remarkably fine.

The ladies here are very fashionable I assure you. I found several novelties in dress since I quitted England which a good deal surprised me, as I had no idea that fashion travelled so fast. It is customary to take the air in carriages every evening in the environs of Madras; for excursions in the country these are commonly used, but in town they have palanquins carried by four bearers which I prefer. They are often beautifully ornamented and appear in character with the country and with the languid air of those who use them which though very different from anything I have been accustomed to admire in a woman, as you well know, yet is not unpleasing in a country the charms of which are heightened by exhibiting a view of society entirely new to me.

Mr. Popham is one of the most eccentric beings I ever met with. Poor man, he is a perpetual projector—a member of a race whose exertions have frequently benefited society but seldom, I believe, been productive of much advantage to themselves or their families. He is at present laying plans for building what is called the Black Town to a great extent, and confidently expects to realise an immense fortune, but others foresee such difficulties in the way that they fear he may be ruined by the undertaking. The pleasure he takes in his visionary scheme should not be omitted in the account as of some value, for it really seems to be an uncommon source of enjoyment.

The Black Town is that part of Madras which was formerly inhabited wholly by the natives, but of late many Europeans have taken houses there, rents being considerably lower than in Fort St. George, which is a very strong garrison built by the English, and where since have been constructed many fine houses, etc. This is considered, of course, a more fashionable place to reside in. Between the Black Town and the Fort lies Choultry Plain, which, being covered entirely with a whitish sand, reflects such dazzling light and intolerable heat as to render it a terrible annoyance, especially to strangers. Mr. Fay has been exceedingly pressed to take up his abode here, and really many substantial inducements have been held out to him; but as his views have been all directed to Calcutta, where knowleledge and talents are most likely to meet encouragement, he cannot be persuaded to remain. A capital objection besides is that, no Supreme Court being as yet established, he could be only admitted to practise as an attorney, no advocates being allowed in the Mayor's Court, so that his rank as a barrister would avail nothing here. I most cordially acquiesce in this determination. But I must suspend my scribbling. Mr. Popham is waiting to take me to St. Thomas' Mount.

17th April 1780.

I resume my pen, resolved to devote this chapter to my dear friends, as it is likely to be the last I shall spend in Madras. I found St. Thomas' Mount a very beautiful place. It is a high hill of conical form crowned at the top with white houses and a church built by the Portuguese in memory of some St. Thomas, who they say was murdered on this spot by a Brahmin. The road to this place is delightful, being a complete avenue of the finest trees I ever saw, whose intermingling branches are absolutely impervious to the sun. Not far from hence, I was shown a prodigiously fine Banian tree, the singular nature of which is that its branches bend down to the ground, take root and thence spring out anew, thus forming innumerable arches. I call it a vegetable cathedral, and could not help fancying that Banian groves were formerly appropriated to idolatrous worship, since they are admirably calculated for the celebration of any mysterious and solemn rites from which the uninitiated are excluded, and may be properly described as "temples not made with hands." On the whole I felt highly gratified by my little excursion, which was, I believe, not more than seven miles from Madras.

I must now assure you that I have actually seen with my own eyes several of those things which we girls used to think poor Captain S——took travellers' liberty in relating, such as dancing snakes, jugglers swallowing swords, etc. The snakes were to me somewhat alarming, the other a very disgusting spectacle. When they are become familiar, I may be amused with the one, since the various forms, the prismatic colours and the graceful motions of the snakes may give pleasure which the other exhibitions never can. When you have seen a man thrust a sword down his throat, and are fully convinced that there is no deception, you feel that you have beheld a wonder, and there the gratification ends, for the sight is unnatural and disgusting. With some other tricks of the juggler I was, however, much pleased. He had a manner of throwing four brass balls up and catching them with such amazing rapidity that they perpetually encircled his head, forming a kind of hat around it. He likewise threaded small beads with his tongue, and performed a number of very curious sleights of hand. Dancing girls are a constant source of amusement here, but I was much disappointed in them. They wrap such a quantity of muslin round them by way of petticoat, that they almost appear to have hoops: their motions are so slow, formal and little varied that you see the whole dance (as it were) at once. They are very inferior to those of the same profession at Grand Cairo, though I never saw any there out in the streets. However their dancing is certainly less indecent, at least as far as I could witness it.

There seems to be a strange inconsistency in the character of the natives. They appear the most pusillanimous creatures in existence, except those employed on the water whose activity and exertions are inconceivable. They will encounter every danger for the sake of reward with all the eagerness of avarice and all the heroism of courage ; so that if you have occasion to send off a note to a ship, no matter how high the surf may run, you will always find some one ready to convey it for you and generally without being damaged, as their turbans are curiously folded with waxed cloth for that purpose. So off they skip to their catamarans, for the prospect of gain renders them as brisk as the most lively Europeans.

The Hindus have generally their heads shaved, but they preserve a single lock and a pair of small whiskers with the greatest care. Their manner of writing is curious: they write with iron needles on palm leaves, which are afterwards strung together and form books. Boys are taught to write on the sand—a very good plan as it saves materials and a number can be instructed at the same time. For teaching arithmetic great numbers of pebbles are used : so that every part of the apparatus is cheap.

The natives of India are immoderately fond of an intoxicating liquor called *Toddy*, which is the unfermented juice of the cocoanut or Palmyra tree : suggar and water is also a favourite beverage. Butter is very scarce and not good. What they call *ghee* is butter boiled or clarified in order to preserve it, and is very useful for many purposes, such as frying, etc. On the whole one may live very well at Madras. To me it appears a land of luxury, as you may suppose, when you recollect how I had been accustomed to fare. We may think ourselves very well off in escaping from the paws of that fell tyger, Hyder Ally, as we did, for I am assured that the threat of sending us up the country to be fed on dry rice was not likely to be a vain one. It is thought that several of our countrymen are at this very time suffering in that way. If so, I heartily wish that the war he has provoked may go forward, till those unhappy beings are released and the usurping tyrant is effectually humbled.

Mr. O'Donnell has just called and desired me to prepare for an early summons to-morrow. I have ever found him friendly and attentive, and must always deem myself highly obliged to him, as he certainly had too much occasion to feel hurt by the behaviour of Mr. Fay, whose temper, you must know, is not the most placid in the world. He quarrelled with both him and Mr. Moore during the passage about the merest trifles (wherein he was most palpably in the wrong), and challenged them both. Judge what I must have suffered during these altercations, vainly endeavouring to conciliate, and in agonies lest things should proceed to extremities. On our arrival here, I prevailed on Mr. Popham to act as mediator between the parties; he at length, though with great difficulty, convinced Mr. Fay that he had been to blame, and induced him to make a proper apology to both gentlemen. Thus ended the affair, but I have reason to think that, had I not been with him, he would not have been invited to proceed farther on the ship. Nor am I free from apprehension at present. Yet Mr. O'Donnell has proved himself so true a friend, and has so materially served my husband, that I trust our short trip from hence to Calcutta will prove a pleasant one. I understand that several additional passengers are to join us—which may operate as a check on *fiery spirits*.

18th April.

Mr. and Mrs. Popham have completed their hospitable kindness by insisting that we should partake of an *early* dinner (at one o'clock), after which we immediately proceed on board, and heartily rejoiced shall I be when once over the terrific surf. I leave Madras with some regret, having met with much civility and even sympathy here. I must now bid you adieu. In my next, I hope to announce that my long pilgrimage is ended. I likewise shall expect to find letters from you waiting my arrival at Calcutta. My anxiety at times rises to impatience lest any evil should have befallen you during the long period in which all communication has been suspended between us. My heart, however, yet retains its power of conversing with you. Whenever I see anything new or entertaining, I directly imagine how *you* would have looked and what *you* would have said on the occasion; and thus cheat myself into a pleasing dream of social intercourse with those most dear to me.

Our stay at Madras has been the means of procuring us some respectable recommendations to persons in Calcutta, for we have made several desirable connections here. Hope again smiles on us, and I endeavour to cherish her suggestions: for it is as much my *duty* as my *interest* to keep up my spirits, since, in my present state of health, without them, I must wholly sink, and now more than ever I feel the necessity of using exertion.

The hot winds prevail here at present which renders the weather peculiarly oppressive, but a few hours will change the scene. Adieu. Remember me in your prayers, my beloved parents, my dear sisters, and rest assured of the unalterable affection of your own

ELIZA.

LETTER XV.

CALCUTTA, *22nd May 1780.*

MY DEAR FRIENDS,—I may now indeed call for your congratulations since, after an eventful period of twelve months and eighteen days, I have at length reached the place for which I have so long sighed, to which I have looked with innumerable hopes and fears, and where I have long rested my most rational expectations of future prosperity and comfort. I must now, in order to keep up the connection of my story, return to Madras, and from thence conduct you here regularly.

Mr. Fay and Mr. Popham both assured me that a massulah boat was engaged, but on arriving at the beach none could be had. So, there being no remedy, I went off in a common cargo boat, which had no accommodation whatever for passengers, and where my only seat was one of the cross beams. How I saved myself from falling Heaven knows. Mr. Fay was under the necessity of exerting his whole strength to keep me up, so he suffered *a little* for his negligence. It is what is called a black surf and deemed very dangerous. There were some moments when I really thought we were gone, for how could I, in my weak state, have buffetted the waves, had the boat overset? When once on board, our voyage passed comfortably enough. Our society was pleasant: indeed Mr. O'Donnell is ever a host to us in kindness. Mr. M., our supercargo, was, however, more strict in his enforcement of rules than was agreeable to most of us. We were kept more orderly than so many children at school, for if we were in the midst of a rubber of whist, he would make us give over at nine precisely, and we were obliged keep our score till the following evening. But this was of little moment, for as we advanced towards the place of our destination, we were too much interested to think of anything else. We had a distant view of the pagodas of Jaggernath, three large pyramidical buildings, very famous temples among the Hindoos, who there worship the images of Jaggernath and keep a splendid establishment of the priesthood attendant on the idols in the manner of the ancient heathens. I am credibly assured that, at stated intervals, the principal figure is taken out in an enormous car with a great number of wheels, beneath which his votaries prostrate themselves with the most undaunted resolution, firmly persuaded that, by thus sacrificing their lives, they shall pass immediately after death into a state of everlasting felicity. Well may we say that "life and immortality were brought to light by the Gospel," since in these regions, where its sacred influence is unknown, or unattended to, we see such gross acts of folly and superstition as these sanctioned by authority. May it please the Almighty disposer of events to hasten the period of their emancipation that all mankind may hail each other as brothers, and we may be brought together "as one fold under One Shepherd."

Calcutta, you know, is on the Hooghly, a branch of the Ganges ; and, as you enter Garden Reach, which extends about nine miles below the town, the most interesting views that can possibly be imagined greet the eye. The banks of the river are, as one may say, absolutely studded with elegant mansions called here, as at Madras, garden-houses. These houses are surrounded by groves and lawns, which descend to the water's edge, and present a constant succession of whatever can delight the eye or bespeak wealth and elegance in the owners. The noble appearance of the river also, which is much wider than the Thames at London Bridge, together with the amazing variety of vessels continually passing on its surface, add to the beauty of the scene. Some of these are so whimsically constructed as to charm by their novelty. I was much pleased with the snake boat in particular. Budgerows, somewhat resembling our city barges, are very common: many of these are spacious enough to accommodate a large family. Besides these, the very different kinds of pleasure boats intermixed with the mercantile vessels and ships of war, render the whole a magnificent and beautiful moving picture, at once exhilarating to the heart and charming the senses: for every object of sight is viewed through a medium that heightens its attraction in this brilliant climate.

The town of Calcutta reaches along the eastern bank of the Hooghly. As you come up past Fort William and the Esplanade it has a beautiful appearance. Esplanade Row, as it is called, which fronts the Fort, seems to be composed of palaces. The whole range, except what is taken up by the Government and Council houses, is occupied by gentlemen in the settlement. No person being allowed to reside in Fort William but such as are attached to the Army gives it greatly the advantage over Fort St. George, which is so incumbered with buildings of one kind or other that it has more the look of a town than of a military Garrison. *Our* Fort is also so well kept, and everything in such excellent order, that it is quite a curiosity to see it. All the slopes, banks, and ramparts are covered with richest verdure, which completes the enchantment of the scene. Indeed the general aspect of the country is astonishing, notwithstanding the extreme heat (the thermometer seldom standing below ninety in the afternoon). I never saw a more vivid green than adorns the surrounding fields—not that parched miserable look our lands have during the summer heats, large fissures opening in the ground as if all vegetation were suspended. In fact, the copious dews, which fall at night, restore a moisture to the ground and cause a thick short grass to spring up which makes the finest food imaginable for the cattle. Bengal mutton, always good, is at this period excellent. I must not forget to tell you that there is a very good race ground at a short distance from Calcutta which is a place of fashionable resort for morning and evening airings.

Through Mr. O'Donnell's kindness, we were introduced to a very respectable Portuguese family, who received us with the greatest civility, inviting us to take up our abode with them, until we could provide ourselves with a house. Mr. Da C. was a widower, but his late wife's sisters, who resided with him, were born at Chandernagore (a French settlement between twenty and thirty miles higher up the river), but from long disuse they had lost the habit of *speaking* their native language, though they *understood* it perfectly. So I was forced to make out their Portuguese in the best manner I could, constantly answering in French. In this way we frequently conversed, and I gained much information respecting the customs of the place, the price of provisions, and many other useful matters.

Fortunately, throughout all our difficulties we had preserved our letters of introduction by keeping them always concealed about us, together with Mr. Fay's admission to the Bar and other credentials which were essentially necessary to his establishment here : so that my husband immediately became known to Sir Robert Chambers, who behaved to him with utmost attention, and whose lady after hearing a little of my melancholy story, and finding I was too much indisposed to admit of my paying my respects to her, had the goodness to waive all ceremony and, accompanied by her husband, to visit me at the house of the Portuguese merchant which was a condescension that I certainly had no right to expect. She is the most beautiful woman I ever beheld—in the bloom of youth, and there is an agreeable frankness in her manners, that enhances her loveliness and renders her truly fascinating. Her kindness towards me daily increases, and she seems never weary of listening to my sad story. "She loves me for the dangers I have passed, and I love her that she does pity them."

29th May.

I have delivered my letter of introduction to Mrs. Hastings, on whom I should have waited long ago had the state of my health admitted of the exertion. She resides at Belvedere house, about, I believe, five miles from Calcutta, which is a great distance at this season and for an invalid. The lady was fortunately at home, and had three of her most intimate friends with her on a visit—one of them, Mrs. Motte, a most charming woman. Mrs. Hastings herself, it is easy to perceive at the first glance, is far superior to the generality of her sex, though her appearance is rather eccentric, owing to the circumstance of her beautiful auburn hair being disposed in ringlets throwing an air of elegant, nay almost infantine simplicity over the countenance, most admirably adapted to heighten the effect intended to be produced. Her whole dress too, though studiously becoming, being at variance with our present modes, which are certainly not so, perhaps for that reason, she has chosen to depart from them. As a foreigner, you know, she may be excused for not strictly conforming to our fashions; besides her rank in the settlement sets her above the necessity of studying anything but the whim of the moment. It is easy to perceive how fully sensible she is of her own consequence. She is indeed raised to a "giddy height," and expects to be treated with the most profound respect and deference. She received me civilly and insisted on my staying to dinner, which I had no inclination to refuse: but she seemed not to evince much sympathy when I slightly touched on the misfortunes which had befallen me. Nay, she even hinted that I had brought them on myself by imprudently venturing on such an expedition out of mere curiosity. Alas! Mrs.

HASTINGS' HOUSE, ALIPUR.
(Photo by C. F. Hooper, Esq.)

Hastings could not know what you are well acquainted with—that I undertook the journey with a view of preserving my husband from destruction; for, had I not accompanied him, and in many instances restrained his extravagance and dissipated habits, he would never, never, I am convinced, have reached Bengal, but have fallen a wretched sacrifice to them on the way, or, perhaps through the violence of his temper, been involved in some dispute, which he was too ready to provoke.

But to return, I could not help feeling vexed at Mrs. Hastings' observation; to say the best of it, it was unfeeling—but I excuse her. Those basking in the lap of prosperity can little appreciate the sufferings or make allowance for the errors of the unfortunate, whom they regard as almost beings of another order.

You will expect me to say something of the house, which is a perfect *bijou* most superbly fitted up with all that unbounded affluence can display, but still deficient in that simple elegance which the wealthy so seldom attain, from the circumstance of not being obliged to search for effect without much cost, which those but moderately rich find to be indispensable. The gardens are said to be very tastefully laid out, but how far this report is accurate I had no opportunity of judging, the windows being all (as it were) hermetically closed—sashes, blinds and every opening, except where *tatties* were placed, to exclude the hot wind. This surprised me very much, but I understand no method is so effectual for that purpose. I was not permitted to take my departure till the evening, when the fair lady of the mansion dismissed me with many general professions of kindness, of which I knew how to estimate the value.

Next morning we received an invitation to the ball annually given on the King's birthday. This, however, I was under the necessity of declining on the plea of ill health, and Mr. Fay could hardly ever be persuaded to attend such formal assemblies.

When my husband waited on Sir Elijah Impey, the Chief Justice, to show his credentials, he met with a most flattering reception. It so happened that he was called to the Bar from Lincoln's Inn itself, and seemed quite at home while perusing the papers, being acquainted with the handwriting of the officers who prepared them, and perhaps that circumstance might render him more partial. On Mr. Fay's expressing some apprehensions lest his having come out without leave of the E. I. Company might throw obstacles in the way of his admission to the Bar here, Sir Elijah indignantly exclaimed: "No Sir, had you dropped from the clouds with such documents, we would admit you. The Supreme Court is independent and will never endure to be dictated to by any body of men whose claims are not enforced by superior authority. It is nothing to us whether you *had* or *had not* permission from the Court of Directors to proceed to this settlement. You come to us an authenticated English barrister, and as such we shall on the first day of the next term admit you to *our* Bar." Sir Elijah also offered to introduce him to Mr. Hyde which Mr. Fay thankfully accepted. Do you not admire the high tone in which Sir Elijah delivers his sentiments? There exists, it seems, a strong jealousy betweent he Government and the Supreme Court, lest either should encroach on the prerogatives of the other. The latter not long since committed Mr. Naylor, the Company's Attorney, for some breach of privilege, who, being in a weak state of health at the time, died in confinement. This has increased the difference. I mention this *en passant*, for it regards us not: let them quarrel or agree, so the business of the Court be not impeded, we cannot suffer. Mr. Fay is already retained in several causes. His whole mind will now, I trust, be occupied with his profession; and, as his abilities have never been questioned, I flatter myself that he has every reason to look forward to ultimate success.

20th July.

Hyder Ally has at length thrown off the mask and commenced hostilities in good earnest. How providential was our liberation at this most critical juncture! My gratitude to heaven was lately called forth in another instance. I recently conversed with a gentleman, who crossed the Great Desert by way of Aleppo. He assures me that, besides the danger from the Arabs, there is so much more from other causes than in going over that to Suez, that he is quite confident I never could have survived the journey,——"or," he added, "any European woman." Therefore, on the whole, we seem to have experienced the lesser evil, though the alternative of falling into the hands of the enemy was horrible! I am concerned to say that dreadful reports are in circulation respecting the excesses committed by Hyder's troops in the Carnatic, but the particulars are too shocking to be repeated.

You have no idea how busy I am. Lady Chambers has been kind enough to lend me some of her dresses for mine to be made by. I have commenced house-keeping, and am arranging my establishment, which is no little trouble in a country where the servants will not do a single thing but that for which you expressly engage them or even that willingly. I just now asked a man to place a small table near me; he began to bawl as loud as he could for the bearers to come and help him. "Why don't you do it yourself?" said I, rising as I spoke to assist. "Oh! I no English: I Bengal man. I no estrong like English: one, two, three Bengal man cannot do like Englishman." Adieu. Remember, you must write me long letters. You see even the heat has not reduced mine to a single sheet. I trust I shall never be incapable of addressing *you*. Mr. Fay unites with me in kind remembrances.

I am ever most affectionately yours,

E. F.

LETTER XVI.

CALCUTTA, *29th August, 1780.*

MY DEAR FRIENDS,—Ten thousand thanks for the precious packet of letters I yesterday received. You can form no idea of the eagerness with which I flew from my dressing room, and Mr. Fay from his study, at the joyful sound of letters from England. But my very eagerness wrought for a little while its own disappointment; for, when I laid my hand on the prize, I fell into a kind of hysteric, and it was some time before I could break the seals, and yet would not suffer Mr. Fay to deprive me of the gratification for which I had so long panted. Over such treasures who would not be a miser? I would not permit a single scrap to escape me till I had devoured the whole. Those only know what that impatient hunger of the heart is after information, and the intercourse of affliction, and who have been debarred so long as I have been from objects so dear.

I rejoice to find that the Chevalier de St. Lubin performed his promise, and that you are now in possession of every event that occurred to us till our arrival at Mocha. To know that we had passed the Desert, that object of my mother's dread and apprehension, must have set her mind comparatively at ease! Alas! Little did she suppose how far more terrible were the miseries that we still had to undergo! Thank Heaven they are past. I will quit the subject which agitates me too much.

I am happy to say that our house is a very comfortable one, but we are surrounded by a set of thieves. In England, if servants are dishonest we punish them or turn them away in disgrace: and their fate proves, it may be hoped, a warning to others: but these wretches have no sense of shame. I will give you an instance or two of their conduct that you may perceive how enviably I am situated. My *Khansaman* (or house-steward) brought in a charge of a gallon of milk and thirteen eggs for making scarcely a pint and a half of custard. This was so barefaced a cheat that I refused to allow it: on which he gave me warning. I sent for another, and, after I had hired him, said I: "Now take notice, friend, I have enquired into the market price of every article that enters my house and will submit to no imposition. You must, therefore, agree to deliver in a just account to me every morning." What reply do you think he made! Why, he demanded double wages. You may be sure that I dismissed him, and have since forgiven the first, but not till he had *salaamed* to my foot: this is the most abject token of submission. Alas! How much better should I like a little common honesty. I know him to be a rogue, and so are they all: but, as he understands me now, he will perhaps be induced to use rather more moderation in his attempts to defraud. At first, he used to charge me with twelve ounces of butter a day for each person: now he grants that the consumption is only four ounces. As if these persons were aware that I am writing about them, they have very obligingly furnished me with another anecdote. It seems my *Comprodore* (or market man) is gone away. He says poor servants have no profit by staying with me. At other gentlemen's houses he always made a rupee a day at least besides his wages, but here, if he only charges an anna or two more, it is sure to be taken off. So you see what a terrible creature I am! I dare say you never gave me the credit for being so close. I find that I was imposed on in taking a *comprodore* at all: the *khansaman* ought to know the business. Judge whether I have not sufficient employment amongst these harpies, feeling as I do the necessity of a reasonable economy? It is astonishing, and would be amusing, if one did not suffer by it, to see the various arts they will practise to keep a few annas in their hands. Though the lawful interest of money is but 12 per cent.—enough you will say—yet 24 is given by the shopkeepers, who will lend or borrow the smallest sums for a single day, and ascertain the precise interest to the greatest exactitude, having the advantage of *cowrees*, 5,120 of which go to make one rupee. The foolish custom, which subsists here, of keeping banians gives rise to a thousand deceptions as no one pays or receives money but through the medium of these people, who have their profit on everything that comes into the house.

In order to give you an idea of my household expenses and the price of living here, I must inform you that our house costs only 200 rupees per month, because it is not in a part of the town much esteemed; otherwise we must pay 300 or 400 rupees. We are now seeking a better situation. We were very frequently told in England, you know, that the heat in Bengal destroyed the appetite. I must own that I never yet saw any proof of that: on the contrary, I cannot help thinking that I never saw an equal quantity of victuals consumed. We dine too at two o'clock in the very heat of the day. At this moment Mr. Fay is looking out with an hawk's eye for his dinner; and, though still much of an invalid, I have no doubt of being able to pick a bit myself. I will give you our bill of fare and the general prices of things. A soup, a roast fowl, curry and rice, a mutton pie, a fore-quarter of lamb, a rice pudding, tarts, very good cheese, fresh churned butter, fine bread, excellent Madeira (that is expensive, but eatables are very cheap). A whole sheep costs but 2 rupees, a lamb one rupee, six good fowls or ducks ditto, twelve pigeons ditto, twelve pounds of bread ditto, two pounds of butter ditto, and a joint of veal ditto. Good cheese two months ago sold at the enormous price of two or three rupees per pound, but now you may buy it for one and a half. English claret sells at this time for sixty rupees a dozen. There's a price for you! I need not say that much of it will not be seen at our table. Now and then we are forced to produce it, but very seldom. I assure you that much caution is requisite to avoid running deeply in debt. The facility of obtaining credit is beyond what I could have imagined. The European shopkeepers are always ready to send in goods, and the banians are so anxious to get into employment that they outbid each other. One says: "Master had better take me: I will advance five thousand:" another offers seven, and perhaps a third ten thousand rupees. A Company's servant particularly will always find numbers ready to support his extravagance. It is not uncommon to see Writers withina few months after their arrivals dashing away on the course four-in-hand. Allowing for the inconsiderateness of youth, is it surprising if many become deeply embarrassed? Several have been pointed out to me who in the course of two or three years have involved themselves almost beyond hop of redemption. The interest of money being twelve per cent., and the banian taking care to secure bonds for whatever he advances, making up the account yearly and adding the sum due for interest, his thoughtless *master* (as he calls him—but in fact his slave) soon finds his debt doubled, and dares not complain unless he has the means of release which alas! are denied him.

I should have told you before that Mr. Fay was admitted as an advocate in the Supreme Court, on the 16th June. He has been engaged in several causes, wherein he acquitted himself to general satisfaction, and is at present as busy as can be desired. Everyone seems willing to encourage him, and, if he continue but his own friend, all will go well with us, and we shall collect our own share of gold mohurs, as well as our neighbours. I like to see the briefs come in well enough The fees are much higher here than in England: so you will say "they ought," and I perfectly agree with you.

Sir R. Chambers met with an accident some weeks ago by jumping out of a carriage when the horses were restive, which confined him to his house a long while, but he is now recovering. I was a good deal vexed both on his account, poor man, and because Mr. Fay was deprived of his kindly aid. I have seen little of my kind patroness since, for she goes scarcely anywhere without her husband. We were to dine wlth them the very day the circumstance happened. They are gone up-country and will not return for some months.

31st August, 1780.

I have received another packet, and rejoice to hear you are all going on so well. They talk of a frigate being soon to sail, in which case I shall close and despatch this. As I propose sending you a regular supply of *Calcutta Gazettes*, there can be no necessity to fill my letters with political information. I trust that in a short time Hyder will be effectually humbled.

Mr. Hare has visited us several times and is now quite complaisant to Mr. Fay. This is the way of the world you know, and, of course, to be expected from such a slave to outward circumstance—such a mere summer friend as this man ever evinced himself. By his account the hardships they underwent would have very soon destroyed so poor a creature as I was at that time, so that the difficulties we fell into, though at the moment of suffering so deplored, proved eventually our safeguard in more respects than one. Had we not touched at Callcut, I am fully persuaded we should have been shipwrecked, and had not my illness furnished a pretext for detaining us there after the rest, I should have died among those cruel people in the most shocking way imaginable, since they were for a longw hile absolutely destitute of every necessary. What short-sighted beings we are! How futile, how defective our best formed calculations! I have sometimes pleased myself (I hope not improperly) with the idea, that the power of discerning clearly the beneficent designs of Providence during our earthly pilgrimage, and of perceiving that in a thousand instances like these, a rough and stony path has led to safety and ultimate happiness, may be intended to form part of our enjoyment in a future state, wherein we are taught that to contemplate the Supreme Being in His perfections will constitute theh eight of bliss. Let me have your sentiments on the subject; its discussion can do neither of us any harm and may lead to improvement.

8th September, 1780.

I have nothing particular to add. My health continues very good considering all things. This is a very dull time—vacations are always so to professional people. God bless you and grant us a happy meeting. Our prospects are good. Nothing but the grossest misconduct can prevent our success. Adieu!

Yours most affectionately,

E. F.

LETTER XVII.

CALCUTTA, 27*th September*, 1780.

MY DEAR FRIENDS,—The bad news I hinted at some time ago is already avenged, and a more serious affair has happened since ; but for the present I must relate what has occupied a great deal of attention for some days past—no less than a duel between the Governor-General and the First in Council, Mr. Francis. There were two shots fired, and the Governor's second fire took place. He immediately ran up to his antagonist and expressed his sorrow for what had happened, which I dare say was sincere, for he is said to be a very amiable man. Happily the ball was soon extricated ; and, if he escape fever, there is no doubt of his speedy recovery. What gave occasion to the quarrel is said to have been an offensive minute entered on the Council books by Mr. Francis which he refused to rescind. Being unacquainted with the particulars, I have as little right as inclination to make any comments on the subject. It always vexes me to hear of such things. What a shocking custom is that of duelling ! Yet there are times when men may be so situated that, as the world goes, one knows not how they could act otherwise. Much may be effected by the judicious interference of friends, but those qualified for the task are rarely to be met with. Mr. Francis is highly respected here, and being now at the head of what is called the Opposition Party, his death would be severely felt by many who affect great indifference about the event.

Since I wrote last, we have had a good deal of trouble with our Mahomedan servants on account of an old custom. Not one of them would touch a plate in which pork had been laid. So that, whenever we had any at our table, our plates remained till the cook or his mate came up to change them. This being represented as a religious prejudice, I felt it right to give way, however ridiculous it might appear. In fact it was an inconvenience we felt in common with the whole settlement, except the gentlemen of the Army who had long emancipated themselves from any such restraint. Finding this really to be the case, the whole of the European inhabitants agreed to insist upon their servants doing the same as those of the officers at the Fort or quitting their places. They chose the latter alternative; and, as their prejudices run very high in all religious matters, we were in doubt whether they would not prefer suffering the greatest extremity rather than touch the very vessels which contained this abhorred food : but behold, in about four days, they came back again asking to be reinstated, acknowledging that the only penalty incurred by touching the plates was the necessity of bathing afterwards. From this you may judge of their excessive idleness. However, all now goes on well, and we hear no more of their objection.

The serious affair, at which I hinted at the beginning of this letter, was the cutting to pieces of Colonel Baillie's detachment with dreadful slaughter. I trust we shall soon have ample revenge, for that fine old veteran Sir Eyre Coote is about to take the field, and his very name will strike those undisciplined hordes with terror. Oh! how I feel interested in the event!

Nothing surely can be more disagreeable than the weather here at present. It is very hot with scarcely a breath of air stirring: and such swarms of insects buzzing about. Beyond all the bug fly is disgusting: one of them will scent a room. They are in form like a ladybird, but their smell is a thousand times more offensive than that of our bugs. A good breeze would disperse them all, but that we must not expect till the monsoon changes, and that is about the middle of the month.

I never told you that one of the captains who had charge of us at Calicut made his escape some months ago, and came to ask our assistance till he could get employment up the country. Mr. Fay gave him a lower room, and he remained with us several weeks. His name is West. This is the man from whom we collected intelligence of the plots laid against us there which nearly proved so successful. West is a stout fellow accustomed in his early days to labour and seasoned to the climate. He is gone up to Patna in charge of some boats, and is to remain there. Ayres used to treat him very ill at times, and *he* says attemped more than once to assassinate him, because he refused to concur with a party that Ayres headed, consisting of six or eight abandoned wretches, whose intention it was to cut off several of the more opulent natives secretly, and possess themselves of their effects, while they should contrive to fix the guilt of the transaction on some persons who were obnoxious to them. West threatened to reveal the whole plot, on which they pretended to abandon it; but he soon found their object was to rid themselves of him, and he effected his escape in a canoe, at the utmost risk of perishing in the attempt, to Cochin, from whence he easily got to Bengal. What a horrible fellow is that Ayres! Surel he will meet with his desserts; should the English take him, he will be shot instantly as a deserter.

We have found out a nephew of Isaac's named Daniel. He is a man of no great consequence here, either in point of situation or circumstances, though not absolutely poor. We asked him to dinner, and endeavoured by every means in our power to evince the grateful sense we entertain of his worthy uncle's kindness and beneficence.

3rd November, 1780.

Since my last date, I have the pleasure to acknowledge the receipt of another packet from England with the gratifying intelligence that you are all well on the 7th of April.

MRS. FAY'S HOUSE IN CALCUTTA.

My time has passed very stupidly for some months, but the town is now beginning to fill: people are returning for the cold season. Term has commenced, and Mr. Fay has no reason to complain of his business falling off. If *he* fall not from it, all will be well. My first patroness, Lady Chambers, has returned from her tour, but Sir Robert, having purchased an elegant mansion in Calcutta (for which he is to pay £6,000 in England), her Ladyship has full employment in arranging and fitting up her new abode, so that I see very little of her. She is, however, always kind and full of condescension towards me, when we do meet.

19th December.

Mr. Fay has met with a gentleman here—a Dr. Jackson, who comes from the same part of Ireland and knows many of his connections. They soon became intimate. Dr. Jackson is physician to the Company and in very high practice besides. I have been visited by the whole family. The eldest son, a fine noble looking young man, is a Lieutenant in the army, and has lately married a very pretty little woman, who came out, in the same ship, under the protection of his mother, as did Miss C——y, a most amiable and interesting young lady who now resides with them. They have not been long arrived. The Doctor's lady is a native of Jamaica, and, like those "children of the sun," frank and hospitable to a degree, fond of social parties in the old style, "where the song and merry jest circulate round the festive board"—particularly after supper. Dinner parties they seldom give: but I had been present at several elsewhere since the commencement of the cold season. The dinner hour as I mentioned before is two, and it is customary to sit a long while at table, particularly during the cold season: for people here are mighty fond of grills and stews, which they season themselves and generally make very hot. The Burdwan stew takes a deal of time: it is composed of everything at the table, fish, flesh and fowl—somewhat like the Spanish Olla Podrida. Many suppose that unless prepared in a silver saucepan it cannot be good. On this point I must not presume to give an opinion, being satisfied with plain food, and never tasting any of these incentives to luxurious indulgence. During dinner a good deal of wine is drunk, but a very little after the cloth is removed, except in bachelor's parties as they are called. For the custom of reposing, if not sleeping after dinner, is so general that the streets of Calcutta are from four to five in the afternoon, almost as empty of Europeans as if it were midnight. Next come the evening airings. To the Course every one goes, though sure of being suffocated with dust. On returning from thence, tea is served and universally drunk here even during the extreme heats. After tea, either cards or music fill up the space till ten when supper is generally announced.

Five-card Loo is the usual game, and they play a rupee a fish limited to ten. This will strike you as being enormously high, but it is thought nothing here. Tré dille and whist are much in fashion, but ladies seldom join in the latter, for, though the stakes are moderate, bets frequently run high among the gentlemen—which renders those anxious who sit down for amusement lest others should lose by their blunders.

Formal visits are paid in the evening. They are generally very short, as perhaps each lady has half a dozen to make and a party waiting for her besides. Gentlemen also call to offer their respects, and if asked to put down their hat, it is considered as an invitation to supper. Many a hat have I seen vainly dangling in its owner's hand for half an hour who at last has been compelled to withdraw without any one's offering to relieve him of the burden.

Great preparations are making for Christmas and New Year public balls. Of course you will not expect me to write much till they are over: nor, to own the truth, am

I in spirits, having great reason to be dissatisfied with Mr. Fay's conduct. Instead of cultivating the intimacy of those who might be serviceable, or paying the necessary attention to persons in power, I can scarcely prevail on him to accompany me even to Dr. Jackson's, who is generally visited by the first people. He cannot endure being subjected to the forms of society. Sometimes he has called on Sir Robert Chambers, but the other Judges he has never *seen* except on the bench since his admission. He did not even accept Sir Elijah Impey's obliging offer to introduce him to Mr. Hyde, but suffered Mr. Sealy to perform that ceremony; and, when the Chief Justice advanced to accompany him, he was forced to acknowledge that he had been already introduced: upon which the great man turned on his heel and hardly ever noticed him afterwards. This happened on the day Mr. Fay was admitted to the Bar at Mr. Hyde's public breakfast, at whose house the professional gentlemen all meet on the first day of every term and go from thence in procession to the Court House. I will now close this letter in the hope of having better accounts to give you in my next.

Yours affectionately,

E. F.

LETTER XVIII.

CALCUTTA, *27th January, 1781.*

MY DEAR SISTER,—Since my last we have been engaged in a perpetual round of gaiety. Keeping Christmas, as it is called, though sinking into disuse at home, prevails here with all its ancient festivity. The external appearance of the English gentlemen's houses on Christmas Day is really pleasing from its novelty. Large plantain trees are placed on each side of the principal entrances, and the gates and pillars, being ornamented with wreaths of flowers fancifully disposed, enliven the scene.

All the servants, from the Banian down to the lowest menial, bring presents of fish and fruit; for these, it is true, we are obliged in many instances to make a return perhaps beyond the real value, but still it is regarded as a compliment to our *burrah din.* A public dinner is given at Government House to the gentlemen of the Presidency, and the evening concludes with an elegant ball and supper for the ladies. These are repeated on New Year's Day and on the King's birthday. I should say *have been*, for that grand festival happening at the hottest season, and every one being obliged to appear full dressed, so much incovenience resulted from the immense crowd, even in some cases severe fits of illness being the consequence, that it has been determined to change the day of celebration to the 8th of December which arrangement gives general satisfaction. I shall not attempt to describe these splendid entertainments further than by saying that they were in the highest style of magnificence. In fact such grand parties so much resemble each other that a particular detail would be unnecessary and even tiresome.

I felt far more gratified some time ago, when Mrs. Jackson favoured me with a ticket for the Harmonic, which was supported by a select number of gentlemen, who each in alphabetical rotation give a concert, ball and supper during the cold season—I believe once a fortnight. That I attended was given by a Mr. Taylor and closed the subscription, which I understand will not be renewed—a circumstance generally regretted as it was an elegant amusement and conducted on a very eligible plan. We had a great deal of delightful music, and Lady Chambers, who is a capital performer on the harpsicord, played, among other pieces, a Sonata of Nicolai's in a most brilliant style. A gentleman, who was present and who seemed to be quite charmed with her execution, asked me the next evening if I did not think that the *jig* Lady Chambers played the night before was the prettiest thing I ever heard? He meant the rondo which is remarkably lively, but I daresay "Over the water to Charley" would have pleased him equally well.

Mrs. Hastings was of the party. She came in late, and happened to place herself on the opposite side of the room, beyond a speaking distance: so strange to tell, I quite forgot she was there! After some time had elapsed, my observant friend, Mrs. Jackson, who had been impatiently watching my looks, asked if I had paid my respects to the Lady Governess? I answered in the negative, having had no opportunity, as she had no chance to look towards me when I was prepared to do so. "Oh!" replied the kind old lady, "you must fix your eyes on her, and never take them off till she notices you. Miss C——dy has done this and so have I. It is absolutely necessary to avoid giving offence." I followed her prudent advice, and was soon honoured with a complacent glance, which I returned, as became me, by a most respectful bend. Not long after, she walked over to our side, and conversed very affably with me, for we are now, through Mrs. Jackson's interference, on good terms together.

She also introduced me to Lady Coote and her inseparable friend, Miss Molly Bazett. It was agreed between them when they were both girls, whichever married first, the other was to live with her: and accordingly when Sir Eyre took his lady from St. Helena, of which place her father was Governor, Miss Molly, who is a native of the island, accompanied them to England and from thence to India, where she has remained ever since. Thus giving a proof of steady attachment not often equalled and never perhaps excelled.

19th February, 1781.

Yesterday being the Anniversary of our release from imprisonment, we invited Dr. Jackson's family, Mr. O'Donnel and some friends to assist in its celebration. I call it my "Jubilee Day," and trust my dear friends at home did not forget the occasion.

This reminds me to tell you that Sudder Khan and Ayres, our chief enemies, have both closed their career of wickedness. The former died of wounds received before Tellicherry; and the latter, having repeatedly advanced close to the lines of that place, holding the most contemptuous language and indecent gestures towards the officers, setting every one at defiance, and daring them to fire at him—I suppose in a state of intoxication, miserable wretch!—was at last picked off (to use a military phrase). Too honourable a death for such a monster of iniquity! My hope was that he would have been taken prisoner and afterwards recognised and shot as a deserter.

Poor West is also dead. He never reached his destination. The boat he went up in by some accident struck on a sand bank and nearly all on board perished.

26th March, 1781.

A Frigate being ordered to sail for Europe with despatches from Government, I shall avail myself of the occasion, and close this letter with a few remarks on our theatrical amusements. The house was built by subscription. It is very neatly fitted up, and the scenery and decorations quite equal to what could be expected here. The parts are entirely represented by amateurs in the drama; no hired persons being allowed to act. I assure you I have seen characters supported in a manner that would not disgrace any European stage. *Venice Preserved* was exhibited by Captain Call (of the Army), Mr. Droz (a member of the Board of Trade) and Lieutenant Norfar, in Jaffier, Pierre, and Belvidera shewed very superior theatrical talents. The latter has rather an effeminate appearance off the stage, yet I am told that he is a very brave officer when on service; and though always dressed as if for a ball, when he makes his appearance, is among the most alert in a moment of danger. I cannot imagine how he contrives it, for the present mode of arranging the hair requires a great deal of time to make it look tolerable: however, this is said to be the case. One of the chief inconveniences in establishments of this kind is that the performers being independent of any control will sometimes persist in taking parts to which their abilities are by no means adequate. This throws an air of ridicule over the whole as the spectators are too apt to indulge their mirth on the least opening of that kind. In fact many go to see a tragedy for the express purpose of enjoying a laugh, which is certainly very illiberal and must prove detrimental to the hopes of an infant institution like the one in question. For my own part, I think such a mode of passing an evening highly rational, and, were I not debarred by the expense, should seldom miss a representation; but a gold mohur is really too much to bestow on such a temporary gratification. Adieu! I shall write again soon.

Yours most affectionately,

E. F.

LETTER XIX.

CALCUTTA, *20th May, 1781.*

MY DEAR SISTER,—You must have perceived that the style of my letters for some months past has been constrained, nor could it possibly be otherwise. Not wishing to grieve your affectionate heart by a recital of the melancholy change in my prospects occasioned by Mr. Fay's imprudent behaviour, I was reduced to enlarge on less important subjects. Some hints, however, escaped me which must have led you to suspect that all was not going on properly, but his conduct of late has been such that no hope remains of his *ever* being able to prosecute his profession here.

Ever since his arrival he has acted in every respect directly contrary to my advice. By constantly associating with persons who had distinguished themselves by thwarting the measures of Government he soon became equally obnoxious. On one occasion when a tax was proposed to be levied on houses, several meetings were held at our house wherein he openly insisted on the illegality of such a procedure and encouraged his *new* friends to assert their independence. I remonstrated in the strongest terms against measures so pregnant with evil which must terminate in utter ruin, if not speedily abandoned: the character of our *chief ruler* being well known—he will never *desert* a friend or *forgive* an enemy. What chance then, has an individual, who rashly incurs his resentment, of escaping its baneful effects? All this and more I repeatedly, but also *vainly,* urged. My representations were, as heretofore, treated with contempt. He still persevered, giving himself entirely up to low and unworthy pursuits, while his professional duties were wholly neglected and his best friends slighted.

We were frequently invited to parties which he has constantly evaded, leaving me to make what excuses I could for his absence. My dear kind patroness, Lady Chambers, still continues on my account to shew him attention as do the Jacksons and some few others. She has lately added a son to her family. I was with her at the time, and the sweet infant seems to have formed closer ties between us. On a late occasion, however, she was compelled to speak plainly. The Christening is to take place in a few days. Sir Elijah and Lady Impey have offered to stand for the child, and Lady Chambers wishes me to be present, but Sir Elijah positively refuses to meet Mr. Fay, who, of course, cannot be included. So, unless I can reconcile him to the omission, I must remain at home also.

3rd June, 1781.

The grand ceremony is over. I had no difficulty with Mr. Fay. He declared himself pre-engaged the instant I mentioned the subject, and insisted that I should make some apology for him which was readily promised. You may suppose that I could not under such circumstances enjoy much pleasure, though Sir Elijah and his Lady behaved very graciously. But the idea that my husband was so totally proscribed where he might have figured among the foremost pierced my very soul. Yet I was forced to put on the appearance of cheerfulness that I might receive as a compliment what was certainly so intended. The public countenance of Lady Chambers and being admitted to such a select party cannot but operate favourably for me at this crisis, when I shall stand so much in need of support.

24th June, 1781.

Though the term is now advanced, Mr. Fay has scarcely a brief. The attorneys are positively afraid to employ him, and causes have actually come on with two advocates on one side and one on the other, rather than permit him to appear in them. What a noble opportunity of making an ample fortune is thus wantonly thrown away. Heaven grant me patience. I have only this reflection to console me that every effort in my power has been made to ward off the blow which is now inevitable.

I yesterday confided to Lady Chambers my real situation. She, on my stating that Mr. Fay must certainly be obliged to quit the settlement very shortly, with the utmost kindness insisted on my making her house my home whenever that event should take place, and Sir Robert has in the most cordial way inforced the invitation. Thus, through the goodness of Providence, am I provided with a secure and highly respectable asylum, till a passage to Europe can be obtained on moderate terms—a difficult matter to accomplish.

17th July, 1781.

On the last day of the present month we must quit our house, and when my husband and I may reside under the same roof together again, Heaven alone can tell. It is astonishing to see with what apparent unconcern he supports the shock, but the acquisition of a new patron has raised his spirits. Colonel W——, a man of superior abilities and immense fortune, has long been a determined opposer of Government and the bitter enemy of Sir Elijah Impey, against whom he has set an impeachment on foot, to prosecute which it is requisite that a confidential agent should serve the process on the defendant here and proceed to England with the necessary documents. Mr. Fay has contrived to get himself appointed to this office. He has drawn up a set of articles, many copies of which are prepared by Bengalee writers, who though they profess to understand English and are tolerably correct in copying what is put before them, know not the meaning of what they write—a great convenience this to such as conduct affairs that require secrecy, since the persons employed cannot, if they were so disposed, betray their trust. Colonel W——. never comes here. All is carried on with an air of profound mystery. I like not such proceedings and doubt if any good can come of them, but I dare not interfere nor drop even a hint which might lead to suspicion that anything extraordinary is going on. The duty of a wife, which is paramount to all other civil obligations, compels me silently to witness what is beyond my power to counteract, although the character of a highly revered friend is obliquely glanced at, and may be in the future more seriously implicated in the business. You will guess to whom I allude. Adieu! You shall hear from me again when I change my abode.

Yours affectionately,

E. F.

LETTER XX.

CALCUTTA, *28th August, 1781.*

MY DEAR SISTER,—Since I wrote last my feelings have been harassed in various ways almost beyond endurance. Mr. Fay quitted me on the 31st ultimo, and the rest of the day was devoted to the distressing (however just and necessary) task of delivering such articles of furniture as had not been paid for to the persons who supplied us with them, and also returning what had been borrowed of different friends for our convenience. What remained was taken possession of next morning by a man to whom my unfortunate husband had given a bond for money advanced on the most exorbitant terms to support his extravagance. Thus I am left, destitute of everything but my clothes, to endure the wretched effects of his imprudence, with a constitution weakened by the sufferings and privations I underwent during my eventful journey added to the dread which I cannot avoid feeling lest that unlucky blow I received in Calicut should be productive of serious consequences.

Lady Chambers welcomed me as a sister. She wishes me to accompany her everywhere. Time alone can reconcile me to general society. The very day of my removal here, a circumstance was disclosed that determined me no longer to bind my destiny with that of a man who could set thus at defiance all ties divine and human. After consulting my legal friends, I demanded a separation, to which he having consented, a deed was drawn up by Mr. S——under the inspection of Sir Robert Chambers, in the fullest manner possible rendering me wholly independent of Mr. Fay's authority, with power to make a will, etc.—in short conceived in the strongest terms our language could supply. I have appointed Mr. G. Jones, Solicitor of Lincoln's Inn, and Mr. McVeagh, one of the masters in Chancery here, to act as my trustees. Two more respectable men I could not have chosen. You, my dear sister, who know better than any one what exertions I have used and what sacrifices I have *vainly* made for this most ungrateful of beings, will not be surprised to find that even *my* patience was not proof against this last outrage.

But let me dismiss the hateful subject, merely stating that the deeds were signed on the 11th instant. His secret is safe with me, though, when we met on that occasion, he had the insolence to hint his belief that out of *revenge* I should divulge it. So let him *still* think, for I deigned no reply except by a look, when I, with secret triumph, beheld his hitherto undaunted eye sink beneath the indignant glance of mine.

" 'Tis Conscience that makes cowards of us all."

5th September, 1781.

Sir Robert, being appointed President of the Court at Chinsurah, is gone up to take possession of his charge, accompanied by Lady Chambers and the family. So here am I left alone to ramble over this great house and to meditate on irremediable evils. Sir Robert has, however, kindly entrusted me with the keys of his immense library, which will furnish a rich treat when my mind acquires sufficient calmness to look beyond itself in search of amusement.

The acquaintance of Mrs. Wheler I have found a most invaluable acquisition. I went with Lady Chambers to pass a day with her at the gardens, and have been treated with the utmost attention ever since. She has authorised me to look up to her as a steady patroness on all occasions. Mr. Hastings being gone up-country on political business, Mr. Wheler, of course, takes the chair during his absence, so you may judge what influence Mrs. Wheler possesses : but she bears her honours so meekly and contrives to soften the refusals, which she is frequently compelled to give, by so much affability and sympathy, as to conciliate all parties and render herself generally beloved.

I have never mentioned yet how indifferently we are provided with respect to a place of worship, Divine Service being performed in a room (not a very large one) at the Old Fort—which is a great disgrace to the settlement. They talk of building a church, and have fixed on a very eligible spot whereon to erect it, but no further progress has been made in the business.

I now propose, having full leisure, to give you some account of the East Indian customs and ceremonies, such as I have been able to collect, but it must be considered as a mere sketch to point your further researches. And first for that horrible custom of widows burning themselves with the dead bodies of their husbands. The fact is indubitable, but I have never had an opportunity of witnessing the various incidental ceremonies, nor have I ever seen any European who had been present at them. I cannot suppose that the usage originates in the superior tenderness and ardent attachment of Indian wives towards their spouses, since the same tenderness and ardour would doubtless extend to his offspring, and prevent them from exposing the innocent survivors to the miseries attendant on an orphan state, and they would see clearly that to live and cherish these pledges of affection would be the most rational and natural way of shewing their regard for both husband and children. I apprehend that as personal fondness can have no part here at all,—since all matches are made between the parents of the parties, who are betrothed to each other at too early a period for choice to be consulted,—this practice is entirely a political scheme intended to insure the care and good offices of wives to their husbands, who have not failed in most countries to invent a sufficient number of rules to render the weaker sex totally subservient to their authority. I cannot avoid smiling when I hear gentlemen bring forward the conduct of Hindoo women as a test of superior character, since I am well aware that, so much are we the slaves of habit *every-where*, that were it necessary for a woman's reputation to burn herself in England, many a one who has *accepted* a husband merely for the sake of an establishment, who has lived with him without affection, perhaps thwarted his views, dissipated his fortune, and rendered his life uncomfortable to its close, would yet mount the funeral pile with all imaginable decency, and die with heroic fortitude. The most specious sacrifices are not always the greatest. She who wages war with a naturally petulant temper, who practises a rigid self-denial, endures without complaining the unkindness, infidelity, extravagance, meaness, or scorn of the man to whom she has given a tender and confiding heart, and for whose happiness and well-being in life all the powers of her mind are engaged—is ten times more of a heroine than the slave of bigotry and superstition, who affects to scorn the life demanded of her by the laws of her country or at least that country's custom. Many such we have in England, and I doubt not in India likewise : so indeed we ought : have we not a religion more pure than that of India?

The Hindoos, or Gentoos, are divided into four castes or tribes called the Brahmin, the Khutree, the Buesho, and the Shodor. Their rank in the land declines gradually to the last named, and if any one of them commit an offence which deprives them of the privileges that belong to their respective castes they become Parias, which may, therefore, be called a filthy tribe formed, as it were, of the refuse of the rest. These are indeed considered the very dregs of the people, and supply all the lowest offices of human life. They profess what is called the religion of Brahma. From the caste which bears his name all priests are chosen who are treated in every respect with the distinguished honour and reverence. Their religious code is contained in a book called the Veda, which only Brahmins are allowed to read. It is written in a dead language called Sanscrit. They worship three deities, Brahma the Creator, Vistnoo the Preserver, and Sheevah the Destroyer, but they profess to believe them to be only the representations or types of the great spirit Brahma (the Supreme God) whom they call the Spirit of Wisdom and the Principle of Truth. None but Hindoos are allowed to enter temples, but I am told the idols worshipped here are the ugliest forms that imagination can conceive, and to whom Pope's description of the heathen deities may, in other respects, be strictly applied.

> " Gods changeful, partial, passionate, unjust,
> Whose attributes are rage, revenge, or lust."

I lament to add that to such wretched objects as these numbers of the deluded natives are devoted in the strongest and most absolute manner possible. A certain sect named Pundurams live in continual beggary. Extreme beggary alone induces them to ask for food, which when granted, they only take just what will preserve life; and spend all their days in singing songs in praise of Sheevah. Another sect add a tabor and hollow brass rings about their ancles to increase the noise with which they extol their deity. I consider both these as a species of monks, but believe the holy fathers fall far short of the Jogees or Seniases of India in their religious austerities. These not only endure all possible privations with apparent indifference, but invent for themselves various kinds of tortures which they carry to an astonishing length: such as keeping their hands clenched till the nails grow into them, standing on one foot for several days and even weeks together, and hiring people to support their hands in a perpendicular position.

Their expiatory punishments are some of them most dreadful. I myself saw a man running in the streets with a piece of iron thrust through his tongue which was bleeding profusely. On the Churuk Poojah (swinging feast) hundreds, I have heard, are suspended at an amazing height by means of hooks finely fixed in the flesh of the back, to which sometimes a cloth is added round the body to afford the miserable victim a chance of escape, should the hook give way. I, by accident (for voluntarily nothing should have tempted me to witness such a spectacle), saw one of these wretches who was whirling round with surprizing rapidity, and at that distance scarcely appeared to retain the semblance of a human form. They firmly expect by this infliction to obtain pardon of all their offences ; and, should death be the consequence, they go straight to heaven, thus changing the horrid state of privation and misery in which they exist here for one of bliss. If such be their real persuasion, who can condemn the result ?

Indeed, under other circumstances, it is found that, notwithstanding their apparent gentleness and timidity, the Hindoos will meet death with intrepid firmness. They are also invincibly obstinate, and that they will die rather than concede a point—of this a very painfulinstance has lately occurred. A Hindoo beggar of the Brahman caste went to the house of a very rich man but of an inferior tribe requesting alms. He was either rejected or considered himself inadequately relieved, and refused to quit the place. As his lying before the door and thus obstructing the passage was unpleasant, one of the servants first entreated, then insisted on his retiring, and, in speaking, pushed him gently away. He chose to call this push a blow, and cried aloud for redress, declaring that he would never stir from the spot till he had obtained justice against the man. The latter now endeavoured to sooth him, but in vain. Like a true Hindoo, he sat down, never moved again, and thirty hours afterwards expired, demanding justice with his latest breath, being well aware of this—the master would have an enormous fine to pay, which accordingly happened. I am sure that such evidences of the surprising indifference to life, the inflexible stubbornness and vindictive dispositions of these people are by no means rare. It seems extraordinary, though, that sentiments and feeling so contrary to each other should operate on the same minds. Seeing them so quiet and supine, so (if it may be so expressed) only half-alive as they generally show themselves, one is prepared for their sinking, without an effort to avert any impending danger. But that they should at the same time nourish so violent and active a passion as revenge, and brave even death so intrepidly, as they often do in pursuit of it, is very singular. But enough of these silly enthusiasts !

I had lately the opportunity of witnessing the marriage procession of a rich Hindoo. The bride, as I was told, sat in the same *palanquin* with the bridegroom which was splendidly ornamented. They were accompanied by all the relations on both sides, dressed in the most superb manner —some on horse back, some on elephants. Bands of dancing girls and musicians (I understood) preceded them. In the evening there were fire-works at the bride's father's house, and the appearance of much feasting, but no European was present. This wedding was of a nature by no means uncommon here. A rich man had an only daughter, and he bargained to dispose of her, or rather to take for her a husband out of a poor man's family, but of his own *caste:* for this is indispensable. In this case the bridegroom is brought home to his father-in-law's house and becomes a member of the family. So that, although the law prohibits a man from giving a dowry with his daughter, yet, you see, he does it in effect, since he gives a house to a man who wants one—in fact a fortune saddled with an encumbrance. In a few years perhaps the old man may die, and the young one having fulfilled the wishes of his parents, and provided for his own wants may employ some of his female relations to look round the poorer families of his caste for a pretty girl, whom he will take as a second wife, tho' the first always retains the pre-eminence and governs the house; nor can the husband devote more of his time to one than the other, the law compelling him to live with them alternately. You may be sure the account is strictly kept. My banian, Dattaram Chuckerbutty, has married between twenty and thirty years without taking a second lady, and he boasts of being much happier with his old wife (as he calls her) than the generality of his friends are with the charms of variety. For my own part, I have not a doubt but he is in the right.

The Hindoo ladies are never seen abroad. When they go out, their carriages are closed covered with curtains, so that one has little chance of satisfying curiosity. I once saw two apparently very beautiful women: they use so much art, however, as renders it difficult to judge what claim they really have to that appellation. Their whole time is taken up in decorating their persons. The hair, eye-lids, eye-brows, teeth, hands, and nails all undergo certain processes to render them more completely fascinating. Nor can one seriously blame their having recourse to these or the like artifices, the motive being to secure the affections of a husband, or to counteract the plans of a rival.

27th September, 1781.

The Hindoos who can afford to purchase wood for a funeral pile burn their dead. One cannot go on the river without seeing numbers of these exhibitions, especially at night, and the most disgusting spectacles they are. I will not enlarge on the subject. This mode, however, is far superior to that practised by the poor of throwing them into the river, where they offend more senses than one. I have been frequently obliged to return from a walk along the river side by the noisome exhalations which arose from these wretched objects.

Some of the Hindu customs respecting the sick are really shocking. When a person is given over by the Brahmins, who are physicians as well as priests, the relations immediately carry him, if within a reasonable distance, to banks of the Ganges, where he is smeared with mud, quantities of which I am told are thrust into his mouth, nose, and ears. This treatment soon reduces him to a dying state, nor is it desirable that he should recover, since he must in that case lose caste ; for it is an established rule that whoever removes from the spot where the sacred rites have been performed, becomes an outcaste. Dr. Jackson was once fortunate enough to be called in to attend the wife of a Hindu Rajah whom they were on the point of taking to the river when he arrived. He assured the Rajah that he perceived no dangerous symptoms and would answer for her doing well. Luckily the tremendous ceremonies had not commenced. The event justified our good Doctor's predictions. The lady is still living, and his success in this instance has led to several others, highly gratifying to the best feelings of humanity, and certainly beneficial to his fortune.

This letter has run to such an enormous length that I must now conclude with wishing that I may soon hear good news of you.

I remain,
Yours most affectionately,
E. F.

LETTER XXI.

CALCUTTA, *17th December, 1781.*

MY DEAR SISTER,—Sir Robert Chambers and Lady Chambers have been down since I wrote last, and remained here during the term, but are now gone up again, though much distressed. Mrs. Chambers prefers staying here. A melancholy event has occurred in the family. The sweet little boy (just turned six months old), to whom I was so fondly attached, died a few weeks ago. Dear interesting child! I shall long lament his loss. He was not ill more than three days, so rapid is the progress of disease in this country.

Mr. and Mrs. Hosea are arrived in town and have taken accommodations on the *Grosvenor*, Captain Coxon. I was in the hopes of being able to take my passage with them but am disappointed. Mr. Hosea was resident at one of the upper stations. He is a man of high character and generally esteemed, and his wife one of the most amiable women I ever knew. It is impossible to do otherwise than love her. As she daily looks to be confined, her leaving Calcutta till after that period is out of the question : so they must suffer the *Grosvenor* to proceed without them to Madras, where she is expected to remain a month at least. The family and baggage of Mr. Hosea are to follow in a country ship at the risk of arriving too late. The agreement is that, if she sails from thence before a certain day a small sum is to be forfeited ; but after that day, should Captain Coxon be compelled to proceed on his voyage without them, he is still to receive ten thousand rupees, that is half the passage money by way of compensation. I state these particulars to show what large sums are exacted of passengers.

The society of Mrs. Chambers, who is a fine looking respectable old lady, well informed and cheerful, with that of Mrs. Hosea, who has chaiming spirits, enables me to pass the time far more pleasantly than when I was left here during the rains. Besides, I often visit at Dr. Jackson's, and have made acquaintance with several agreeable families, who allow me to call on them, without any formality, the very idea of which is hateful to me at present, so cruely fallen are my once highly and justly raised expectations. For what place do I now hold in the society with which I am permitted to mix? Alas! none except by sufferance: but most ardently do I wish to escape from this fatal spot, the scene of so many severe afflictions, and seek comfort with those who have never failed to afford it. There I shall not be constantly reminded of past hopes—now alas! sunk in disappointment. Think not these observations proceed from a repining spirit or unmindfulness of favours received. I have been most beneficently treated, and my views have been furthered in a way which I had no right whatever to expect. Can attentions like these be forgotten? No! It forms my proudest boast that *I have* such friends, and while life remains, I must ever cherish the remembrance of their generous exertions. The appr aching season always inspires melancholy reflections. I will, therefore, pass it over, and look forward to the next, when, by the blessing of Providence, I hope to be with my beloved family.

27th January, 1782.

My dear Mrs. Hosea has, thank Heaven, got happily over her confinement, which took place three weeks ago, and all now is bustle and preparation for their departure. Sir Robert's eldest son, Thomas, goes under their care. He is a charming boy, nearly seven years of age, which is rather late, but no good opportunity has occurred till now. A Miss Shore (the daughter of an intimate friend), about the age of Thomas, also proceeds with them. Mrs. Hosea takes one little girl of her own, sixteen months old. The baby is to be left with Lady Chambers. She promises to be a lovely child.

We are to have the Christening to-morrow, when I shall take my leave of large parties except one which I must attend. Mrs. Hosea's infant daughter is to be christened next month and Sir Robert's whole family is invited. At present I devote myself entirely to Mrs. Hosea, who I really think has a friendship for me. Would it were in my power to accompany her, but that for many reasons is impossible.

Another *Indiaman*, the *Dartmouth* (Captain——Thompson), has just sailed, but she too is absolutely crowded with passengers : so I must have patience. It is almost incredible what quantities of baggage people of consequence invariably take with them. I myself counted twenty-nine trunks that were sent on board for Mr. and Mrs. Hosea exclusive of chests-of-drawers and other packages, with cabin stores, etc., and more still remain to be shipped. This separate passage to Madras will greatly add to the expense, for Captain Coxon would not have charged a rupee more had they embarked with him at Bengal. Even removing so much baggage from one ship to another will occasion no small inconvenience.

CHINSURAH, *10th February, 1782.*

My time has been taken up for this fortnight past to afford leisure for writing. I have another melancholy event to record. But let me proceed regularly.

Our friends left us on the second instant. Poor Mrs. Hosea was dreadfully affected at parting with her infant. It seemed cruel for a mother to abandon her child only twenty-five days old : but it must in all probability have fallen a sacrifice. Her anxiety in other respects was great. Admiral Suffrien is said to keep a sharp look out after English ships going down the Bay, but I trust Sir E. Hughes will find the French fleet better employed than cruizing about after our vessels.

Sir Robert and Lady Chambers felt severely the shock of their son's departure, but poor Mrs. Chambers, whose very soul seemed treasured up, if I may so express myself, in her grandson, sunk under the blow. On the fifth she was seized with a violent illness, of which on the seventh she expired. Sir Robert is deeply affected. I should be surprised if he were not, for to him she was an ever exemplary parent, and gave an irreparable proof of strong maternal affection by accompanying him to this country at her advanced period of life. Her death is generally lamented as that of a most charitable humane good woman. "Let her works praise her." She was in her seventieth year.

We came up here, immediately after the funeral, which took place the next day, and was most numerously attended, I may say, by the whole Settlement—gentlemen as well as ladies. Her character demanded this testimony of respect, and that it was paid affords me pleasure.

You will expect me to give you some account of this place. But after having told you that it contains many very fine houses, is regularly built, and kept remarkably clean, nothing more remains to be said. One cannot expect much cheerfulness among the inhabitants, though they are treated with the utmost kindness, and all private property is held sacred.

A strange circumstance occurred at the time of its capture which will probably become a subject of litigation. A King's ship, either a frigate or a sloop of war, was lying off Calcutta when the news arrived that the Dutch had commenced hostilities. The Captain, accompanied by a party of his officers and seamen, proceeded with all expedition to

Chinsurah, which he reached about 2 A.M. next day, and summoned the place to surrender to His Majesty's arms. The Governor, being totally unprovided with the means of resistance, complied. So that when a detachment of the Company's troops marched in at 7 o'clock to take possession, they found the business already settled, and had the laugh against them. The Captain was soon induced to relinquish his capture, but insisted that his people were entitled to prize money, and has put in his claim accordingly. Is not this an odd affair ?

21st February, 1782.

Sir Robert is going to dispatch some letters for England, and I will profit by the occasion, having nothing at present further to communicate, all remains in uncertainty.

I am,
Your affectionate,
E. F.

LETTER XXII.

CALCUTTA, *17th March*, *1782*.

MY DEAR SISTER,—This is in all probability the last letter I shall write from Bengal. Mrs. Wheler has been indefatigable in her exertions, and has at length secured a passage for me on the *Valentine* (Captain——Lewis), a fine new ship. This is her first voyage. I shall have a female companion too, which is certainly desirable. Colonel and Mrs. Tottingham with their family accompany us. Besides these we shall have several military men, two of the Company's civil servants, and thirteen children under Captain Lewis' immediate protection. The ship is expected to sail in the beginning of next month. I dined in company with Captain Lewis yesterday at Mrs. Wheler's, and we were both much pleased with his behaviour. When we retired, after dinner, my good friend congratulated me on the prospect of sailing under such a commander. Many of them assume airs of consequence, but Captain Lewis does not seem at all that way disposed, and, should the passengers prove agreeable, I really think we may promise ourselves a comfortable voyage.

I am using every effort in preparing my baggage, and Lady Chambers, with her usual kindness, renders me every assistance. Nor have my other friends been neglectful of anything that can contribute to my comfort both on the passage and after my arrival in England, till my health shall, with the blessing of Providence, be restored, when I may be enabled to seek out some decent means of support.

I had a very eligible proposal made me of entering into partnership with a most amiable lady, who was lately engaged in the school line, but was compelled to decline it, my complaints requiring a change of climate, and that I should consult those medical friends who have been accustomed to prescribe for me. I much regret this circumstance, having no doubt but we might well have suited each other extremely well, for she has proved herself a sincere friend in many instances and must ever receive my grateful esteem.

28th March, 1782.

I had the pleasure last evening of being present at the marriage of Captain P. M——and my young friend Miss T——: the wedding was kept at Dr. Jackson's and, of course, they intended to have a small ball, but hardly anyone could be induced to dance so late in the season. I had given a solemn promise that nothing should induce me to run the risk: so to comply was out of the question. At length Mrs. Jackson senior, who is turned of sixty-five, opened the ball with a very good minuet, and afterwards footed it away for about two hours as gaily as the youngest. Her example took effect, and they made up a tolerable set. The dance was succeeded by a magnificent supper to which nearly thirty persons sat down. After the customary toasts, we retired, and I reached home before one. May they be happy is my sincere wish.

This is a terrible season for reaching the ships: none but stout vessels can venture down. Colonel Tottingham pays seventy pounds for a sloop to convey his family. I am in this respect fortunate. Sir Robert and Lady Chambers are going to a place called Bearcole for the benefit of sea-bathing, and I shall accompany them to Ingellee, which is within a tide of the *Valentine.* My friends will then proceed by land to the bathing-place, and one of the sloops, by Sir Roberts' orders, will convey me and my luggage to the Barrabola Head, where the ship is lying at anchor to complete her cargo.

5th April, 1782.

I have everything now ready and only wait for the completion of Sir Robert's preparations. I feel very impatient to get to sea being persuaded that it will have a salutary effect on my health. Change of scene and company will also be of service. I have taken leave of everyone, and for many shall preserve sentiments of the most grateful esteem.

ON BOARD THE "VALENTINE,'
Barrabola Head, 14th April, 1782.

I left Calcutta on Tuesday, the 9th instant, with Sir Robert and Lady Chambers. The latter, I am concerned to say, is in a very weak state, but trust sea-bathing will be beneficial. We had a boisterous trip of it down to Ingellee, and every one but myself was dreadfully sea sick.

My kind friends quitted me on Saturday evening. I felt quite forlorn at our separation. To be thrown among strangers after experiencing for near nine months the attentive hospitality of such a family as I was torn from, almost overcame my fortitude, but I soon lost every other sensation in that overwhelming one of sea sickness, which lasted the whole way, nor could I go on board till the afternoon. I shall keep this open till the Pilot goes, that you may have the satisfaction that we have passed the first dangers.

20th April, 1782.

Our Commander is by no means the placid being we supposed. I doubt he will prove a very tyrant. Instead of paying attention or shewing respect, he *exacts* both, and woe be to those who fail in either. We are still waiting for the remainder of our cargo, and Captain Lewis vents his rage in drinking "Confusion to the Board of Trade" every day.

28th April, 1782.

We had a narrow escape last evening, though I knew not of the danger till it was over. I was seized after tea with severe spasms in the stomach and had the doctor with me. When suddenly the ship began to pitch and toss violently, I heard Captain Lewis call out in a voice of thunder: "Stand by the sheet anchor : heave the lead." Presently all was quiet again, nor had the least suspicion till next morning of our having been *adrift* on the Barrabola sand. What might have been our fate, Heaven knows, had not the sheet anchor brought us up, for it is a most dangerous place, surrounded by shoals, and out of sight of land.

It is pleasant to see Captain Lewis so alert on perilous occasions. He appears to be an excellent seaman, but the roughest being surely that nature ever formed in language and manners. The oaths he swears by are most horrible, and he prides himself on inventing new ones. How were Mrs. Wheler and I mistaken ! I see he must be humoured like a child, for the least contradiction makes him almost frantic.

2nd May, 1782.

Now I must indeed say farewell. The Pilot is just quitting us, and has promised to put this on board the first vessel that sails for England. There is one under despatch. God bless you. Within six months I trust we shall all meet in health and safety.

I am,
Yours affectionately,
E. F.

LETTER XXIII.

ST. JAMES' VALLEY, ST. HELENA, *24th September, 1782.*

MY DEAR SISTER,—A more uncomfortable passage than I have made to this place can hardly be imagined. The port of my cabin being kept almost constantly shut, and the door opening into the steerage, I had neither light nor air but from a scuttle. Half the space was occupied by a great gun, which prevented me from going near the port when it was open.

Mrs. Tottingham at first took her meals in the cuddy, but the gentlemen were in general too fond of the bottle to pay us the least attention. After tea we never asked to cut in at cards, though they played every evening. Captain Lewis swore so dreadfully, making use of such vulgar oaths and expressions, and became so rude and boisterous, that Mrs. Tottingham finally withdrew entirely from the table, and never left her cabin for thirteen weeks; but the Colonel took care to send her whatever was necessary. I had no one to perform the like kind office for me, and was therefore forced to venture up among them, or risk starvation below.

The table was at first most profusely covered, being our Captain's favourite maxim "Never to make two wants of one." Everyone foresaw what must be the consequence, but he would not listen to reason. Thus we went on till the beginning of August, when he declared that we had rounded the Cape of Good Hope, offering to back his opinion by receiving twenty guineas and return a guinea a day till we reached St. Helena. No one accepted the bet; yet doubts seemed to hang on the minds of many. However on the 5th, at noon, hearing that we were in Latitude 33, 32, S., I began to think with the Captain that it was needless to *spare* our stock, since a few days would bring us a fresh supply. But, alas! at 4 P.M. land was perceived on the East Coast of Africa, so near, that before we backed, *flies* were seen on the shore. Had this happened during the night, nothing could have saved us from shipwreck. Can I sufficiently bless Providence for this second escape?

On examining the state of our water and provision, after the error was discovered, we were put on allowance of a quart of water a day for all purposes, and, for nearly a month before we arrived here, we were forced to live on salt provisions. Even the children and the sick had no better fare.

While off the Cape, we encountered very stormy weather, but happily sustained no injury, except the loss of a fore-top-mast, which was very easily replaced. Captain Lewis, one day, thought fit to refuse me a passage through his cabin for which I had expressly stipulated. I retired, and in a few minutes, he came down to apologise for his behaviour, and a most curious apology he made. He began by saying that he had been beaten at *piquet* and that losing always made him cross. "Besides," said he, "to tell you the truth, I do not like ladies. Not (with a great oath) that I have any particular objection to you. On the contrary, I really think you are a quiet good sort of woman enough: but I cannot *abide* ladies, and I declare that sometimes when you come up to me upon deck and say 'How do you do, Captain Lewis?' it makes my back open and shirt (*sic*) like a knife." So much for this gentleman's respect and politeness. I was forced to appear satisfied, and he seemed very penitent for some days, till another cross fit came on.

Judge if I did not rejoice at the sight of this romantic island, though its appearance from the sea is very unpromising—inaccessible rocks and stupendous crags frowning every side but one, nor is there any anchorage except at that point. The town is literally an ascending valley between two hills, just wide enough to admit of one street. The houses are in the English style with sashed windows and small doors. Here are back-gardens but no gardens which makes the place intensely hot for want of a free circulation of air ; but when you once ascend Ladder Hill, the scene changes and all seems enchantment. The most exquisite prospects you can conceive burst suddenly on the eye, fruitful vallies, cultivated hills and diversified scenery of every description. The inhabitants are obliging and attentive, indeed remarkably. So altogether I find it most welcome resting place. After being kept on salt provisions for a month, one is not likely to be very fastidious, former abstinence giving more poignant relish to the excellent food which is set before us.

The *Lord North* and the *Hastings*, China ships, arrived soon after us, but we were detained for convey. How vexatious !

18th October, 1782.

Yesterday Captain Lewis gave a grand entertainment on board the *Valentine*. I was obliged to preside, for Mrs. Tottingham would not venture on the water till there was necessity for it. We had a most brilliant party. I danced a good deal, but find no inconvenience from it. It is odd enough that he should have fixed on your birthday. You may be sure I silently drank my own toast. Mrs. Comettee and the other ladies seemed highly gratified, and well they might, for no expense was spared to render it completely elegant.

20th October, 1782.

The *Chapman* is just arrived in a most dreadful state, having lost near fifty of her crew in her passage from Madras, from whence she sailed in company with the *Dartmouth* which was wrecked off the Carnicobar Island, the *very ship*

I was, as I *then* thought, so *unfortunate* in missing. So that, in this instance as in so many others, I may justly impute my safety to that Providence which—

> " From hidden dangers, snares and death
> Has gently steered my way."

11th November, 1782.

Among the passengers in the *Dartmouth* were Mrs. I—n and her infant son (a most interesting child, three years of age), who were wonderfully preserved through sufferings enough to overwhelm the strongest constitution, and proceeded to St. Helena on the *Chapman*, on board which were Mr. Casamajor and his mother, who secured accommodations on the *Lord North*. Not choosing to venture farther on the *Valentine*, upon which I was applied to accompany Mrs. I—n, who could not well proceed without a female companion, and who was not able to procure accommodations on the other ships, I instantly determined on accompanying her for the express purpose of endeavouring to soften the inconveniences under which she laboured, and to soothe her mind harassed by the many hardships of her distressing voyage.

28th November, 1782.

This day we left St. Helena in company with the *Lord North*, *Valentine* and *Hastings*. The *Chapman* sails very ill and cannot keep up with the other ships. Captain Lewis told me at St. Helena, in order to prevent me quitting the *Valentine*, that we should be left in the lurch the first fair opportunity. And so it happened long ere we reached England.

Our passage was tremendous, the sea breaking over the ship and continually carrying something or the other away: nor had we any naval stores to replace what was lost.

Captain Walker and Mr. Gooch, the second officer, were daily employed with the people repairing the sails and the rigging, nor did they shrink from any labour. I never beheld such exertion. Very frequently they were obliged to take the wheel, for scarcely a sufficient number could be found to keep watch.

On entering the channel, the weather was so thick that no observation could be taken for five days. One night, after remaining in dreadful suspense respecting our situation, Captain Walker came down, about half-past ten o'clock, to tell us that we were off Scilly. What a declaration! Off Scilly on a stormy night at the beginning of February! This intelligence was not likely to tranquilise our feelings. Mrs. I—n and myself passed a sleepless night. In the morning one of the sailors ascertained the place we were driven in to be St. Ives' Bay—a most dangerous place. Thanks to Providence, we sustained no injury, except being forced round the Land's End which was to us a serious misfortune, we being utterly unable to beat back into the English Channel, our men being worn out with illness and exertion and our stores of every kind nearly exhausted.

No pilot would venture to stay on board. The *Chapman* having no poop looked so unlike an Indiaman that she was taken for an American, and we forlorn creatures set down at once as prisoners. "Why don't you release those women?" said they, "we will have nothing to do with you: we know better." We found afterwards that, although the preliminaries of peace had been some time signed, no account of the important event had reached this remote spot. Captain Walker now proposed proceeding to Milford Haven to refit, but the indraught, as it is called, having brought us off Lundy, he changed his resolution and took a pilot for King Road, where we anchored at 7 A.M. on the 7th February 1783.

THE END OF THE FIRST PART.

PART SECOND

CONTAINING AN ABSTRACT
OF THE AUTHOR'S
THREE SUBSEQUENT
VOYAGES TO INDIA.

LETTER I.

To Mrs. L.——

Blackheath, *12th February*, *1815*.

My Dear Madam,—The interest which you are pleased to take in my welfare and the kind inquiries you make respecting the voyages I have performed since my first memorable one, induce me to offer you a simple statement of facts relative to them, though to accomplish this, even in the briefest manner, some circumstances must be revealed which I would rather consign to oblivion, and some wounds must be reopened which time has mollified, if not healed. The manuscript submitted to your perusal closes with an account of my arrival in England, and thus ended my first eventful visit to India, a period which, according to my estimation, had comprised a whole life of suffering and anxiety, and dissolved for ever the strongest tie the human heart can form for itself—a period in which physical and moral evils had alike combined to inflict whatever can wound the heart to its inmost core and destroy that confidence in our fellow creatures without which the world seems indeed "a howling wilderness" peopled with terrific monsters, each prowling either by violence or fraud for his defenceless prey.

Happily for me gentler beings had blended in my path their benign influences. My sorrows had been cheered and consoled by many. I was still young; and, with buoyant spirits relieved in some degree from their late pressure, hailed my native land. Yet a sigh of regret would mingle my joyful anticipations at quitting the society, wherein, though assailed by tempestuous winds and mountainous seas, I had so frequently enjoyed "the feast of reason and the flow of soul" amidst congenial minds.

For ever blest be the moment when I quitted the *Valentine.* From that circumstance arose a friendship, which constituted one of the sweetest enjoyments of my life, and which still remains unbroken, though my friend and I seldom meet. But her letters are invaluable: few possess such epistolary talents: they have been my chief solace and consolation in distress.

Mrs. I—n, her little boy, and myself went on to town, where a dreadful shock awaited me. My dear mother was no more. The tie to which a daughter most fondly clings was rent asunder. Though I had still a father and two most affectionate sisters remaining, it was long ere I could justly appreciate their worth or draw consolation from their society. For nearly a year I laboured under very severe indisposition and incurred great expense for medical attendance—not less than £150. I was several times considered in imminent danger. Mrs. I—n too was, long after her arrival, affected with the most distressing nervous debility. All this is not to be wondered at, for, during the passage from St. Helena, both of us were in an unfirm state, and our health had suffered much from the circumstances in which we were placed. It is true we experienced all possible relief from the kindness of those around us whom we daily beheld subjected to privations and exertions the most trying yet ever affording us comfort and attention. In each benevolent act Captain Walker was amply assisted by Mr. Gooch and the Surgeon, Mr. Crawfoot—a most worthy and scientific young man, to whose skill I was probably more indebted for the prolongation of a precarious existence than I was aware of at the time. My health being in some measure restored, I tried various plans in pursuit of independence, but none seemed to promise success. My friends wished me to remain at home, but Calcutta appeared the most likely theatre of exertion. You cannot wonder that my heart warmed to a place where I had met such friendship and generosity, and where so much general encouragement was given to the efforts of respectable individuals. I still bore in mind the offer which had been made to me in Bengal, and determined to pursue this plan ; and, having become acquainted with a Miss Hicks, a young woman of the strictest integrity, who possessed many valuable qualifications, I engaged her to accompany me as an assistant. Captain Walker, who was about to proceed to Bombay as commander of the *Lord Camden*, offered me a passage on very moderate terms, provided I took charge of four ladies who wished to have a protectoress during the voyage. Being desirous of seeing Bombay, I felt very little reluctance to comply, especially as my friend Mr. Gooch held the same situation in the *Camden* as he had so meritoriously filled int he *Chapman*. The passage to be sure would be rather circuitous, but in a fine new ship, navigated by persons of whose nautical abilities I had such indubitable proofs, that appeared of little moment. The prospect of strengthening my connection with India influenced me still further. Having, therefore, arranged my plans on a general ground, allowing for the deviations, which in such a case as mine might be allowed to arise from circumstances, I embarked on the *Lord Camden*, and sailed from the Downs for India on the 17th March 1784. Here let me pause for the moment ; I will soon resume my pen.

I am, etc.,
E. F.

LETTER II.

To Mrs. L.——

15th February, 1815.

My Dear Madam,—For some days we had rather boisterous weather, but this subsided as we passed the Canary Islands, where (to my great mortification) we did not stop. On the 3rd April we had a view of Teneriffe which is said to be 2,000 feet high perpendicularly. It must have been formerly a considerable volcano. So lately as the year 1704 there was an irruption from it which did immense damage. On the 10th we passed the Cape de Verde Islands, but, to my regret, without touching at any; for curiosity was ever with me a predominant feeling. The island of Fogo has a volcano, which sometimes flames out in a terrible manner, and discharges pumice stones to a great distance. The weather at this time was intensely hot, but we had plenty of apples on board which afforded great refreshment. Soon after they were finished, we spoke a Danish ship, whose Captain made the ladies a handsome present of oranges and fine apples. It is not easy for you, my dear Madam, to conceive the importance of such accommodations, but those who have been many weeks, perhaps months, shut up in a floating prison, without the power of procuring refreshments which even health demands, will be well aware of their value. At length the trade winds visited us, "and bore healing on their wings." We passed the Tropic of Capricorn very pleasantly, but soon afterwards a change took place. Such are the vicissitudes of a sea life! I have not yet mentioned the names of the ladies who accompanied me: there were Mrs. Pemberton and Misses Turner, Bellas, and Fisher, who, with Miss Hicks and myself, occupied two-thirds of the round house. I note it, as rather a singular circumstance, that we were only five times on deck during the passage, which was owing to a previous arrangement between the Captain and me to guard against imprudent attachments, which are more easily formed than broken, and I am happy to say the plan succeeded to our wish. About this time, Captain Walker fell dangerously ill, but fortunately recovered before the 8th June, when the birthday of Miss Ludlow, a Bristol lady, who subsequently became Mrs. Walker, was celebrated in high style. All the ship's company had a dinner of fresh provisions, and we sat down to a most sumptuous repast, vegetables and fruit having been provided in England, and salad raised purposely for the occasion.

We were now going at the rate of eight knots an hour, off the Cape, with a heavy swell: but the young folks nevertheless so earnestly solicited for a dance that the Captain could not refuse. So all the furniture being removed out of the cuddy, I led off, by particular request, but had only gone down one couple when a tremendous lee lurch put us all in confusion. I declined standing up again, butt he rest during three or four hours tumbled about in the prettiest manner possible; and when no longer able to dance, made themselves amends by singing and laughing; no serious accident occurred to any one, and the evening concluded very agreeably.

On the 11th June we struck soundings at 7 A.M. off Cape l'Aguillas. This exactly confirmed Captain Walker's observations, and was matter of greater rejoicing to me than can be imagined by persons who were never brought into danger by the ignorance and inattention of those entrusted with the command. The next day we shipped so many seas from the heavy land-swell as to extinguish the fire. We were, therefore, constrained to put up with a cold dinner. However our good Captain, ever provident, produced a fine round of beef, preserved by Hoffmann, which well supplied the deficiency.

On the 24th June, we anchored in the Bay of Johanna, one of the African isles to the north of Madagascar. It is a fertile little spot. We here met with plenty of refreshments and very cheap. The oranges are remarkably fine; I took a good quantity of them. Their beef is pretty good. Captain Walker purchased several bullocks for the ship's use and to supply our table. The inhabitants are very civil, but are said to be the greatest thieves in existence. We were much amused with the high titles assumed by them. The Prince of Wales honoured us with his company at breakfast, after which Mr. Lewin, one of our passengers, took him down to his cabin, where, having a number of knick knacks, he requested His Royal Highness to make choice of some article to keep in remembrance of him. To Mr. Lewin's astonishment he fixed on a large mahogany bookcase which occupied one side of the cabin; and, on being told that could not be spared, went away in high displeasure, refusing to accept anything else. The Duke of Buccleugh washed our linen; H.R.H. the Duke of York officiated as boatman; and a boy of fourteen, who sold us some fruit, introduced himself as the Earl of Mansfield. They seem very proud of these titles. We all went ashore; and while those who were able to walk rambled about to view the country, which they described as very delightful, I awaited their return in a thatched building erected for the accommodation of strangers. We were careful to return before sunset, the night air being reckoned very pernicious to Europeans. These people are almost constantly at war with those of the adjacent Isles. Being in great want of gunpowder, they prevailed on Captain Walker to give them the quantity that would have been expended in the customary salutes.

On the 2nd July we left Johanna with a pleasant breeze, but were soon driven back and experienced great fatigue for many days from a heavy rolling sea, but on the 20th, at day-break, we saw Old Woman's Island, and at 11 A.M. cast anchor at Bombay. An alarming accident occurred while saluting the Fort. The gunner's mate reloaded one of the guns without having properly cleansed it : in consequence of which he was blown into the water. Never did I behold a more shocking sight. The poor creature's face was covered with blood, yet he swam like a fish till a boat reached him. Thank God he escaped with some slight hurts, and to my surprise was upon deck next day.

On the 21st, we went on shore with Mr. Coggan, the Naval Storekeeper, who was Miss Turner's brother-in-law. We landed in the dockyard, where the many fine ships building and repairing, with the number of Europeans walking about, almost persuaded me that I was at home, till the dress and dark complexion of the workmen destroyed the pleasing illusion. Mrs. Coggan received me very kindly ; and, by her hospitable treatment, rendered my stay at Bombay as agree-able as possible. On Saturday, the 24th, we received a visit from the Governor (Mr. Boddam) which I find is considered as a great compliment. We went to Church on the 25th and in the evening sat up to receive company, as also on the two following evenings—a tiresome ceremony to me, who detest parade and was merely a traveller. But Mrs. Coggan assured me it would be an affront to the Settlement if I submitted not to the established custom. The like usage formerly prevailed in Bengal but is now abolished. On the 29th, we went to pay our respects to the Governor at Parell, his country seat—a delightful place and a charming ride to it. Indeed all the environs are beautiful : in this respect it has greatly the advantage of Calcutta, but the town itself is inferior. They have a handsome church and a good assembly room, where they dance all the year round.

We dined one day at Mr. Nesbit's, Chief of the Marine, who gave us a repast in true *old* Indian style. "The tables they groaned with the weight of the feast." We had every joint of a calf on the table at once, nearly half a Bengal sheep, several large dishes of fish, boiled and roast turkeys, a ham, a kid, tongue, fowls, and a long train of etceteras. The heat was excessive, the hour two, and we were thirty in company in a lower roomed house: so you may conceive what sensations such a prodigious dinner would produce. It is, however, the fact that they ate with great appetite—to my astonishment who could scarcely touch a morsel.

On the 1st August, the *Camden*, being ordered to Madras without any prospect of proceeding from thence to Bengal, Captain Walker secured a passage for Miss Hicks and myself on the *Nottingham*—Captain Curtis, who offered us the best accommodation, and refused to accept of any remuneration. He afterwards disposed of his ship, but under the express stipulation that we should retain our cabin. I dined, on the 8th, at Mr. D. Scott's with our fellow-passengers Mr. and Mrs. Lewin, and a very agreeable day we passed, the whole of the cuddy passengers being invited, so that we sat down once more together, assuredly for the last time. On the 23rd, I dined with Miss Bellas at her uncle's gardens, where I met with a most cordial reception, and was introduced to Captain Christie, whom she married before I quitted the settlement, and alas! I must add, survived her marriage only thirteen weeks. She died, as I afterwards heard, of a confirmed liver complaint. Her health was very bad during the whole passage; for on the least motion she constantly became sea-sick and never overcame it. She was a most amiable young woman and generally beloved. I shall ever cherish her memory with affection. On the 25th, Captain Curtis introduced the new Commander to me and made as many apologies for quitting the ship, as if he had been accountable to me for his conduct. "But, however," said he, "go when you will, I will see you safe on board and clear over the Reef," which is a ridge of rocks at the entrance of Bombay harbour. This promise he performed on the 4th September, when, having taken leave of our friends, he accompanied us on board the *Louisa*, for so was the *Nottingham* named in honour of the new owner's wife. He staid until seven in the evening, and then went on shore with the Pilot, first calling up all his late servants, whom he charged to pay me the same attention as if he were present. I shall ever esteem him. Our friendship continued unabated while I remained in India. He afterwards commanded the *Swallow Packet*, and mine was the first and last house he entered on each voyage. Since my return home I have seldom seen him : but that alters not my sentiments. It was natural that I should quit Bombay with favourable impressions. I had been treated with much kindness, and mixed with the first society on the Island. I refer you to other travellers for descriptions, observing only that provisions of all kinds are good, but rather dear, except fish which is here in high perfection and very plentiful.

On the 15th September, we anchored in Anjengo Roads to take in coir, rope and cables for which this is the great mart. They are fabricated out of the outer rind of the cocoanut, whose quality is such that the salt nourishes it, and it possesses also an elasticity which enables it to contract or dilate itself in proportion to the strain on it. This property is particularly useful in these seas, where squalls frequently come on with frightful violence and rapidity, and the preservation of an anchor is an object of importance. The surf runs very high here, and is at times extremely dangerous. Captain Ross brought off an invitation from Mr. Hutchinson, the Chief, to dine with him : but no one chose to venture on shore. I have not forgotten the fate of Mrs. Blomer, who was drowned same years ago with seven others in attempting to land on the beach.

Here is a pretty strong Fort on the seaside. Every one who went ashore spoke with great rapture of the country. The vicinity of the great chain of mountains, which separated the coast of Malabar from that of Coromandel, and which are said to be the highest in the world (the Alps and Andes excepted) gives an awful termination to the prospect. The water here is so indifferent that few Europeans attempt to drink it. Formerly Anjengo was famous throughout India for its manufacture of long cloth and stockings, but these have fallen into decay. We left this dangerous place on the 22nd. The wind several times blew so strong, we had great apprehensions of being driven on ashore, and a very narrow escape we had : for on examining the anchor, only one fluke was found remaining : the other must have been so nearly broken by the strain on it, that it would not bear heaving up. Our passage was remarkably tedious though we had a pleasant man in command who kept an exceeding good table. Not expecting to be more than five or six weeks at sea, *instead of twelve,* our stock of fresh provisions was quite exhausted long ere we reached Calcutta, and only distilled water to drink. On the 27th November, we arrived, and, to my great surprise, after all that had been said against the probability of such an event taking place, found the *Camden* had been some time in the river. Mr. Baldwin, the Chief Officer, died soon after and my friend, Mr. Gooch, succeeded him. In this situation he remained for several voyages with Captain Dance, till he obtained command of the *Lushington,* and I frequently had the pleasure of seeing him during my residence in Bengal. Being now about to enter on a new scene, I will take leave for the present and remaln.

Yours, etc.,

E. F.

LETTER III.

To Mrs. L.——

BLACKHEALH, *19th February, 1815.*

My dear Madam,—At Calcutta I met with great kindness from many whom I had formerly known, and who now appeared desirous of forwarding any plan I might adopt. At length, with the approbation of Captain Walker and several other friends, I determined on placing Miss Hicks in business as a milliner. It was agreed that my name should not appear, although I retained in my hands the entire management of the concern, allowing Miss H. one-third of the profits. Mr. Barry, purser of the *Camden*, had the goodness to open a set of books, and to give me every necessary instruction how to set them in proper order, which afterwards proved very advantageous in the prosecution of my concerns. You are quite aware how many difficulties, both from within and from without, must have opposed themselves to this design, and how much the same feeling operated in contrary directions—at least, if the wish for independence may be determined pride, to which it was certainly allied. Soon afterwards, a proposal was made to me to engage in a seminary for young ladies on so liberal a plan that I have since frequently regretted not having complied with the solicitations of my friends, but I had in fact gone rather too far to recede, having made several large purchases, which could not be disposed of suddenly but at a considerable loss. Within four months after our arrival, Miss Hicks married Mr. Lacey, and the following Christmas lay in of a fine boy, but unfortunately lost him at the end of six weeks. After which her health declined so fast as to render it absolutely necessary that she should proceed to Europe. I took that opportunity of sending home for education a natural child of my husband's whose birth had caused me bitter affliction : yet I could not abandon him, though he was deserted by his natural protector. They, accordingly, embarked on the 5th September 1786 on the *Seven Packet* (Captain Kidd), with every prospect of a favourable passage, but on the 9th, the vessel struck on a sand, called the Broken Ground, just below Ingellee, and every European on board unhappily perished, except the second officer in whose arms the poor little boy expired. Mrs. Lacey supported herself in the forechains with exemplary fortitude, till a tremendous sea broke over them and he saw her no more, but by a great exertion he reached the shore on a broken spar. I felt her loss severely, for she possessed a mind and spirit that would have graced any station.

After this melancholy event, I was compelled to conduct business in my own name, but on a more extensive scale, and succeeded tolerably well, till the unlucky year 1788, when such immense investments were brought out, that nearly all concerned in that branch of commerce were involved in one common ruin. Yielding to the strain, for I had large consignments, which I was compelled to receive, my brother having become security for them at home, I solicited and obtained the indulgence of my creditors for eighteen months, under four trustees, Messrs. Fairlie, Colvin, Child, and Moscrop, whose names were sufficient to sanction any concern. Such was the confidence reposed in my integrity that everything remained in my own hands as formerly. Never, I am proud to say, was that confidence abused. Pardon the seeming vanity of this assertion. In justice to my own character, I must say this much, and can boldly appeal to those who are best acquainted with the whole transaction for the truth of my statement. Having received large consignments from my kind friends at home which sold to great advantage, and various other means suggesting themselves, wherein I was benevolently assisted by many who saw and compassionated my arduous struggles after independence, I succeeded in settling, either in money or goods, every claim on me, and again became possessed of a little property, when in the beginning of 1794 anxiety to see my dear friends led me to resolve on returning to Europe. I must here mention what operated as a strong encouragement to prosecute the plan immediately. In May 1791, Mr. Benjamin Lacey, brother of my lamented friend's husband, came to Bengal, bringing out a small investment for me. I received him into my family, and although only nineteen years of age, he evinced such abilities that I soon obtained a situation for him, where he conducted himself so much to the satisfaction of his employers as to be intrusted with confidential commissions to Madras and elsewhere, which he executed with judgment and integrity. This young man, happening to be in Calcutta, I embraced the opportunity of leaving to him the management of my concerns. As a proof that my confidence was not misplaced, allow me here to notice, that although my stock and bills were delivered over to him without inventory or engagement on his part, when I left India, he in the course of *eleven* days after, transmitted regular accounts of the whole and where they were placed, making himself responsible for the proceeds in the strongest manner: so that had we both died, my friends would have found no difficulty in claiming my effects. Having by his assistance, laid in a small investment, I embarked on 25th March on board the American ship *Henry* (Captain Jacob Crowinshield) bound for Ostend, and on the 29th the pilot quitted us. I found the *Henry* a snug little vessel, Captain C. a well behaved man, and his officers, though not of polished manners, yet in their way disposed to offer me every attention that could render the passage agreeable. I suffered at times from the heat, but on the whole enjoyed better health than during my former voyage. Having only one passenger besides myself, but little occurred to relieve the monotony of a sea-life. I frequently played chess, and was almost constantly beaten. Cards and backgammon had their turn, but I grew tired of all, till at length, on the 2nd of July, we anchored off St. Helena.

I went on shore in the afternoon and learnt with some vexation that a large fleet sailed only the day before. I wished to have written specially as we were not bound direct to England. Many changes had occurred in this curious little Island during my twelve years of absence. Few recollect me, but Captain Wall of the *Buccleugh*, formerly chief officer of the *Valentine*, behaved with the greatest attention. I shall ever acknowledge his kindness. Fresh provisions were very scarce. A drought had prevailed until this season for four years, and it would require three good seasons to repair the damage sustained by their stock perishing for want of water. A circumstance happened during our stay of which the like was not to be remembered by the oldest inhabitant, though, from the appearance of the place, one could conclude such events were common. A large fragment of rock, detatched by the moisture, fell from the side of Ladder Hill on a smallo uthouse at the upper end of the valley in which two men were sleeping in separate beds. The stone broke through the top and lodged between them. The master of the house was suffocated, it is supposed, by the rubbish, as no bruises were found on his body. The other man forced his way through, and gave the alarm, but had not enough time to save his companion. This accident has caused many to tremble for their safety, since, all the way up the valley, houses are built under similar projections, and will, some time or other, probably experience the same fate. Among the Alps such things are common.

An unpleasant affair also occurred to me. I had, when last here given a girl, who attended me from Calcutta, and behaved very ill, to Mrs. Mason, with whom I boarded, under a promise that she should not be sold, consequently no slave paper passed. Mr. Mason, however, in defiance of this prohibition disposed of her for £10. This act militating against the established regulations, not only advantage was taken of my return to the Island to call upon me as the original offender for that sum, but a demand was made of £60 more to pay the woman's passage back to Bengal with her two children !! After every effort, I could only obtain a mitigation of £10, being forced to draw on my brother P. at sixty days sight in favour of the Court of Directors for £60, a sum that I could ill-afford to lose, but the strong hand of power left me no other alternative.

On the 6th July, we quitted St. Helena, and, on the 11th, anchored off Ascension. Our Captain and the gentlemen went on shore to look at the Island. The following remarks I extract from his journal: "The soil near the sea appears dry and barren in the extreme like cinders from a fire ; indeed, the whole Island bears evident marks of the former existence of volcanoes, several craters still appearing on the hills. Perhaps it owes its origin to some great convulsion of nature, as I am persuaded does St. Helena. Although the sea coast presents a dreary view, yet on walking farther the prospect becomes enchanting. A most delightful verdure covers the smaller hills and the valleys, and no doubt they afford plenty of water, though, not being very well, I was too much fatigued to examine. The Second Officer saw five or six goats, but could not get near enough to fire at them."

Numbers of man-of-war birds and eggs were taken, which proved to be good eating. They likewise caught the finest turtle I ever saw weighing near 400lbs., but, by an act of unpardonable negligence in people so situated, it was suffered to walk overboard in the night. We had, however, the good luck to catch a fine albercuor, which weighed near 100lbs.; its flesh when roasted resembled veal. We were fortunate in having an excellent cook on board, who really made the most of our scanty provisions. On the 3rd August, three large ships hove in sight, one of which bore down towards us, and fired several guns to bring us to. They sent a boat on board with orders for our Captain to attend the Commander. He, to our great joy, came back in about half-an-hour, having been treated with much civility by the French Captain. It was now we heard the distressing news of Ostend being in the hands of the French. Indeed they boasted of having gained the advantage everywhere except in the West Indies. These were three frigates mounting from 28 to 32 guns. They had been 20 days from Brest and had taken 22 prizes. We had been assured by Captain Wall that the French dared not show their *noses* in the Channel, but I now with sorrow beheld the contrary, not on my own account (being safe enough on board an American), but Captain Crowinshield told me there were more than 200 English prisoners on board these ships. He now acquainted me with his determination to proceed to America, and very politey offered me a passage that I might witness the disposal of my property, which I, of course, declined, not feeling the least desire to prolong my voyage. So having arranged my affairs in the best manner possible, under existing circumstances, I took a final leave of the *Henry* on the 4th September, and landed with my luggage at Cowes in the Isle of Wight. From this place I soon reached London, pleased as I went to behold scenes from which I had been so many years banished, and anticipating the delight with which my dear father would receive his long absent child. Alas! I was doomed to behold him no more. He expired only four moths before my arrival. The remainder of my family I had the happiness of finding in perfect health. The property sent to America came to a tolerable market, but Captain Crowinshield, instead of making the returns in cash, sent a ship called the *Minerva* with his young brother, Richard Crowinshield, in command of her. This ship it was proposed that I should take out to India under certain conditions. She was a fine new vessel of about 300 tons burthen. I had her coppered, and proposed her first making a voyage to America, and, on her return, sailing for Bengal about Christmas : but, when completely fitted out for sea, with a picked cargo on board for Boston, she took fire by the bursting of a bottle of aquafortis, which had been negligently stored among other goods ; and, though immediately scuttled and every precaution taken, sustained material damage. This involved me in a series of misfortunes. Mr. P. Wynne, who had shipped to the amount of £428 on the *Minerva*, by mere accident discovered that, contrary to the general opinion, the Captain was responsible for all goods committed to his charge under regular bills of lading ; and, accordingly commenced an action against him. In this he was successful, the whole debt and costs near £6,000 falling on the Captain, and, from his inability to pay, on me. This decision caused a change in the tenor of bills of lading, which now contain clauses against fire and several other casualties, whereas before the "dangers of the seas" were alone excepted. Thus did my loss operate to the advantage of others. To prevent the total wreck of my little property, I was compelled to proceed immediately on the original plan as affording the only chance of attaining independence, and ultimately securing a home in my native country.

Having resolved never again to travel alone, I engaged a Miss Tripler as a companion for two years, at £30 per annum, but had soon cause to regret the agreement. A proposal being made by my dearest friend Mrs. I—n to take out a young lady, who had been educated in England

and was going to rejoin her friends in Bengal, I felt no inclination to refuse, having frequently seen Miss Rogers and knowing her to be a most amiable little girl. Besides, as I had a pianoforte and a pair of globes with me and a good collection of books, I was pleased with the idea of contributing to *her* improvement, and amusing myself at the same time. The ship being obliged to touch at Guernsey, I determined to join her there. So on the 17th July [1795] she sailed for that place, Miss Tripler and my Bengal servant proceeding on her as the most saving plan. Here let me pause, reserving the account of my third voyage for another letter.

I remain truly yours,

E. F.

LETTER IV.

To Mrs L.——

BLACKHEATH, *24th February, 1815*.

My Dear Madam,—On Sunday, the 2nd August 1795, at 5 A.M., Miss Rogers and myself, accompanied by Captain Richard Crowinshield, quitted London for Southampton, from whence the packets sail for Guernsey. I did not leave my sister and nieces without regret. They were *always* very dear to me; but now, having lost my parents, the tie was drawn still closer. Abstracted from this consideration, I rather rejoiced at quitting England, as the whole tone of my stay had been embittered by a succession of losses and disappointments, arising partly from my individual misfortune respecting the ship and partly from the general state of commerce at this inauspicious period. Alas! in the number of wretched emigrants whom I saw crowding the port of Southampton, I felt I had but too many fellow-sufferers, and it was easy to read in many a sorrowful countenance that "the times were out of joint."

On arriving there, we were advised to go to Lymington and embark from thence. This gave me an opportunity of passing a few hours at Newtown park, a short mile from Lymington, the residence of Miss I—n's sister, Mrs. P—n. The house and grounds are strikingly beautiful, and an observatory on the top of the former commands an extensive view over the Isle of Wight and great part of the Channel. Mrs. P.—n assured me that, not long before, she saw from thence near four hundred vessels sail together. The wind becoming fair, we embarked on the 5th August, and next evening safely reached the *Minerva* at Guernsey. We found all on board greatly fatigued, the ship having arrived only the night before after a harassing passage of eighteen days. What an escape we had! On the 8th we went on shore; passed through the market, which appears to be well supplied, particularly with fruit, vegetables, poultry, and butter. We took a quantity of the latter, which lasted perfectly good all the way out. I was pleased with the market people, they were so remarkably clean and civil. The women wore bonnets with enormous stiffened crowns; underneath they had becoming laced mobs. Provisions are in general good and cheap: the fish excellent; such delicious soles I never tasted anywhere. We went to Church and heard prayers both in French and English. A dialect of the former prevails here, but it is a vile jargon. I could scarcely understand one word in ten. This must be a very healthy place. I saw here a lady who at the age of ninety-four had full possession of her faculties, and I heard there were several others on the island of nearly the same age. Mr. Tupper, a gentleman, to whom I had a letter, was in his 76th year. He and his whole family paid Miss Rogers and myself the greatest attention. I was surprised to see the magnificent style in which their house was fitted up. The drawing room stove was of silver, the curtains rich silk with gilt cornices: the chimneypiece cost eighty pounds, and every other article corresponding. Even these were trifling when compared with the many capital paintings which adorned every room in the house. I afterwards found that the prevailing taste with the wealthy here is for expensive houses; for the roads are so bad and steep that single horse chaises are the only carriages in use. On the 17th August, Mr. S. Tupper came by appointment to show us the Island, of which we almost made the tour. The lands are highly cultivated, but such roads I never saw; they are barely wide enough to admit a single chaise. Fortunately we only met one, which backed for us to pass. I admire the exact manner in which the hedges are kept: they add great beauty to the prospect. I have seldom seen more picturesque views; the land and sea valluys are particularly striking. Their parties thoughly elegant, are by no means expensive: for liquors are duty free and the best wines do not cost more than 16*s*. per dozen, except claret, which is at from 25 to 28*s*. The hospitality with which we were all treated by this worthy family, excited the most grateful emotions, and I bade them adieu with the most sincere regret.

I am yours truly,

E. F.

LETTER V.

BLACKHEATH, *25th February, 1815.*

MY DEAR MADAM,—We were a pretty large party on board. Mr. Campbell, fresh from the Highlands of Scotland, on whom the officers were continually playing their jokes; Mr. Smith, a youth going to the Madeiras, and Mr. Reigail, who was one of the most interesting young men I ever met with,—his mind highly polished and his disposition placid and benevolent, but he appeared bending beneath a deep dejection. He never joined in conversation if it were gay; he ate no more than barely sufficed nature, and though from politeness and native suavity, he never refused to join our evening parties at cards, yet his depression was visible even in the moments of amusement. He had been brought up in Russia, and had, for his age (which could not be more than 24) seen much of the world, and evidently mixed in the first society. I apprehend some singular blight had happened in his fortunes.

On the 7th September, we landed at Funchall, the capital of Madeira. I was exceedingly delighted with our approach to the Island. The town is built on rising ground; and, as you draw near to it, appears imposing and magnificent, having several churches and convents. Behind the town, the ground rises abruptly into steep hills covered with vineyards, and ornamented with pleasure houses, at once exhibiting the appearance of prosperity and cultivation, and the charms of picturesque and romantic scenery. A Mr. L.—, to whom I had letters, went with us to a hotel; for, unfortunately his lady being in England, he could not entertain us at his own house. Living in this manner was very expensive and disagreeable also. We paid 5*s.* each for dinner, exclusive of wine. Neither the waiter nor any other servant understood a word of English or any other language we could speak. It was only with the landlady we could have any communication. We found Funchall much less beautiful than its appearance promised. The streets were ill paved, narrow, dirty, and solitary ; but the great Church is a handsome building, and the Hospital is a very excellent one. Before it is a fine fountain—always a refreshing sight in a country like this.

The American Consul visited us next morning and invited us to his country house, for which we sat out at 5 o'clock. Miss Rogers and I were in silk-net hammocks, slung upon poles. We were each carried by two men, who went at a great rate. The road lay up a steep hill. This is the only mode of conveyance, except riding on horse-back, as no wheel carriages can be used in a country so hilly. They employ a kind of dray or sledge drawn by oxen to transport goods.

We found a large party assembled. The lady of the house, a pleasant Irish gentlewoman, had all the frankness and hospitality of her country ; and, with her husband, a most amiable and companionable man, made us quickly forget that we were strangers. Even the Portuguese ladies seemed familiar with us, though unluckily we could not converse with them. We had a ball at night, but the weather being too warm for dancing, we exchanged it for whist. I could not help observing here how frequently people who travel will find an advantage in knowing something of this game, as they may sit down with persons of different nations and languages, and enjoy with them an amusement that, for the time, admits of an interchange of ideas and facilitates good will, even where conversation is denied. We down above thirty to an elegant supper. The grapes I found delicious here, but the season for other fruits was over. The vineyards are tended with unusual care. The grapes, of which wine is made, are not suffered to ripen in the sun, which they told me is the reason of the superior flavour in Madeira wine. The Consul's house was most delightfully situated. It overlooked the whole town of Funchall, the surrounding country, and the wide spreading ocean. It had a beautiful garden, quinces, apples, pears, walnuts, bananas, guavas, and pine-apples. I quitted this Paradise with regret, and found my road—down hill very fatiguing and disagreeable.

We stayed here till the 21st, and, by means of our first friend, spent several pleasant days and gay evenings; but the weather was so hot and other travelling so disagreeable that, if I had not been detained by business, I would much rather have passed my time on board. One day we went with the American Consul to visit a convent of Ursulines. We found the chapel door open, but were not suffered to pass the threshold. The nuns were very chatty and, like most ignorant persons, very curious, asking a hundred ridiculous questions. How very differently do human beings pass the time allotted them in this probationary existence! Surely, to consume it in supine indolence or "vain repetitions" can never render us more acceptable to Him who is the Fountain of Light and Knowledge. We ate some preserved peaches with them, which the Consul paid for, and then took our leave, but were forced to submit to a salute from the sisters which we would gladly have dispensed with, for they all took an enormous quantity of snuff. These are the only nuns I ever saw who do not conceal their hair. On leaving these pious ladies, we went to Golgotha, or the chapel of skulls (as it is called), being entirely lined with skulls and other human bones. What an idea!

We drank tea, the same day, with Signor Esmerado, whose large house and extensive grounds once belonged to the Jesuits. This is one of the richest families in the Island. The display of plate surprised me. The tea tray was the largest I ever saw and of massive silver. Wine and sweetmeats were served in the same costly style. Afterwards there were several minuets danced. They, with difficulty, suffered us to depart, and were the means of introducing us to another pleasant evening party, when the lady of the house played remarkably well on the pianoforte and sang in a style of superior excellence.

One day we went on horseback to visit the Church of Nossa Senhora de La Monte (Our Lady of the Mount), about three miles from Funchall, upon a very highly ground, which must have cost a large sum in building. The ascent to it is by at least one hundred steps. The Church is not large but richly ornamented. There is a wonder working image of the Virgin, in a crystal shrine, very small—not more than two feet high. It looks exactly like a doll, but her little Ladyship, however insignificent her appearance, had more votaries than any other saint in the Island. Here we saw some paintings, which considered as the work of a self-taught genius (I was assured this was a fact) had extraordinary merit. In this little excursion, I was surprised to see the diversity of climate exhibited in a short distance. The vintage was riper below: while the grapes around us were like bullets, and I am told they never completely ripen. We observed the same effect in Mr. Murray's plantation half a mile lower. This gentleman, who was the English Consul, had laid out above £20,000 in improving a spot, which, after all, will never bring anything to maturity. Yet it is a most charming place. There are three ranges of gardens, one above another, the lower are very large and well laid out on a level artificially formed, in the midst of which stands a good house, but not sufficiently elegant to correspond with such extensive grounds. In these there are several reservoirs, containing gold and silver fish, which are supplied with water by small cascades, so as to be kept constantly full.

Nor are Mr. Murray's improvements confined to his own estate. The road up to the Mount and the wall which secures it, with many fountains, conduits, and reservoirs, were made by him. He has also opened many cross-paths winding round the hill in the prettiest manner imaginable, with stone seats and alcoves to rest on from time to time, and has planted the hollows with chestnut trees, entirely at his own expense. Poor man! he had been obliged by ill heath to abandon his little Paradise, and was at this time in Lisbon. We afterwards called upon the British Vice-Consul, Mr. C——k, at his country seat, which was remarkable for its extensive prospect. We thought him and Mrs. C. very good kind of people but were surprized to find that, although the latter was English, she had resided abroad from infancy and knew scarcely a hundred words of her native language.

Although we were certainly treated with much kindness and hospitality at this place, yet were we assured that the inhabitants had little enjoyment of society with each other; that, being all engaged in one line of merchandize, the pursuits of interest were found to jar with those of good-fellowship, and that, on the whole, Madeira was an unpleasant residence, except to the sick and the wayfaring.

I am yours truly,

E. F.

LETTER VI.

To Mrs. L——.

BLACKHEATH, *28th February, 1815.*

My dear Madam,—We were as might be expected much tossed about by the equinoctial gales on quitting Madeira ; but on the 23rd September, we obtained a sight of the Peak of Teneriffe. All that day we kept standing in for the land, but to little purpose, as the mountains are too high to admit of approach except in a calm. On the 26th, we cast anchor in the road of Oratavia. The visit boat came out, and, as soon as our bill of health had been examined, the Captain was permitted to go ashore. I sent by him a letter which Mr. P——, the American Consul at Madeira, had given me, and received in reply a most cordial invitation from Mr. and Mrs. Barry for Miss Rogers and myself to take up our abode with them during our stay, with which we thankfully complied in the evening. The appearance of this country pleased me much better than Madeira, as it is more cultivated and better inhabited. The city of Oratavia constitutes a fine feature in the beautiful scene. We were received most kindly by the worthy country people, who invited us, and at whose house we met with the best society in the Island. I greatly prefer the Spanish ladies to the Portuguese, finding them more easy in their manners and much better educated. Many spoke French and Italian with facility, and several had been so connected with the English as to have attained enough of the language to be tolerably intelligible in it. Their persons were pleasing, and some would have been handsome, but for the presence of Mrs. Barry, who although in her thirty-fourth year, I thought the most beautiful woman I ever beheld. She was in England just before Sir Joshua Reynolds' death, and he declared repeatedly that would his health permit him ever to take another picture, it should be Mrs. Barry's. Her height was commanding with just enough *embonpoint* to be agreeable. Dimples have been called "the first of the graces." I never saw a countenance display more of them : her smile was perfectly fascinating.

I was disappointed in my intention of ascending the Peak of Teneriffe, the season being too far advanced, and I was assured by many that I was quite unequal at any time to have endured the fatigue. After travelling 15 miles over loose stones and rugged ascents, you find yourself still at the foot of the Peak. Here it is necessary to remain till two in the morning, when the task of clambering begins over pumice stone and ashes, and should you reach the top by sunrise, you may esteem yourself very fortunate. Four hours are generally allowed for the ascent, and after all, should the Peak be enveloped in clouds, which is frequently the case, you have your labour for your pains. But, on a clear day, the view is truly sublime. You can distinctly see the seven Canary Islands. Some assert that both the continent of Africa and the Island of Madeira have been seen from hence; but, I cannot suppose the human vision capable of extending so far, though I do not doubt that both places are comprehended within the immense horizon such a prodigious height may command. Having heard a very good account of Santa Cruz, which is between 20 and 30 miles across the Island, we determined to visit it, little aware of the roads we must encounter. Ladies here travel on asses, on which are placed a sort of armed chair with cushions and a footstool. This plan appeared to be easy, but we soon found that the roads at Madeira were bowling greens compared with these. How the poor animals that bore us contrived to keep their legs, clambering over the rocks that from time to time had fallen in the path I know not: the shocks they gave me I shall never forget. Mr. Barry had provided a cold turkey, wine, etc., for a repast; and, when ready for it, we went into a peasant's cottage, and dined comfortably, endeavouring to laugh away our fears and fatigues. The remains of our meal afforded a feast to the peasants, who live in a most wretched style, seldom tasting either meat, eggs or milk. The mother of the mistress of the cottage was near eighty, and to see with what eagerness the poor old creature watched every morsel we put to our mouths was really affecting. Notwithstanding their coarse fare, the common people here are a stout hardy race: fair complexioned, well featured, and remarkably lively, as we found by our attendants, for as each animal has a man to guide it, we were almost stunned by their incessant chatter. Soon after dinner we renewed our journey. My animal fell down, but I was not hurt. For the next five miles our road was easy, and lay over a delightful plain, which brought us to the ancient city of Laguna, the Capital of the Island, which is tolerably large, well inhabited and has two good churches with several convents. From thence the road to Santa Cruz lay entirely on the descent over large stones and fragments of rock. The jumbling was horrible, and *pour surcroit de malheur*, so strong a wind blew from the sea, that my whole strength was scarce sufficient to hold my umbrella; yet I did not dare give it up, the rays of the sun were so powerful, and the reflection from the stones intolerable. I was at one time so exhausted that I declared I must give up the journey, but the creature I rode carried me on in spite of me and stopped not, till we arrived at the house of Mr. R——y in Santa Cruz who gave us all a hearty welcome. This gentleman lived in a most delightful situation fronting the Mole, where notwithstanding our fatigue, we walked in the evening, when our good host got tipsy for joy, and with great difficulty allowed us to retire. Alas! weary as we were, the mosquitoes would scarcely permit us to sleep. My companion suffered terribly from them.

Santa Cruz is indeed a fine place, and the country around well deserves the pen of Mrs. Ratcliffe to celebrate its cloud-capt mountains, valley teeming with abundance, that, in the language of Holy Writ, they seemed to "laugh and sing" beneath the eye of their majestic mountains. To render every *coup d'œil* complete, the vast Atlantic occupies the front and offers its immense world of waters to our contemplation.

The most curious, perhaps I ought to say the most *interesting*, circumstance that happened to me in this expedition was the violent passion our kind entertainer conceived for me, which was certainly opened in a manner perfectly new. "My *dare* soul what shall I do to *plase* you? Is it fifty pipes of wine you would like? But *why* will I talk of wine? You shall have my house, my garden, all I have in the world! At 9 o'clock to-morrow I will resign everything up to you, and by [both] if you'll consent to marry me, I'll be drunk every day of my life just for joy." Irresistible as the last argument was, my heart of adamant withstood it. Poor R——y! never did a kinder heart, a more generous spirit exist, and, but for a fault which proceeded really from the warmth of his heart, he would have been a most agreeable companion. He was beloved by everyone. Poor man! let me here close his history by recording that he was killed by a shot in the streets of Santa Cruz at the time of Lord Nelson's attack against it. We returned soon after this declaration, and found the road present objects of new beauty, because we were from habit a little more at ease in our conveyance.

We found a new guest with Mrs. Barry, a Mr. Edwards, who was just arrived from Turkey and attended by a native of that country. He was completely a citizen of the world, held a commission in the service of the Grand Signor, had been everywhere and seen everything. He was elegant, accomplished, and in every way 'agreeable. Our fellow voyager, Mr. Campbell, during all the time we were at Teneriffe, continued the butt of the Captain's jokes, in which others were too ready to join him. On our return, they persuaded him that his legs were swelled (which was ever the precursor of mortal disease in the Island), and the poor fellow submitted to be swathed in flannel and dosed with every nauseous mess they gave him, with the utmost patience, until Mr. Barry's good nature released the victim, who was to be sure the most ignorant creature in the ways of the world I ever met with.

I cannot omit to mention that when we left Santa Cruz, one of Mr. Barry's servants walked over from Oratavia, that morning, and returned with us apparently without fatigue, as he laughed and talked all the way home, though the real distance was fifty miles, and the badness of the roads, of course, rendered the exertion much greater. I was assured this was not remarkable.

On the 6th October, after breakfast, we took leave of our kind hosts ; and here, instead of putting on a semblance of concern, I was obliged to stifle my actual emotions lest they should appear affected. I never recollect being equally moved at a separation after so short an acquaintance. But Mrs. Barry is so truly amiable, and we were treated with such generous hospitality by both parties, that it seemed more like a parting between near relations than casual acquaintances. Since then oceans have rolled between us, and time and sorrow have combined to efface the traces of recollection in my mind of a variety of circumstances, yet everything I then saw and enjoyed is still fresh in my memory. Adieu, my dear Madam, for a while. Believe me

Yours truly,

E. F.

LETTER VII.

To Mrs. L.——.

BLACKHEATH, 1st *March*, 1815.

MY DEAR MADAM,—On the 7th October, 1795, we set sail from Oratavia with a fair wind, and, as it continued, I was sorry we were obliged to stop at St. Iago, where we anchored, on the 13th, in Port Praya Bay. This Bay makes a noble appearance, the surrounding hills rising like an amphitheatre from the sea. The next morning we went on shore about eight o'clock, but were excessively incommoded by the sun, which in these climates rises very rapidly when once above the horizon. Signor Basto, the Commandant of the Island, received us very politely, and most of the principal inhabitants came out to pay their respects to, and gazed at the strangers—among the rest a tall negro priest whose shaven crown had a strange appearance. Signor Basto led us to a summer house, which he had built for the sake of *coolness* and where there was indeed wind; but the air from a brick-kiln would have been equally pleasant and refreshing, while the glare was insupportable, as the place was open on all sides. Fortunately I had brought a pack of cards, so to whist we sat. His Excellency, the Governor, joined us and did us the honour to play several rubbers; and, as he spoke neither English nor French, I knew not, as I have observed before, how we could have amused each other better. An elegant dinner was provided for us at which I was obliged to preside. In the evening we walked out to see the country, which is well cultivated and highly picturesque, but the inhabitants make a wretched appearance, generally living in huts, even when they are rich. The sugarcane raised here is remarkably strong : they have also very good cotton, which they manufacture into a pretty kind of cloth, but it is very dear and exceedingly narrow, being only about a quarter wide. After tea we returned on board, though Signor Basto offered to accommodate us with a house to ourselves ; but, as it is considered dangerous to sleep ashore, we declined his offer and bade him adieu with many thanks for his civilities. In the course of the day we learned that this place is so unhealthy that out of twenty who land here fifteen generally die within six months. What a pity ! Every production of warm countries thrives here in abundance : but man, who cultivates them, sickens and dies.

Our Captain here laid in a stock for a long voyage, and we set sail with a pleasant gale. The day following we caught a fine dolphin. I never saw anything so beautiful as the colours it displayed when dying. On the 29th October we crossed the Line, and again poor Mr. Campbell was the butt of the party. He had been taught to express a great shock on passing it, and really stepped forward to look at it, but the boatswain, who was his countryman, advised him to keep aloof ; he, however, declared very seriously that "he felt a very great shock, he must say, at the time." Nothing further occurred worthy of notice till our arrival at Madras, which took place on the 25th January 1796. I found this town much improved since my former visit, and was particularly pleased with the Exchange, which is a noble building, ornamented with whole length pictures of Lord Cornwallis, Sir Eyre Coote, and General Meadows. The Theatre and Pantheon, where the assemblies are held, are three miles from Madras. At this place we parted with poor Mr. Campbell. I shall never forget the agony of tears I one day found him in. "What is the matter?" said I. "Miss Rogers is going away and I am *here*," answered he. The words were very comprehensive : many young people will be aware that they express love and misery in the extreme. Poor Mr. Campbell must mourn in vain, for, alas! "his love met no return."

On the 6th February, we again set sail, and were fortunately but little annoyed by the surf. On the 22nd, we reached Fulta, where the Pilot, being ever anxious to get forward, made sail at night, when the soundings suddenly shallowing, he found it necessary to cast anchor, though not quite early enough, for in swinging round the ship struck. At first she lay easy, having made a bed in the sand; but, when the tide came in, she heeled terribly, and it was the opinion of most on board that she would never be got off. The chief officer advised us to secure whatever valuables we had about our persons for fear of the worst (which precaution I had already taken), and himself used all possible means for the preservation of the vessel. Happily the rising tide floated her off. You cannot judge of the acuteness of my feelings on this occasion: to see all my hopes and cares frustrated, and the quick transition from sorrow and distress on seeing the ship afloat again, without having sustained the least injury, can only be imagined by those who have experienced such changes.

On Wednesday, the 24th February, we reached Calcutta in safety, where we remained several months. Here we found a resting place after a long voyage, diversified by many pleasant and perilous occurrences, and here, therefore, I shall make a pause in the narrative.

I remain,
My dear Madam,
Yours truly,
E. F.

LETTER VIII.

To Mrs. L——.

BLACKHEATH, *3rd March, 1815.*

My dear Madam,—On Wednesday, the 24th February, 1796 (as I mentioned in the conclusion of my last letter), my feet once more pressed the ground of Calcutta. Miss Rogers, Miss Tripler, and myself went directly to the large house, which Mr. Benjamin Lacey had taken for us by my desire. We procured a freight for the *Minerva* and sent her off within a month after her arrival. The ship, from various causes, had been detained so long on her passage that our goods came to a very bad market. We were compelled, therefore, to sell part by retail, and dispose of the remainder by auction. A small copper bottomed ship, the *Rosalia*, a very fast sailer, was purchased, and the command given to Captain Robinson, an American, who came out with us; and, on the 26th August following, I embarked on her, with Mr. Benjamin Lacey and Miss Tripler for the United States, after bidding painful adieu to my dear young friend and companion, Miss Rogers, whose place Miss Tripler had neither inclination nor ability to supply; but having fettered myself by an engagement I was forced to submit: besides I could not well have proceeded alone. We set sail with a fair wind, but a very strong current running astern. On the night of the 29th, the water broke with such violence against the ship that I called for dead-lights, but was assured by the Captain that there was not the *least* occasion for them. Loth to be thought cowardly or an ignorant sailor, I instantly gave up the point, but had great reason to lament my acquiescence

In less than a quarter of an hour, a most tremendous sea broke in at the starboard side of the cabin and half-filled it with water, which soaked both a bale of valuable muslins and me their unfortunate owner. On this the Pilot bawled out that, if the dead lights were not put up instantly, he would cut cable and get under weigh: so at length they were fixed. In the morning we had the mortification to find that the ship had sprung a leak, and, what was worse than all, that she appeared generally too weak to support the voyage; but, as it would have been wrong to give her up without a trial, we proceeded with the tide to Ingillee, in the faint hope of the leak closing. On the 30th we reached the lower buoy of the Barabulla. Our leak still continuing to increase, on the 1st September, we were obliged to put back for Calcutta. In the evening of the 4th, we anchored off Cooly Bazar, and the next day went on shore at Calcutta, where the *Rosalia* was examined, and pronounced totally unfit for the voyage.

On the 11th September, I went on board the *Swallow Packet* with Captain Simson, who was a guinea pig (as it is called) on board the *Camden* when I came out in 1784. He has been a very fortunate young man so early in life to obtain a command. We had a very elegant repast or tiffin, and I must say Captain Simson seemed heartily glad to receive his old shipmate. Mr. Lacey and Miss Tripler having accompanied me, the former was suddenly taken ill with an ague and fever. This, added to the fatigue, loss, and the disappointment I had so lately endured, was too much for me. I brought him back, procured the best advice for him; and, in a few days, he was relieved: but, before he was able to crawl out, I was in the same situation with a similar intermittent, but escaped the cold fit. I was exceedingly reduced but restored by the free use of bark and other prescriptions from Dr. Hare, who never failed to relieve me.

On the 22nd October, Mr. Lacey engaged for our freight and passage on board the *Hero*, Captain Jackson, bound to New York, to sail between the first and tenth of December. As soon as my strength returned, I bustled about my business, endeavoured to repair my losses, visited my friends, and bade them farewell; and, every necessary preparation being completed, on the 18th of December, we went on board at Garden Reach, and reached Culpee on the 22nd, after a tedious passage kedging all the way. Here we went on shore and laid in provisions. On Christmas day we anchored off Kedgeree. On New Year's day we got under weigh: but unfortunately the wind failed us; and, at six in the morning, the Pilot received instructions not to take us out till further orders. This was a sad beginning of the New Year. The embargo lasted 18 days, after which we proceeded, though very slowly, and on the 30th arrived at Vizagapatam, where we ran some risk from the *Hero*, being mistaken for a French frigate. On the Captain's going on shore, I sent a letter from my good friend Mrs. Child to Captain Hodson, who returned me a pressing invitation, and the next day I found him on the beach with four palanquins for me and my friends. We proceeded to Waltair, where Mrs. Hodson, Mrs. Child's sister, gave us a most cordial reception and insisted on our staying till the ship was ready to sail. The next morning I breakfasted with Captain Pitman, one of the most elegant young men I ever met. He obligingly drove me in his curricle round Waltair, and showed me *Sardinia Bay*, and several other spots remarkable for their beauty.

His own house was charmingly situated on a hill, half-way between Vizagapatam and Waltair. Land here is considered of so little value that every person who built took in as much as he could employ. To one whose eye has been fatigued with viewing the flat country of Bengal this place appears delightful; but yet diversified prospects do not repay the want of fertile plains. Here I bought some beautiful sandal-wood and ivory boxes, for which this place is famous.

Captain and Mrs. Hodson behaved to us with unbounded kindness. In the evening we quitted Vizagapatam. The town makes an agreeable appearance from the sea, not unlike St. James Valley in St. Helena. All who can afford it live at Waltair, which, however, does not contain above ten houses.

On Friday, the 24th February (1796), I once more landed on Madras Beach, and the day following saw many of my friends, amongst others Captain Gooch, who looked remarkably well. There is nothing more pleasant than to meet unexpectedly an old friend, after a long absence and in a foreign country. He dined with us, and everyone was charmed with his behaviour, so different from many who on getting into command, fancy that insolence establishes superiority.

On the 27th, we dined at St. Thomé with Mr. Stevens, Mr. B. Lacey's agent. In the evening we set down to vingt-un, at a rupee a fish, which Mr. Stevens assured was very low. I lost only two dozen. We rose from the card table at half-past eleven ; and, for the honour of Madras hospitality, were suffered to get into our palanquins at that time of night, without the offer of a glass of wine to support us during a four-mile jumble, or a shawl to keep us from the damp air.

On the 2nd of March, Captain Gooch paid us a farewell visit. I was a good deal affected at parting. How many thousand miles had each to traverse before we meet again ! At 5 P.M. we left Madras. There was scarce any surf, but the sea ran high. I found everything very dear here, and consequently made few purchases.

On the 4th of March, we got under weigh at daybreak, and set sail for a new country towards which I now looked with eager expectation. On the 15th, I had the misfortune to fall into the after-hold, which opens into the great cabin, the steward having carelessly left the scuttle open, while he went for a candle. I was taken up senseless, having received a severe blow on the head and many bruises, but, thank Heaven, no material injury. There was a large open case of empty bottles under the opening ; and, had I fallen the other way, I must have gone directly on it. Judge what the consequences must have been.

About the 20th, we began to be troubled with calms and southerly winds, when our Captain politely accused Miss Tripler and me of being two Jonahs, saying he never knew a good voyage made where a woman or a parson was on board. I had a very agreeable revenge, for that very afternoon a breeze sprang up which proved to be the trade wind, and for some time we enjoyed a fine run : but the ship was the most uneasy I ever sailed in, rolling and pitching on every occasion. On the 23rd of April, a violent gale came on, and for several days we had very unpleasant weather. I was in great fear of the passage round the Cape, and we were all in trouble, as provisions ran very short. All our wine and spirits were expended, and we had neither butter, cheese, nor coffee remaining. On the 18th of May, we arrived off False Bay ; and, on the 20th at noon, Mr. D. Trail, the Harbour Master, came on board. Mr. Lacey wrote to Lord Macartney for leave to proceed to Cape Town, as, without his permission, no passengers are suffered to land. We received a visit from Mr. Gooch, First Lieutenant of the *Jupiter*, an elder brother of Captain Gooch, of whose arrival at Madras we brought the first news. I called by invitation on Captain, Linzee to look at the *Dort*, late Admiral De Lucas' ship. Captain Linzee has been three years a Post-Captain, though not yet four and twenty. When in command of the *Nemesis*, he cut out two French vessels from some Mahomedan port in the Mediterranean, and was afterwards taken himself. He but just saved his distance now, for hearing at Cape Town on his arrival ten days ago, that the *Dort* was under sailing orders, he set off on horse back, an arrived but twelve hours before she was to have sailed. Mr. Gooch brought Mrs. Losack, the wife of the Captain of the *Jupiter*, to visit me, and they took us with them on board that ship, where we drank tea and supped.

On Monday, the 22nd, we went on shore at noon, and were received by Major Grimstone, the Commanding Officer, who politely apologised for detaining us so long. At one, six of us mounted a waggon with eight horses, which to my great surprise were driven by one man in hand, at the rate of six miles an hour, over loose stones or whatever else came in the way: so that we were almost jumbled to death. We passed three beaches; and, to avoid quick-sands, they drove through the surf, the roaring of which,—the horses splashing as they galloped along, added to the crack of the driver's long whip, formed altogether a charming concert. As the driver cannot wield these enormous instruments with one hand, another man sits by to hold the reins, while by lengthening or shortening his arm he dexterously contrives to make every horse in turn feel the weight of the lash. At length we reached Cape Town in safety, but were terribly tired and bruised. Between the beaches, the road (such as it is) passes along stupendous mountains, from whose craggy tops masses of stone are continually falling, some of them large enough to crush a church. Many have rolled into the sea, where they form a barrier against the surf, and may defy its force for ages.

We heard that the former Governor, General Craig, sailed from thence on Tuesday preceding. He was once forced to put back, but the second attempt succeeded.

There were no less than six vessels here. The flag was struck on the 15th, and would not be hoisted again until the 15th August, during which interval the Dutch suffered no ships to remain in Table Bay. Our people are not so cautious: perhaps experience may render them so. I like the appearance of the place; for, although the houses are generally low, they occupy much ground, being built of stone or covered with plaster, and containing five or six rooms, they look well; and, though with only one story, yet the ceilings being lofty, they do not seem deficient in height. The Church is handsome. The service is performed in Dutch and English: there are no pews, but benches and chairs, which I greatly prefer, as it gives the idea of social worship more, and is consistent with that equality, which in the more immediate presence of God becomes His creatures, as being equally dependent on Him. It is true this was partly lost here, because the Governor and his family use benches covered with crimson velvet. We set off after service, for St. Simon's Town, and reached the ship about 4 P.M. On Monday, Mr. Gooch took us in the morning to see the *Tremendous*, Admiral Pringle's ship. Here we saw furnaces for heating balls.

On Wednesday, the 31st, we dined on board the *Dort*, where we met Captain and Mrs. Losack, Lord Augustus Fitzroy, Captain Holles of the *Chichester*, and Captain Osborne of the *Trusty*. We went and returned in Captain L.'s barge. Next day we dined on board *L' Imperieuse* with Lord Augusus Fitzroy. In addition to our yesterday's party were Captain Stevens of the *Rattle Snake*, Captain Grainger of the *Good Hope*, Captain Alexander of the *Sphinx*, Mr. Pownall, Naval Officer, and his wife, and Mr. Trail. His Lordship gave us a most magnificent dinner; and, to my great joy, was too much the man of fashion to urge the gentlemen to hard drinking, as had been the case on board the *Dort*. He has an excellent band. When we retired, Mrs. Losack and Mrs. Pownall entered into conversation about the Cape, which they both agreed was the vilest place imaginable. Mrs. Losack is a fine dashing lady. Since her marriage, the *Jupiter* has been on a cruise. I asked her if they were ever fired upon. "Oh, yes, from a battery, and returned the fire." "Did you go below?" "Not I indeed." "Then I suppose you must have been greatly alarmed for fear of being shot?" "Why, to tell you the truth, I was so much engaged in observing how they loaded the guns that I *never* once thought of danger." There is a courageous lady for you.

We played at whist in the evening, and retired at eleven. Captain Alexander took us on board his barge. On the 4th of June, the Admiral, at one, fired two guns, then all the Men of War followed with twenty-one each. The effect produced by the reverberation from so many stupendous rocks was noble! Mr. Gooch and the Doctor came on board to take leave; and, on going away, the boat's crew gave us three cheers, which our people returned. On the whole, our time here passed pleasantly. The politeness of my countrymen, contrasted with the manners of our American officers, served to soothe the irritation of our minds, and teach us to endure for a season with patience that which we had often found to be a trial of our spirits and our temper, in the hopes of meeting by-and-by with gentlemen.

On the 5th of June the wind was as foul as it could blow, and split our only main sail. It is a great misfortune to sail in a vessel ill-provided with stores and necessaries. We had the opportunity of observing this day what a good ship can perform. *L'Imperieuse* Frigate, being ordered on a cruise, got under weigh at noon, passed us at 3 P.M., and was safely out before night. Lord Augustus was polite enough to hoist his colours while going by, and struck them immediately afterwards. Our Captain was too much of a Yankee, however, to return the compliment. I forgot to mention that yesterday four large ships came in: they proved to be the *Rose*, the *Hillsborough*, and the *Thurlow*, East Indiamen, under the convoy of H. M. 74-Gun Ship *Raisonable*.

On the 8th of June we were still in sight of Simon's Town, though we were out two days. On the 11th of July, we crossed the equinoctial line, and I felt satisfied in thinking that I was once more in my own hemisphere. There are cases in which it is wisdom to please ourselves with trifles. At this time my spirits were very low, and sunk with what I may now term a presentiment, as I approached another people and another world, which was eventually the grave of that property, for which I had toiled so long. On the 28th of August, a Pilot came on board from Philadelphia, and from him we had the mournful account that a sickness raged in the city almost as fatal as that which ravaged it a few years before, and that a general distress prevailed in America—frequent bankruptcies, trade at a stand, and an open war with France daily expected, as they took away everything from America which fell in their way. As we did not like to proceed to Philadelphia, after hearing this account, we tacked and stood to the northward, but we had a succession of vexatious hindrances, having narrowly escaped shipwreck in Egg Harbour, and did not reach New York till the 3rd of September, where we landed at six in the evening, and went immediately to a house recommended by my friend Captain Crowinshield, most happy to part with the strange beings with whom we had been so long and painfully immured.

Now having arrived in the land of Columbia, I will bid you adieu for a while.

I am, my dear Madam,
Yours truly,
E. F.

Advertisement.

The work had been printed thus far when the death of the author took place. The subsequent parts of her journal, not appearing to contain any events of a nature sufficiently interesting to claim publication, no additional extracts have been deemed necessary by the administrator, who from a view of benefiting the estate has been induced to undertake the present publication.

NOTES.

Page 6.—The Queen.—Marie Antoinette at this time had not reached the age of twenty-four.

Page 20.—Mount Cenis.—The reader would find it interesting to compare Mrs. Fay's account of the crossing of Mount Cenis with that given by Lady Mary Wortley Montague on 25th September 1718. "The first day's journey, from Turin to Novalese, is through a very fine country, beautifully planted, and enriched by art and nature. The next day we began to ascend Mount Cenis, being carried in little seats of twisted osiers, fixed upon men's shoulders; our chaise taken to pieces and laid upon mules. The prodigious prospect of mountains covered with eternal snow, clouds hanging far below our feet, and the vast cascades tumbling down the rocks with a confusing roaring, would have been solemnly entertaining to me, if I had suffered less from the extreme cold that reigns here; but the misty rain which falls perpetually, penetrated even the thick fur I was wrapped in; and I was half dead with cold before we got to the foot of the mountain, which was not till two hours after it was dark. This hill has a spacious plain on the top of it, and a fine lake there; but the descent is so steep and slippery, 'tis surprising to see these chairmen go so steadily as they do. Yet I was not half so much afraid of breaking my neck as I was of falling sick; and the event showed that I placed my fears in the right place. The other mountains are now all passable for a chaise, and very fruitful in vines and pastures; among them is the finest breed of goats in the world. Acquebet is the last, and soon after we reached Pont Beauvoisin, the frontier town of France, whose bridge parts this kingdom and the dominion of Savoy."

Page 30.—Cisibeos.—In August, 1718, Lady Mary Wortley Montague wrote from Genoa: "The ladies affect the French habit, and are more genteel than those they imitate. I doubt not that the custom of cesibeos has very much improved their airs. I know not whether you have ever heard of these animals. Upon my word, nothing but my own eyes could have convinced [me] there were any such upon earth. The fashion began here, and is now received all over Italy, where the husbands are not such terrible creatures as we represent them. There are none among them such brutes as to pretend to find fault with a custom so well established, and so politically founded, since I am assured here that it was an expedient first found out by the senate, to put an end to those family hatreds which tore their state to pieces, and to find employment for those young men who were forced to cut one another's throats *pour passer le temps*, and it has succeeded so well, that since the institution of cesibeos there has been nothing but peace and good humour among them. These are particular gentlemen who devote themselves to the service of a particular lady (I mean a married one, for the virgins are all invisible, confined to convents); they are obliged to wait on her to all public places, the plays, operas, and assemblies (which are here called *conversations*), where they wait behind her chair, take care of her fan and gloves if she plays, have the privilege of whispers, etc. When she goes out, they serve her instead of lacquies, gravely trotting by her chair. 'Tis their business to prepare for her a present against any day of public appearance, not forgetting that of her own name; in short, they are to spend all their time and money in her service, who rewards them according to her inclination (for opportunity they want none); but the husband is not to have the impudence to suppose this any other than pure platonic friendship."

Page 44.—Mr. Baldwin.—George Baldwin was the agent of H.E.I.C. at Cairo. In the Original Consultations of the Supreme Council, date 28th August 1779, may be found a strenuous statement of the hardships to which the English in Egypt were at this time subject.

Page 51.—Mr. O'Donnell.—Presumably John O'Donnell, who had come out in 1771 as a Cadet in the Bombay Service, but under the patronage of John Bristow, obtained the post of Deputy Paymaster to the Nawab of Oudh. On his return to Bengal, after the disaster recorded by Mrs. Fay, he represented his grievances on this Egyptian expedition to the Supreme Council, and they are recorded at great length on the Consultations of the Government, 12th June 1780. According to O'Donnell the names of the two French brothers were the Chevaliers de St. Germaine, and this would lead one to suppose that they were the two sons of Pierre de Renault, the defender of Chandernagore against Clive and Watson in 1757. Until I had seen O'Donnell's petition, I had been led by Mrs. Fay to suppose that one of these brothers was Jean Baptiste Chevalier, who after his escape from Chandernagore had been captured by Alexander Elliot at Cuttack, but allowed by Warren Hastings, despite Francis and Wheeler, to return to Europe on board a Danish ship from Serampore to Suez. The last I hear of O'Donnell is in a letter from General Stibbert recommending the loan to the former of a number of invalid artillerymen to man a privateer to go in search of French craft in Indian waters. See *Bengal: Past and Present*, Vol. II., p. 416.

Page 51.—Vanderfield.—According to O'Donnell the name is Vander Velden.

Page 53.—Of the remaining seven.—O'Donnell gives these five—

Barrington
Jenkins
Vander Velden
Chilly
An Armenian linguist.

One of the "two others" returning to Suez was a Capt. Waugh.

Page 55.—"The Grand Signor sends a Bashaw."—The system of divided rule was inaugurated, after the downfall of the Marmaluke Sultanate in the sixteenth century. In 1768 Ali Bey had driven out the Sultan's Pasha, but was himself supplanted by Muhummed Bey in 1771. The death of the latter was followed by the wildest state of anarchy, and it was into the Egypt of this period the Fays plunged. Basha is the old form of our modern *Pasha* (a corruption perhaps of the Persian Padishah).

Page 58.—Pretended he had orders from Constantinople.—I believe this was the case. Mrs. Fay is in error supposing that the order was due to the initiative of the H. E. I. Co. The Porte had made a general order forbidding European ships to trade with Suez, but the H. E. I. Co. obtained (at least a temporary) permission for their own ships to do so.

Page 65.—By Banians and Rajputs (as they are called though I cannot tell why).—"It is clear, therefore," writes Monier Williams "that even Rajputs, Jats, and other modern castes may represent the ancient Vaisyas, who were originally the great class of agriculturists—the men who settled down (root vis) on the soil as husbandmen and cultivators. In fact, very few of the present Vaisya caste have anything to do with agriculture. Some of them may be of tolerably pure descent, but they are generally merchants and traders forming tribes called Baneyas (Sanskrit *banik*), Bhatiyas.. A large class of traders are called *Khatris*, which name probably shows that they are descended from the ancient Kshatriyas, *i.e.* the military or royal caste from whom the Rajputs are derived." (*Hinduism*, pp. 161-63).

Page 65.—Chevalier de St. Lubin.—The story of his Mission may in part at least be recovered from Mr. G. W. Forrest's *Selections from the Letters, Despatches and other State Papers preserved in the Bombay Secretariat, (Maratha Series, Vol. I.)* His mission was not, as Mrs. Fay states, to Hyder Ally [Haidar Ali] but to the Maratha Durbar at Poona, and its direct object was to secure for France a new footing in India by obtaining the island of Chaul and establishing there not only a Factory, but a Military station in touch with the fleet. "If" writes Mr. Forrest, "he had succeeded, the French would have regained their former importance in India, and the English would have had to battle with them, supported by all the powers and resources of the Maratha Empire for Empire in the East."

Page 68.—Tulloh.—It may be safely conjectured that this was the famous Calcutta Auctioneer, whose portrait, tradition has it, may be found in the Judas Iscarlot of Zoffany's altar-piece at St. John's Church, Calcutta.

Page 95.—Mahé which the French held till we took it from them in March last.—On 7th July 1778 the Council at Calcutta received news *viâ* Suez that in March last war had been declared between England and France. On 10th July Chandernagore surrendered, on the 10th October Pondichery, and in March 1779 Mahé. Mahé, situated on the Malabar Coast, is still a French possession. "Haidar" (Hyder), writes Mr. Bowring, "who was in possession of the whole of Malabar, except the few places occupied by European settlements, was enraged at the seizure of Mahé, which he alleged to be under his protection. His soldiers had in fact assisted at its defence. His main objection to its occupation by the English was that through Mahé he derived his military supplies, and he threatened the British Government that, in the event of Mahé being attacked, he would retaliate by invading Arcot. The capture of the settlement led to an uprising of the Nairs [Mrs. Fay's Nayhirs], who were anxious to throw off Haidar's yoke, but the rebellion was suppressed without difficulty."

Page 98.—"*Journey to Seringapatam.*"—Immediately after Schwartz's Mission, another was despatched to Seringapatam to demand the release of some Englishmen who had been seized at Calicut and sent as prisoners to the capital. Mr. Gray, the envoy, was empowered not only to effect their freedom, but to attempt to resume friendly relations. The prisoners were in fact released before he entered Mysore, but on his proceeding to Seringapatam, Haidar's attitude clearly showed that the time for negotiation was passed." (*L. B. Bowring. Haidar Ali and Tipu Sultan*). ("Rulers of India." *p. 86.*)

Page 134.—*Mrs. Motte.*—A Miss Mary Touchet by birth, and, "Sydney Grier" writes, "sister of Peter Touchet who united with Hastings and other old Westminsters in presenting a silver cup to Westminster School in 1777. In 1779 she married Mr. Motte." Busteed writes: "Mr Motte was a free merchant; in 1766 he undertook a journey to the diamond mines in Orissa by direction of Clive, and wrote an account of it. He afterwards lived at Benares, and moved thence to Hooghly, where the Hastings used to visit Mrs. Motte, who was a great friend of Mrs. Hastings. For sometime Mr. Motte held a police appointment in Calcutta, where his name is still preserved in 'Mott's Lane.' About that time he must have got into financial difficulties, as in 1781 there is an advertisment in the newspaper calling a meeting of his creditors. Amongst the Impey manuscripts in the British Museum, there is a petition from Mr. Motte written from the Calcutta Jail in 1783, in which this friend of the Governor-General's begs that the creditors will assent to his release from prison on the score of humanity. His wife accompanied Mrs. Hastings to England in 1784." Her sister, Miss Sally Touchet frequently appears in Hastings' letters.

Page 134.—*Belvedere House.*—In February 1780, Hastings sold Belvedere, the nucleus of the present Palace of the Lieutenant-Governors of Bengal to Major Tolly, the constuctor of Tolly's *nala.* The "Belvedere House," which Mrs. Fay visited, and quite inaccurately sets at "five miles from Calcutta," was probably the "Hastings House," renovated a few years ago by Lord Curzon, and now used as a guest house for native chiefs of importance. It was of this house that Mackrabie wrote, in February, 1778: "Colonel Monson dined with us in the country: after dinner we walked over to the Governor's new built house. 'Tis a very pretty thing, but very small, tho' airy and lofty. These milk white houses with smooth shining surfaces utterly blind one."

Page 134.—*Her whole dress.*—See Mr. H. E. A. Cotton's note on p. 329 the reprint of *Hartley House.* Mirabeau, during his stay in England, wrote a cruel letter to Sir G. Elliot on the subject of Mrs. Hastings' magnificence. Hastings was noted for his extreme simplicity in the matter of costume.

Page 134.—Mrs. Warren Hastings.—Hastings was twice married: 1st in 1757, to Mary, the widow of Captain John Buchanan (not Captain Dougald Campbell as many authorities alledge). Buchanan was one of those who perished in "the Black Hole." Sydney Grier seems to favour the view that Mary Hastings was a Miss Mary Elliot. She had borne two daughters to her first husband, of whom one was Catherine Caroline recorded in the Baptismal Registers at St. John's, Calcutta, on 1st May 1754, and the other Elizabeth. The first Mr. Hastings is buried at Berhampore and the inscription over her grave reads—

IN MEMORY OF
MRS. MARY HASTINGS
And her daughter
ELIZABETH
Who died in 11th July 1759
in the 2—year of her age.
This monument was erected
by her husband
Warren Hastings, Esquire
in due regard
of her memory.
Restored by the Government
of Bengal, 1863.

The Elizabeth of this grave is not to be confused with the daughter of that name by Mary Hastings' first marriage. The two Buchanan girls seem to have turned out badly. The Elizabeth Hastings of Berhampore died on the 23rd day of her birth. Mary Hastings was the mother of George Hastings who died in 1761. He had been sent home by his father to be brought up by the Rev. George and Mrs. Austen, the parents of the famous novelist. The second Mrs. Hastings,—the Mrs. Hastings of this book—was Anna Maria Apollonia, daughter of Baron Chapuset. She married at Madras, Christopher Adam Carl. V. Imhoff. The sordid tale of her divorce and of her alliance with Hastings is too well known to require elucidation in these brief notes.

Page 136.—There exists, it seems, a strong jealousy between the Government and the Supreme Court.—Mrs. Fay here touches upon what still remains one of the most obscure passages in the history of the Warren Hastings' Administration. The treatment of the subject of "the abuses arising from the Pretensions of the Supreme Court" in Mills' *History* is quite inadequate. The student is referred to Chapter XIV. of Sir J. F. Stephen's *Nuncumar and Impey.* The subject will very shortly be dealt with in the pages of *Bengal: Past and Present.* Until then the best account of poor North Naylor is that given by "Sydney Grier": "North Naylor was the Company's attorney, who had incurred the displeasure of the Supreme Court by advising Hastings and the Council to resist their high-handed proceedings against the Rajah of

Kasi Jara, who was not amenable to their Jurisdiction. The aid of the military, when requested by the sheriff to enforce the jurisdiction of the Court, was refused, but the sheriff assembled a force of his own, which broke into the Raja's house and seized his goods. Returning with their spoil, the sheriff's party were met by troops and taken into custody, whereupon the Court retaliated by granting a rule to show cause why an attachment should not issue against Mr. Naylor, and on his refusal to answer interrogatories, he was committed to prison for contempt. At the same time a summons for trespass was issued against the Governor-General and Council, and on their refusal to plead, they were also declared guilty of contempt. The deadlock which ensued was only terminated by the abrupt withdrawal of the plaintiff, Kassinath Babu, in the action against the Rajah, and the consequent quashing of the proceedings. Mr. Beveridge, from whose *Comprehensive History of India*, these particulars are taken, says, of course, that Kasinath Babu had been bribed by Hastings to withdraw his suit. Here again, a study of the Miscellaneous Correspondence would have been of advantage, for in February, 1784, Hastings writes to Wheler that Kasinath is begging that his business may be brought to a speedy conclusion. He has a claim on both of them, since he withdrew the case from the Court on Hastings' promise that he would see justice done him. Naylor's release appears to have come too late, for he was suffering from dysentery induced by the insanitary condition of the Calcutta Gaol." (*Letters of Warren Hastings to his Wife*, pp. 62-63). If Elijah Barwell Impey, the son and apologist of his father, is to be believed, Naylor was in prison from 1st to 16th March, 1780, and he left the Gaol in very much the same condition in which he had entered it. Mrs. Fay says "he died in confinement." This is clearly untrue. Naylor died on 19th August 1780. But Sir Elijah's son gives his whole case away by attempting to prove an *alibi*. "From the 6th of July 1778 to the 15th March in the following year, my father was with his family at Chittagong, above 316 miles from Calcutta. He was in ill-health, and my mother brought to bed at that place, which will account for so long an absence: and during those seven months, Mr Justice Hyde presided in the Supreme Court. It was Hyde, therefore, and not the Chief Justice who committed Naylor to prison" *Memoirs of Sir Elijah Impey*, p. 196. This *alibi*, which in itself is *nihil ad rem* I am afraid, will not stand proof, for in February 1779, Sir Elijah was in Calcutta presiding over the case of *George Francis Grand, Esq.* versus *Philip Francis, Esq.* See also *The Memoirs of Sir Philip Francis*, Vol. ii., p. 186.—On the other hand, it should be said that Sir Elijah proved himself a very kind friend to Naylor and was the protector of his orphan child.

Page 140.—A *soup*. In *Hartley House* we read "no soup, take notice, is served up at Calcutta." Mrs. Fay gives 2 A.M. as the dinner hour: Sophia Goldborne says 3 A.M.

Page 142.—A regular supply of Calcutta Gazettes.—Mrs. Fay must be alluding to Hickey's *Bengal Gazette*. The rival *India Gazette* did not make its appearance till November, and the official *Calcutta Gazette* commenced in 1784. See Busteed, *Echoes of Old Calcutta*, p. 183.

Page 144.—A duel between.—This historical duel took place on the 17th August 1780. The minute which provoked the duel was, not as Mrs. Fay says, the handiwork of Francis, but of Hastings, and it was written on the 3rd July. For a full account of the duel the reader is referred to Chap. VI. of Dr. Busteed's *Echoes of Old Calcutta.*

Page 145.—Col. Baillie.—The story of Col. William Baillie's defeat, after a most gallant and desperate struggle, will be found in all histories of India. It occurred on 10th September 1780. French authorities assert that 700 British and 5,000 Indian soldiers were slain, and that 2,000 English were taken prisoners. These numbers are absurdly exaggerated. Baillie died in prison at Seringapatam on 13th November, 1782. The gallant Sir David Baird, who was captured, remained in prison for 3½ years. The sufferings of the English prisoners, either at Bangalore or Seringapatam form an oft-told story

Page 147.—Rowland Jackson.—In the South Park Street Cemetry will be found a tomb with the following inscription :—

Within this Tomb reposeth the body of
Doctor ROWLAND JACKSON,
a member of the Royal College
of Physicians, of London ;
who died sincerely lammented
by his family and friends,
on the 29th of March, 1784, aged 63 years.

"Sydney C. Grier" writes :—"From an obituary notice of him in the *India Gazette* of 29th March 1784, we learn that he had studied medicine and natural science at most of the European Universities—at Paris he was the friend of Marmontel and other eminent persons—and practised for a time in the West Indies. Succeeding to an Irish estate, he made himself much beloved by treating the poor gratuitously, but was ousted by a law-suit in favour of a nearer heir. When he applied to the Company for leave to go to India, the doctor who examined him as to his qualifications said that their respective positions ought to be reversed. Lawrence Sulivan recommended him to Hastings in a letter dated 15th November 1777, as one who had fallen from a state of affluence, through no fault of his own, and though universally esteemed, is reduced in life to the disagreeable necessity of a residence in Bengal." (*Letters of Warren Hastings to his Wife*, p. 54). Dr. Rowland Jackson sent in an application to be appointed "Physician" to the Calcutta Hospitals, and, despite the strong recommendation of the Court of Directors, Hastings opposed this on the ground that the distinction instituted between a "Physician" and a "Surgeon" would be unfair to the medical men already in the Company's Service as surgeons. Francis supported Jackson's application ; Barwell sided with Hastings, and Wheler save a non-commital vote. Ultimately Jackson was appointed to attend the Company's servants, with the pay of Rs. 600 per mensem and a house allowance of Rs. 200. Jackson, like his colleague Hare, believed in "bar for fever.

Page 147.—The eldest son.—In the Marriage Register at St. John's we find, date 28th January 1779. "Edward Rowland Jackson, cadet in the Hon'ble Company's Service, to Miss Phœbe Tuting.

Page 147.—Miss C——y. This young lady is probably Miss Maria Chantry, who, on 10th May 1781, was married to Captain Archibald Montgomerie at St. John's Church, Calcutta. She is mentioned in some verses in *Hickey's Gazette* to the toast of "the five girls that grace India's soil."

Miss Chantry (afterward Mrs. Montgomerie).
Miss W. (rangham) (afterwards Mrs. Bristow).
Miss S[adler] (afterwards Mrs. Brewer.)
Miss H—d.
Miss Crisp (afterwards Lady Shee).

Page 149.—Suffered Mr. Sealy to perform that ceremony.—Doubtless Mr. Charles Sealy, last Registrar of the Mayor's Court, and first of the Supreme Court. Sidesman of St. John's Parish, 1787. An original portrait in oils of this gentleman to be seen in the vestry of St. John's Church, Calcutta."

Page 149.—Mr. Hyde's public breakfast at whose house the professional gentlemen, etc.—According to the Rev. J. Long this house was on the site of the present Town Hall. Hyde was one of the first Puisne Judges of the Supreme Court. As Magistrate he committed Nanda Kumar (Nuncumar), and as Judge he tried and sentenced him. He served for 21 years and died on 8th July 1790, and was buried in Calcutta.

Page 151.—The Harmonic.—It stood on Bow Bazar facing the old jail, close to the present headquarters of the Calcutta Police. In its origin "the Harmonic House" was the precursor of the "Saturday Club" of to-day. In 1781 the Harmonic Society seems to have ceased to please, and a little later their house was put up for sale. In the eighties of the eighteenth century it was accounted "the handsomest house in Calcutta." In 1784 the House was turned into the "Harmonic Tavern." "It was held capable of accommodating five or six hundred persons with ease," and here the Provincial Grand Lodge of Masons in Bengal for a time held its "communications." See *Calcutta Review*, Vol, XVIII., *p.* 292, and Cotton, *Calcutta: Old and New*, *p.* 729.

Page 152—Lady Coote.—By birth Susanna Hutchinson, the daughter of a former Governor of St. Helena. "Sidney Grier" writes: "when Coote sailed for the Carnatic for the last time in March, 1783, she was with him, and anxiety for her safety heightened with anguish of mind which brought about his death on being chased by a French fleet. She implies distinctly in a letter to Hastings, that the Madras Government might have rescued him if they wished, and that their animosity continued unabated even after Sir Eyre's death is shown by the Chaplain's letters complaining of their behaviour to Lady Coote. She sailed for England in the *Belmont* on 6th February 1784, taking with her husband's body to be buried at Rockburne."

Page 153.—The house was built by subscription.—The Original Calcutta Theatre stood in the Lall Bazar and played a prominent part in the siege of 1756. The Play House of Mrs. Fay's day, erected in 1775, stood close to the north-west corner of the present Lyon's Range, and as Writers' Buildings kept off the south breezes, it was provided with wind sails on the roof "to promote coolness by a free circulation of air." A recent writer in the *Englishman*, who has got himself into some confusion about dates and places tells us that Garrick "sent out a Mr. Messink for the purpose of regulating this theatre at its outset," and that great actor also superintended the selection of the scenery to be sent out. Mrs. Fay's allusion to Lieutenant Norfar's hair-dressing is puzzling. It may be conjectured the Norfar was a Maccaroni. In *Hartley House*, Miss Sophia Goldborne tells us that the House "consists only of pit and boxes: to be admitted to the first of which you pay eight rupees (twenty shillings): to the last, a gold mohr (forty shillings); it is not, therefore wonderful it should be a brilliant spectacle." [1908 Edition p. 59.] In Hickey's *Bengal Gazette* (1781 No. 11 February) we read "Captain Call play'd Jaffier admirably well and may be styled the Garrick of the East. Mr. Norford played Belvidera with such an amorous glow of features and utterance,—and was so characteristic in the description of madness,—as to procure him (as usual) universal applause." Dr. Busteed writes: "Mrs. John Bristow had the honour of being the first in Calcutta, who brought lady actors into fashion." Mrs. Bristow, it is now known, was the Emma Wrangham of whose beauty so much is to be read in the columns of Hickey's *Gazette*. Dr. Busteed notes that one of Mrs. Bristow's triumphs was in the male part of Lucius in Shakespeare's *Julius Cæsar*. At some time in the thirties of the last century the same play was produced by a distinguished band of Calcutta amateurs, but by a daring innovation the part of Cassius made a female one, was played by an actor *en femme!*

Page 159.—The acquaintance of Mrs. Wheler.—This was Wheler's second wife, as the inscription on his grave in the South Park Street Cemetery shows. He married first of all Harriet Chichely Plowden "descended from the Plowdens of Plowden in Shropshire." This good lady, as Francis records, astounded the ladies of Calcutta by the size of her hoop at the ball given in honour of her arrival. She died within seven months of her arrival, and a few months after her death Wheler married again. The bride was "Charlotte, daughter of George Durnford, of Winchester." Warren Hastings would have agreed with Mrs. Fay as to the second Mrs. Wheler's excellencies. Here are two extracts from "S. Grier's" *Letters of Warren Hastings to his Wife*:—

"I saw Mr. Wheler and Miss D. (Durnford) married last night. How it agreed with them I know not, but it has given me a cold and sore throat. God bless them. Would it not be kind—civil at least, if you were to write a short letter to her—expressing your satisfaction, etc., and regret that you were not present; I did this for you, and she said it was a pity."

And, when Wheler was approaching his death (he died October 10, 1784):—

"God will bless Mrs. Wheler for her successful care and affectionate attention. This is not a new trait of her character. I esteem and respect her for that and her many other domestic virtues."

Page 161.—Brahmin, Khutree, the Buesho. and the Shodor, that is the Brāhmin, the Kshatiya, the Vaisya, the Sūdra. In *Hartley House*, the Gentoos (*i. e.*, Hindus) are divided into "five tribes, *viz.*, the Brahmin, Sithis, Beisa, Sudder, and Atarries." See Monier Williams *Hinduism*. (S.P.C.K. Series of "Non-Christian Religious Systems,') p. 163.

Page 167.—A melancholy event.—This was the death of Edward Colin Chambers. It will be worth while to give here the inscriptions on the Chambers' family tomb in the South Park Street Burial Ground. Sir Elijah Impey, Hyde, and Francis were the godparents of Edward Colin Chambers.

In Memory of
ANNE CHAMBERS,
Who died 7th February 1782, aged 69 years.
And two of her grandchildren,
HENRIETTA CHAMBERS,
Who died 30th of July 1779, aged 4 months,
And EDWARD COLIN CHAMBERS,
Who died 9th November 1781, aged 6 months;
Being children of
Sir Robert Chambers
And Frances his wife.
Also in Memory of
Jane Marriot,
An infant about 18 months old,
Who died 23rd November 1781.

To the Memory of
THOMAS FITZMAURICE CHAMBERS,
Son of Sir Robert and Lady Chambers,
Born on the 28th October MDCCLXXVI,
Who was shipwrecked on the "Grosvenor" and
Perished on the coast of East Africa in August 1782.

MR. WILLIAM CHAMBERS, Prothonotary
And Persian Interpreter to the Supreme
Court of Judicature in Bengal; by
Whose death the interests of
True religion in India and the
Concerns of the Calcutta Mission in
particular experienced a considerable loss
He died on the 22nd August 1793.
And was interred in the above
Tomb of his family.

Page 167.—The *Grosvenor*.—The official account of the loss of this ship, apparently in the neighbourhood of Delagoa Bay, on Sunday, 4th August 1782, has been republished in *Bengal: Past and Present*, Vol. II., No. 3. Captain Coxon's misjudgment was the same in kind as that of Captain Lewis which Mrs. Fay reports. The survivors of the wreck numbered 135 persons, including the ladies and the children. In the terrible attempt to march through a strange country, and escape from the savages who pursued them nearly all the European passengers were left behind with the Captain. Miss Blechynden, in her *Calcutta: Old and New*, narrates that in the Kaffir War of 1838, a tribe offered their services as "brothers to the English," and she conjectures these were the descendants of the ladies who had survived the wreck of the *Grosvenor*. The conjecture is scarcely tenable. Only six ladies were wrecked, and of these two were children. For the story of the wreck of the *Grosvenor* see *Bengal: Past and Present*, Vol. II., No. 3. On the 1st August, 1778, Captain Coxon had married at Calcutta Miss Hariet Sherburne.

Page 167.—Hosea.—In his petition to be allowed to take passage on board the *Grosvenor*, William Hosea states that he had been seventeen years in the Company's service. He was Collector of Hughli in 1772—1773. I fancy he had fallen foul of Warren Hastings in Oudh. He was a nephew, of Orme, the Historian. The Marriage Registers at St. John's, Calcutta, show that Hosea married a Miss Mary Browne on 17th September 1764.

Page 170.—All expedition to Chinsurah.—Chinsurah, the old Dutch Settlement near Hughli, was seized by the English in July 1781; and retained till 1782. For its history see Lieutenant Colonel D. G. Crawford's *Brief History of the Hughli District*, published by the Bengal Secretariat. Chinsurah was finally ceded to England by treaty, dated 17th March 1824.

Page 173.—Sir Robert and Lady Chambers are going to a place called Bearcole for the benefit of sea-bathing.—Birkul, about ten miles on the coast below Contai. Birkul—Beercool as Hastings wrote it—was even more in demand as seaside resort in the latter end of the eighteenth century than Puri is at the beginning of the twentieth. On October 19th, 1780, Hastings writes to his wife: "My Marian, I saw an alligator yesterday with a mouth as large as a Budgerow, and was told that it was of a sort which is very common about Balasore, but this not so large. I shall never consent to your going again to Beercool." See Busteed: *Echoes of Old Calcutta*, Chap. VIII.

Page 176.—St. Helena.—Mrs. Fay, on her return journey was apparently detained for over two months at St. Helena, waiting for a convoy. Sir P. Francis, in the previous year, reached St. Helena on 12th March 1781, and was detained there, for a similar reason, for four months.

Page 179.—Mr. Casamajor.—It may be conjectured that this was the gentleman who, when Chief at Vizigapatam, had been made prisoner by the mutineers of the 1st Circar Battalion.

Page 191.—Anjengo.—This name is familiar as that of the birthplace of the Historian, Robert Orme, and also of Sterne's Eliza (Mrs. Draper). A terrible tragedy took place here in 1721 and is recorded by Colonel J. Biddulph in his

Pirates of Malabar and an English Woman in India Two Hundred Years ago. See also Col. J. Walsh's *Military Reminiscencies.* Vol. II., p. 148 *et seq.*

Page 103.—Miss Hicks married Mr. Lacey.—In the Register at St. John's Church against 19th March, 1785. "John Lacey, a bachelor, shopkeeper, to Avis Hicks, single woman. T. Blanshard Chaplain."

Page 218.—By the free use of bark and other prescriptions from Dr. Hare.—Dr. Hare was the physican who attended Sir W. Jones in his last illness. Curiously enough it was another Dr. Hare who brorght the use of quinine into Indian Hospitals as a substitute for bleeding and this later Dr. Hare, the father of the present Lt.-Col. Hare, I.M.S., of Shillong, was the medical man who nursed back to health, Dr. Brydon the sole survivor, with two natives, of the army which marched 13,600 strong from Jagdallak to Jellahabad. See Lieutenant-Colonel E. C. Hare's *Life of Edward Hare.* Mrs. Fay's Dr. Hare, is with Dr. Hartley, commemorated in some verses cited by Dr. Busteed in Chap. VII of *Echoes of Old Calcutta.* A son of Dr. James Hare is buried in the South Park Street Cemetery.

Page 221.—Cape Town.—On 16th September 1795, the Dutch troops, with all the honours of war, marched out of the Fort and surrendered as prisoners of war. On 17th August 1776, the (Dutch) Admiral Lucas, was trapped in Saldanha Bay and surrendered his fleet and nearly 2,000 soldiers.

Page 221.—Lord Macartney.—The First Earl. He had been Governor of Madras 22nd June 1781 to 8th June 1783. He assumed office as Governor of the Cape in May 1797—the month of Mrs. Fay's arrival at the Cape.

INDEX.